GEORGE WASHINGTON AND HISTORICAL SCENES.

HISTORY
IN THE MAKING

Also by Kyle Ward

History Lessons: How Textbooks from Around the World Portray U.S. History
(with Dana Lindaman)

*In the Shadow of Glory: The Thirteenth Minnesota in the Spanish-American
and Philippine-American Wars, 1898–1899*

HISTORY

An Absorbing Look at How American History Has Changed in the Telling over the Last 200 Years

IN THE MAKING

Kyle Ward

THE NEW PRESS

NEW YORK
LONDON

Requests for permission to reproduce selections from this book should
be mailed to: Permissions Department, The New Press, 38 Greene
Street, New York, NY 10013.
Published in the United States by The New Press, New York, 2006
Distributed by W. W. Norton & Company, Inc., New York

LIBRARY OF CONGRESS CATALOGING-IN-PUBLICATION DATA

Ward, Kyle Roy, 1969-
History in the making: an absorbing look at how American history
has changed in the telling over the last 200 years / Kyle Ward.
p. cm.
Includes bibliographical references and index.
ISBN-13: 978-1-59558-044-3 (hc.)
ISBN-10: 1-59558-044-1 (hc.)
1. United States—History—Textbooks. 2. United States—History—
Textbooks—Evaluation. 3. United States—Historiography. I. Title.
E175.85.W37 2006
973.07—dc22   2006008886

The New Press was established in 1990 as a not-for-profit alternative to
the large, commercial publishing houses currently dominating the book
publishing industry. The New Press operates in the public interest rather
than for private gain, and is committed to publishing, in innovative ways,
works of educational, cultural, and community value that are often
deemed insufficiently profitable.

www.thenewpress.com

Composition by *dix!*
This book was set in Minister Light

Printed in the United States of America

2   4   6   8   10   9   7   5   3   1

To Annika—with all my love

CONTENTS

PART VI
The Great Depression and World War II

PART VII
The Cold War and Postwar America

PART VIII
The Vietnam Era

ACKNOWLEDGMENTS

I would like to thank the following people, who helped me complete this project: Bruce Beesley, Jenni Roman, Dr. Paul Bloom, James Loewen, Adam Clark, and Marita (Bach) Pinkstaff. I also need to thank Melissa Richards and Marc Favreau of The New Press for their extraordinary assistance in putting this project together.

And a very special thanks to Dr. David Vancil and Dennis Vetrovec at the Indiana State University Library (ISU) Special Collections Department. These two men and their department were invaluable to my research, to say the least. The ISU Special Collections Department currently houses thirteen major collections, two of which have international importance: the Eugene V. Debs Collection and the Cordell Collection of Dictionaries. Other collections have a more regional or national focus, such as the Cunningham, the Floyd Family, and the Walker collections. The Cunningham Collection contains early or significant works in American education on practice and theory, while the Floyd Family and Walker collections contain over twenty-five hundred cataloged textbooks. While these collections cover all subject areas, the largest number of books are in the fields of history and English.

EDITOR'S NOTE

It would have been a nearly impossible task to read every U.S. history textbook published between 1794–1999. In some instances, textbooks from certain eras (especially the late 1700s and early 1800s) were chosen simply because I could locate them. Although there are some sketchy accounts as to how popular a textbook might have been (usually determined by how many editions were published), there was no way of knowing how widely used and adopted a textbook was. Rather, I argue that each textbook I looked at had to be accepted and adopted by the author, the publisher, a school administration, at least one teacher, and the parents of at least a few communities. I therefore assumed that the material found in the textbook was approved and accepted as solid historical fact at the time it was published.

There are four major reasons why I undertook this project, and why I believe it is important for people to understand not only our history but also the way this history is presented to students.

First, it is essential to understand that U.S. history textbooks to some extent represent our collective stories, passed down and agreed on by society. When we pick up a U.S. history textbook used today or 150 years ago, we know that people of that time period could read that text and agree that what was written captures what our nation is about. A textbook today that would erroneously discuss how the former Soviet Union used the atomic bomb on Japan to end World War II just would not be accepted, since it is not a socially agreed upon historical story and hence would not be adopted for use.

The second reason for undertaking this research was to see how, or even if, the stories students learn about the past have changed over time. Understanding that our history textbooks reflect society's attitudes and beliefs, and thus hopefully influence future generations, I wanted to see how some of these events were portrayed to American students at different times in our nation's history. If we understand that our history was written about people who had personal biases and by people with these same biases, then we are better able to open up the dialogue and begin to debate these different perspectives as well as their impact on how history is taught and understood.

The third reason for this book is to make people aware of the fact that while history textbooks are written in order to affect how students learn about the past, the textbooks themselves are actually written in the present. In other words, what we find in our textbooks today often tells us more about the time in which they were written than the historical events that they are trying to portray.

One also has to assume that much like students today, students in the past accepted what their textbooks told them as fact, never questioning what the "expert" author is telling them. In her book on history textbooks written in the twentieth century, Frances Fitzgerald claims that "those of us who grew up in the fifties believed in the permanence of our American history textbooks. To us as children, those texts were the truth of things: They were American history."[1] The U.S. history textbook was, and for many still is, the authority in the classroom. There is to be no debate, and no questioning of what the textbook tells us.

The fourth desired aim of this work is to get people to begin to think in a historiographical way. History has to be looked at as if it has layers. First, students of history have to understand that an event took place with real characters, all of whom had their own biases and perspectives. Next, they must appreciate that this event has been studied and analyzed by historians, often writing years after the fact. In order to truly grasp the nuances of history, one needs to understand that while these authors were (and are) doing their research and writing, they were also being influenced by the current social, political, economic, and cultural events taking place in what they considered the "present."

While U.S. history textbooks have been published up until the present day, and they are continually updated, I decided to stop my research at 1999. I discovered that textbook stories usually take at least a decade or more to reflect any substantial change in the historiography; in my analysis, textbooks published in 2005 have changed very little since 1999. Imagine a 2005 textbook discussing the Clinton/Lewinsky scandal and its political impact. In less then a decade, this story has not changed much, if at all. Thirty years from now, in ways that we could not possibly judge with any accuracy, we may look back on this scandal and judge it in a very different light.

Finally, I hope this project will spur much discussion about what our students are learning in their history classes, and encourage people to learn more about what exactly happened and how these events continue to affect our lives.

INTRODUCTION

"WARTS AND ALL"

After a number of years of researching, studying, and teaching history, I can say with a great deal of confidence that history is an incredibly fascinating and important subject, which should not only be studied for civic and societal reasons but also because it can help develop critical thinking and other cognitive skills necessary for people to live a full life. It should therefore be an easy sell to convince people to learn about the past, since the subject of history is filled with stories of political intrigue, murder, scandal, mysteries, conspiracies, sexual liaisons, war, genocide, torture, romance, corruption, heroism, and much, much more.

I am not alone in this belief. By simply going to the local library or bookstore, one can see thousands of books written about a wide spectrum of historical events in U.S. history. One can also go to the local movie theater or video store to check out how many films have been based on historical events. Not only has Hollywood used the historical genre as a staple throughout its existence, but television executives have now gone so far as to create an entire channel dedicated to this one topic. Finally, one has to only look at the popularity of numerous historical museums and historic sites to see that we Americans love our history. By the thousands, we read about it, watch it on television and in movie theaters, go to museums and historic sites, collect antiques, search for our families' genealogy, and watch reenactors portray what life was like any number of years ago—all to get a sense of who we were and who we are.

Ironically, with our seemingly growing infatuation with how life used to be, those of us who teach the subject of history at the elementary, high school, or college level are all too aware of the "curse." Unlike the curse of Howard Carter, who unearthed the tomb of Tutankhamen in 1922 (another one of those interesting historical stories you should read about), our curse is that of the countless number of people who constantly remind us how boring and useless they feel the subject of history actually is.

Case in point: a few years ago I was waiting at Chicago's O'Hare Airport for what turned out to be a long-delayed flight due to a snowstorm. Having plenty of time to kill, I opened a book dealing with what I consider to be a fascinating topic, the Philippine-American War of 1899–1902. Halfway through my reading I caught, out of the corner of my eye, a young man who was desperately looking to talk to anyone. This chatty young man and I unfortunately made eye contact, and he began to talk to me as if we had known each other for years. Finally, after listening to his prattling on about his great job, the countless women who were interested in him, and how incredibly brilliant he was, he asked me what I did for a living. With a great deal of pride, I looked at him and said, "I am a history professor at a college in Indiana." To which he looked at me and with a pained look on his face said, "Man, that must suck! History is like the worst subject ever." Needless to say, our conversation ended immediately and I happily went back to reading my book.

Unfortunately for those of us who teach history, chance encounters at airports are not the only times when we are informed that people do not necessarily like our topic or profession. While many people as adults seem to embrace and love our history, young people (and I would argue that those of us who are now adults also fell into this same trap when we were young) look at the subject of history as boring, mundane, and unnecessary.

Part of the problem, I believe, is that many young people do not understand how history is researched and written about, nor do they see or understand the impact past decisions have on their lives today. Sadly, even fewer students have any concept that history is constantly being affected by individual historians as well as our society's own biases, prejudices, perspectives, and interpretations. All too often, I meet people who believe that history is written in stone and that it never changes—that it is just a series of dates and names one is forced to memorize.

I found proof of this belief while attending a conference at Oxford University. There, I was approached by a fellow attendee who taught a subject matter other than history at a well-known U.S. university. When she discovered that I taught history, the first words out of her mouth were, "It must be nice to teach history since you never have to change anything." Like this college professor, many people have an image of the gray-haired college professor (or the high school history teacher) reading from the same notes written on the same legal pad that they originally used in 1974. The common misperception of the field of history is that once something has been written down it stays that way forever. A book written in 1806 about the American Revolution is, many believe, the exact same book that would be written in 1906 or 2006. This just is not true.

The subject of history is a unique topic in the academic world. History teachers, more times then not, are forced to teach their class within the confines of an academic building; rare is the school administrator who allows history classes to go on archaeological digs, visit museums, bring in guest speakers, or buy the necessary books—which include both primary and secondary sources—needed to get a full grasp of the subject. While the English department can have its students read the great literary works, science courses can perform in-class experiments, and math, physical education, band, choir, and industrial arts all have the opportunity to allow their students to be active and create things, history, on the other hand, tends to be viewed as being more stagnant. Finding it extremely difficult to leave the building, bring in guest lecturers, or reenact the Battle of Gettysburg or the Trail of Tears, most teachers use what is at hand—mainly the U.S. history textbook. Therefore, the textbook becomes an essential part of how U.S. students learn about their past.

While the Internet is beginning to help bring new source materials into classrooms across the United States, most teachers cannot rely on Internet access, sufficient numbers of computers, or financial assistance to truly dive into the work of making their students "junior" historians. Therefore, the enormous modern U.S. history textbook, with its glossy pictures and glossed-over historical content, its formulated "debates" and numerous graphs, pictures, and charts, becomes the essential aid for history teachers to get their students to learn about U.S. history. By no means the perfect solution to all the problems that plague teaching U.S. history, the behemoth U.S. history textbook is arguably the most essential tool in the history classroom today—as it has been for nearly two centuries.

The use of textbooks in high school history classes goes all the way back to the late 1700s. The first U.S. history schoolbooks published in this country were not actually considered "U.S. history textbooks"; rather, books such as Noah Webster's *An American Selection of Lessons in Reading and Speaking* (1794) and Jedediah Morse's *Geography Made Easy* (1798) were both complete schoolbooks that included sections dealing with historical events. Webster's book focused on lessons in reading and rhetoric, and included stories with a historical dimension. In some editions of Morse's book there were sections dealing with a chronology of historical events, but no real research or historical interpretation could be found in any of these passages.

There is little agreement as to when the first proper U.S. history textbook was published. While many give credit to Webster and Morse for incorporating history into their textbooks, others claim that John M'Culloch actually published the first U.S. history textbook, *A Concise History of the U.S. from the Discovery of America till 1795* (1795). M'Culloch's work was basically a series of public papers, a summary of the American Revolution, and a handful of articles, but again was not a history textbook in the sense we mean today. Rather, that title should go to Joseph Worcester and his textbook *Elements of History* (1827), which is considered the "first comprehensive, practical American history school textbook."[1] Worcester's book proved to be popular in the nineteenth century and went through several editions.

The obvious answer to the question of why U.S. history textbooks did not immediately appear in American history classes is that there was little unity among the colonies prior to the American Revolution and the signing of the U.S. Constitution. Instead of a comprehensive history of the United States (since the country was in its earliest stages of formation at this point), Americans in the late eighteenth and early nineteenth centuries seemed to be more interested in reading about their own states. This all began to change in the 1830s when large numbers of European immigrants started to move to the new United States. For many "old-stock"

Americans, it became evident that the Americanization process should be accelerated. How to do this was simple: use the newly formed public tax-supported common schools to teach these new young immigrants what it means to be an American. Some of the first steps in accomplishing this was to make English classes as well as courses on U.S. history and government a mandatory part of the curriculum.[2] Time and again, publishers and authors informed teachers that the role of such a course would be to improve students in the following areas: character training, patriotism, good citizenship, and improved memory and thinking. Textbooks wanted students to become better, more informed citizens, and it was up to the teacher to make sure this was accomplished.

Throughout much of the eighteenth, nineteenth, and early twentieth centuries, most American students were taught by teachers in small, country schools who themselves often lacked anything more than a high school education. The image of Laura Ingalls Wilder's one-room schoolhouse was more often the norm for most American students before the 1940s. With a large number of these teachers having little to no college education, the problem remained that few teachers ever really had an opportunity to study American history in any depth. Rather, like their students, they had to rely on the history textbooks that the local administrators had purchased for them.

Looking at history textbooks written over the past two hundred years, it is obvious that authors and publishers understood this lack of historical knowledge. One frequently finds a number of pages at the beginning of these textbooks for "the teacher," explaining how to go about teaching this subject and what questions to assign. The typical curriculum was either a series of questions (the answers to which could easily be found in the text) or memorizing and reciting passages for the teacher, or the class. In some cases, the textbook authors even suggested that the teacher should bring the community in so they could listen to the students recite passages in order to "prove" that learning had occurred.

Lack of historical education, community pressure, and low pay all hindered the teachers' ability to convey the concepts of historical perspectives, bias, and interpretation to their students. Teachers sometimes had to teach classes with only a dozen textbooks or less, no matter how many pupils they had. In classrooms such as this, it would have been common to see students either sharing their textbooks or working in shifts. This practice was common in the United States well into the twentieth century. It was not uncommon, furthermore to find official directives from administrators or school boards informing teachers that old textbooks should be used as long as possible.[3]

Unfortunately, this may still be the case in some school districts across the United States yet today. In 1992, when I took my first high school history teaching job, I was blessed with nineteen textbooks for nearly ninety students. The textbook I was given to use in this class had actually been published in 1974 and was nearly falling apart. When I questioned the superintendent about the opportunity to update these texts, I was informed that since history never changes, neither should our textbooks.

This concept of holding on to old textbooks is long-standing, tried and true. If it's not an administrator who is holding on to an old textbook in order to save money, it is the publishing firm that is basically reusing the exact same textbook over a long stretch of time. Many of our U.S. history textbooks have gone through numerous editions over the course of the past two centuries. Authors such as Noah Webster, Samuel G. Goodrich, Charles A. Goodrich, and Marcius Willson dominated the textbook market in the 1800s with popular works. In the twentieth century, it was names such as Harold Rugg, David Saville Muzzey, and Charles Beard that became synonymous with history textbooks.

While the history textbook market was predominantly male, a few nineteenth-century textbooks did have female authors. Emma Willard (1787–1870) wrote *Republic of America* (1856), which was a popular textbook for a long period of time. Willard also worked at the Troy Female Seminary and was an early advocate for educational opportunities for girls in the United States.[4] Esther Baker's *A Brief History of the United States* (1871), part of the better-known "Barnes Historical Series," was published well into the 1930s and was also fairly well received.[5] Finally, Mara L. Pratt's *American History Stories* (1889) was a four-volume set that focused a great deal of attention on early American history. These three were the most noted female textbook authors until the 1970s. Since the 1970s, we now see female co-authors on most U.S. history textbooks published in the United States.

The nature of textbook publishing has change dramatically over the years. In the 1800s, there were no large publishing houses, as there are today, and textbook authors typically had to rely on local printing shops that would do the printing, marketing, and selling of a textbook. Also, prior to the standardization of copyright laws in the 1900s, many authors flat-out plagiarized other people's work, and there was sometimes considerable overlap from one textbook to the next.[6]

The late 1890s was a turning point in the way history was taught in the United States. In 1892, the American Historical Association formed the Committee on History, Civil Government, and Political Economy (aka the Committee of Ten), its mission was to solve problems between high school and university programs, and help in standardizing the curriculum. While few schools in the United States actually adopted the committee's recommendations, this group did assist in making history one of the core disciplines in the new field of social studies—which was becoming an essential part of the secondary curriculum in schools all across the United States.[7] By making history one of the core subjects in most high schools, the need for more textbooks obviously followed.

These more general changes strongly influenced the use and writing of history textbooks. Before the 1890s, for example, New England received a great deal of attention in U.S. history textbooks. Not only were most of the largest publishing firms of that time found in New York, Philadelphia, and Boston, but many of the early history textbooks were written by New Englanders.[8] After 1900, this New England stranglehold was loosened, as textbooks increasingly dealt with more national issues and began to portray U.S. history in more of a grand, sweeping narrative, rather then just focusing on a series of individual states. It was no coincidence that textbooks made such a shift soon after the Committee of Ten recommended that every school in the United States incorporate history into its curriculum.

With this need for more textbooks, and following World War I, U.S. history textbooks in the United States began to be mass-produced and marketed nationally (or at least regionally) for high schools. Where plagiarism and copyright laws were all but ignored in the nineteenth century, by the mid-twentieth century smaller textbook publishers were being bought up by larger publishing houses, and issues of plagiarism became more significant and obvious. This trend continued through the 1980s and 1990s when even-larger corporations devoured other publishing firms. Today, all the familiar publishing names of twenty years ago have been swallowed up, to the point that it is now argued that only four major publishing firms control the entire textbook market.[9]

This need for textbooks also caused a new trend starting around the 1920s, when publishing houses typically hired a group of editors to "develop" textbooks, in sharp contrast to the "great author" texts of the 1800s. In many situations, we can find a familiar name (for those in the know) attached to a U.S. history textbook, even though this person may have never worked on this project; or, in some cases, an author actually wrote the textbook but passed away years before the latest edition was published.[10]

Another situation affecting how textbooks are published started in the 1950s, when many U.S. history textbooks had to go through an adoption process in many states.[11] While twenty-eight states presently do not have a formal adoption process—meaning local teachers can choose whichever textbook they think best fits their needs—twenty-two states do have a formal adoption process. Usually set on a six-year buying cycle, a state committee will suggest a textbook (or a series of textbooks), and once adopted the state will purchase these textbooks in bulk to be used by every public school within that state. Obviously, getting the entire textbook market in a state is a financial boom for one publishing firm and can be a financial disaster for those not on the official state committee list. Of all the states that go through this process, California and Texas are of key interest to textbook publishers. Due to the enormous size of these two states (and thus the value of the contract to the publishing firm that gets it), many U.S. history textbooks in the past few decades have been written and marketed specifically with California and Texas in mind. Therefore, if a vocal special-interest group in either of these states does or does not want certain things in their high school history textbooks, publishing companies almost always kowtow to their pressure. What is deemed as "historically accurate and appropriate" in these two states usually then affects what the rest of the country learns about U.S. history.

The impact of textbooks on our society has not escaped the arena of politics. Conservatives and liberals in this country have been fighting over the content of our history textbooks for decades, and it does not seem as if they are going to find any common ground soon. A few years ago, I had the opportunity to listen to a liberal commentator discuss what was wrong with our U.S. history textbooks. His argument was that they glorified the past, and that instead history textbooks should include both the good and the bad, or as he phrased it, textbooks should be written "warts and all." Then, a number of months later, while watching television, I listened to a group of conservatives bemoan the problems in U.S. history textbooks, mostly asserting that special-interest groups on the Far Left have taken over history textbook publishing, and that all U.S. history textbooks do today is glorify minority, ethnic, and socially disadvantaged groups, all the while dwelling on all the negative things that have happened in the past. Textbooks, they contended, should extol the virtues of America's past by emphasizing great leaders and heroic events. Interestingly, one of these conservative commentators also added that our textbooks should be written with both the good and the bad, or as he put it, our textbooks should be written "warts and all."

It is with the concept of textbooks being written warts and all that this project was undertaken. This book is not meant as an attack on U.S. history textbooks or their publishers. Rather, my aim is to help people understand that the U.S. history textbook they are currently using, or the one they had back in high school, was not written by the goddess Clio (the Greek muse of history), who kindly passed her stories from on high to us mere mortals below. My goal is to play the role of a history educator in order to show that history textbooks over the past two hundred years have been written, published, taught, and studied by people with personal biases, perspectives, and interpretations of what our past was like, and the impact that has for us in the modern day as well as the future.

Students of history are rarely, if ever, asked to criticize what they read in their U.S. history textbooks or any historical research, nor do people question a textbook's point of view. We as history educators would be better served if they did. For by forcing people to dissect and question their U.S. history textbooks and their understanding of history, we get closer to lifting the veil off the knowledge we have that our history is not only an important subject for a society but also an intriguing and inspirational story as well. And hopefully, in the long run, we can destroy the curse and let others in on the secret that history is not written in stone but is actually a subject that needs discussion, debate, and research to keep it alive and interesting to all.

After fifteen years of teaching U.S. history at all levels, I must admit that I felt a sense of relief when I discovered that within many textbooks, going as far back as the early 1800s, one could find "graffiti" in the margins of a great many U.S. history textbooks. It was liberating to discover that it was not only my students who found the topic sometimes boring, unfortunately, it has been a problem throughout the ages. All too often, while conducting my research, I would find a message scrawled into a textbook informing me that a student did not particularly like that textbook, the teacher, or the topic of history in general. My personal favorite came from the 1850s, when a student felt the need to write in their textbook, "If poison won't kill ya, try reading this."

Obviously, this student did not appreciate how important the role of bias, interpretation, and perspective are in the study of the fascinating and vital topic of history. Hopefully, future students will.

PART I

Exploration and Colonization

I

Native American Relations
with the New Settlers

Native Americans play an interesting role in most U.S. history textbooks written over the past two centuries. From the founding of the country until approximately the early 1900s, Native Americans were seen as opponents to U.S. progress. American students learned throughout the 1800s that these "savages" consistently fought white Americans and their desire to expand and improve this country.

Then, starting in the late 1800s to early 1900s, U.S. students began to learn about the concept of the "noble savage." This was the belief that although Native Americans could be barbaric in warfare and culture, they were also uncorrupted by civilization.

All of this changed in U.S. history textbooks by the 1960s and 1970s, when students were given both a more anthropological view of Native American society as well as a more balanced version of what life was like when the Native Americans first met their European counterparts.

1844

Place yourself in a school classroom in 1844, when a Native American tribe might well have been a neighbor, and one can only imagine the impact a history lesson such as

this would have had on the young white students who read it, especially the "fact"
that these new neighbors were all cannibals.

In the ancient world, tradition has preserved the memory of barbarous nations of cannibals, who fed on human flesh. But in every part of the New World there were people to whom this custom was familiar. It prevailed in the southern continent, in several of the islands, and in various districts of North America. Even in those parts, where circumstances, with which we are unacquainted, had in a great measure abolished this practice, it seems formerly to have been so well known, that it is incorporated into the idiom of their language. Among the Iroquois, the phrase by which they express their resolution of making war against an enemy is, 'Let us go and eat that nation.' If they solicit the aid of a neighboring tribe, they invite it to 'eat broth made of the flesh of their enemies.' Nor was the practice peculiar to rude unpolished tribes; the principle from which it took rise is so deeply rooted in the minds of the Americans, that it subsisted in Mexico, one of the civilized empires in the New World, and relics of it may be discovered among the more mild inhabitants of Peru. It was not scarcity of food, as some authors imagine, and the importunate cravings of hunger, which forced the Americans to those horrid repasts on their fellow creatures. The rancour [*sic*] of revenge first prompted men to this barbarous action. The fiercest tribes devoured none but prisoners taken in war, or such as they regarded as enemies. Women and children, who were not the objects of enmity, if not cut off in the fury of their first inroad into a hostile country, seldom suffered by the deliberate effects of their revenge.[1]

1856

By 1856, most of the Native Americans who had previously lived east of the Mississippi
River had either been forced off their land—such as the Cherokee (in the infamous Trail
of Tears), Creek, Chickasaw, and Choctaw—or killed by disease and warfare. There-
fore, for students living in the eastern part of the United States who had little contact
with Native Americans, stories like the one below became interesting tidbits of histor-
ical knowledge, while for those white Americans who had traveled west to find land
and gold, many of these stories served as an introduction to their new neighbors.
Without a tinge of sorrow or regret, this passage informed students that in the future,
Native Americans will not really be a concern because "they will entirely disappear."

The Indians were proud and happy when they were engaged in combat with the tribes around them. Next to these wars they were best pleased with hunting, for this was a species of fighting, the wild animals in the forest that they pursued being looked upon somewhat as foes. They, however, despised all labor. They sometimes possessed fields of corn, but they compelled the women to plant and hoe it, and to perform all other domestic labors. They would themselves do nothing when at home except make bows and arrows, or carve ornaments upon their clubs, or fashion other warlike weapons. To hunt and to fight was honorable, but labor in any branch of useful industry they considered beneath them.

When America was discovered and began to be settled by the whites, the Indians were gradually forced to retire from those parts of the country which the white men occupied.

Occasionally quarrels would arise, which would lead to wars between the Indian tribes and the white settlers. In these cases, the Indians would sometimes come rushing into the villages at midnight with dreadful yells and outcries, and massacre the inhabitants and burn the houses. At other times they would lurk in ambush among the tree near the fields where the white men were at work, and shoot them with the guns and gunpowder which they had bought of them before.

Not infrequently it happened that children from the families of some of the settlers were seized and carried off as captives, and kept in the wigwam for many years. Whenever the Indians succeeded in getting a white child in their possession in this way, they usually treated him kindly, and often made him a favorite and pet. They regarded him and treated him much as a boy would treat a young squirrel or young fox that he had succeeded in catching in the woods and bringing home. Still it was a dreadful calamity to the poor child to be taken thus away from his father and mother, and from the comforts and pleasures of his home, and compelled to dwell all his life with these rude and cruel savages.

The chief articles that they bought of the white men were gunpowder and rum, and the rum exerted an awful influence in demoralizing and destroying them. The effect of it upon them was to make them perfectly insane, and the imagination can scarcely conceive the horrors of the drunken orgies, which were sometimes witnessed around the midnight fires.

From these causes the Indians have been gradually melting away and disappearing, until now there are few left on this side of the Mississippi River. Beyond the Mississippi the country is still filled with them, but their numbers are gradually diminishing, and there is no doubt that in time they will entirely disappear.[2]

1874

Written amid the Plains Indian Wars of the 1870s, this excerpt takes great pains to emphasize to students the "warlike" characteristics of Native Americans.

Aborigine

When our ancestors first landed upon the shores of the New World, they found it an almost unbroken wilderness, inhabited by numerous tribes or clans of Indians, each tribe under its own sachem, or chief. Of their number, when the English settled among them, we have no certain estimate. They probably did not exceed one hundred and fifty thousand within the limits of the thirteen original states.

The different tribes within the boundaries of the United States were nearly the same in their physical characteristics. In person the Indians were tall, straight, and well-proportioned. Their skins were red, or of a copper brown; their eyes black; their hair long, black and coarse. The same moral characteristics were common to the different tribes. They were quick of apprehension, and not wanting in genius. At times they were friendly, and even courteous. In council, they were distinguished for gravity and eloquence; in war, for bravery and address. They were taciturn and unsocial, except when roused by some strong excitement. When determined upon revenge, no danger would deter them—neither absence nor time could cool them.

Of their employments, war was the favorite. Their weapons were war-clubs, hatchets of stone called tomahawks, and bows and arrows. Their warlike expeditions usually consisted of small parties, and it was their glory to lie in wait for their enemy, or come upon him by surprise. They rushed to the attack with incredible fury, and at the same time uttered their appalling war-whoop. Their captives they often tortured with every variety of cruelty, and to their dying agonies added every species of insult. Next to war, hunting and fishing were esteemed honorable. In the former, the weapons of war became the implements of the chase; in the latter, they used nets made of thread twisted from bark or from the sinews of the moose and deer; for fish-hooks, they used crooked bones. Their arts and manufactures were, for the most part, confined to the construction of wigwams, bows and arrows, wampum, ornaments, stone hatchets, and mortars for pounding corn; to the dressing of skins, and the waving of mats from the bark of trees, or from a coarse sort of hemp. Their agriculture extended not much beyond the cultivation of corn, beans, peas, potatoes, and melons. Their skill in medicine was confined to a few simple prescriptions and operations. When they knew no remedy, they resorted to their powwow, or priest, who undertook a cure by means of sorcery. The Indians, however, were liable to few diseases compared with the number that prevails in civilized society. Their women, or squaws, tilled their scanty fields. And performed the drudgery connected with their household affairs.

They had no books, or written literature, except rude hieroglyphics; and education was confined to the arts of war, hunting, fishing, and the few manufactures which existed among them. Their language was rude, but sonorous, metaphorical, and energetic, and well suited to the purpose of public speaking.[3]

1880

It is important to note that over the last two hundred years, U.S. history textbooks have loved the concept of "progress." A vast majority of the textbooks looked at for this study spend at least part of their time discussing America's newest technology and improvements in society. Within this context, this passage, found in the Barnes Historical Series, one of the more popular U.S. history textbook publishers in the 1800s, explains to students exactly what Native Americans are like and, in the end, offers the best solution as to how to save these people from utter destruction.

The Indians were the successors of the Mound Builders, and were by far their inferiors in civilization. We know not why the ancient race left, nor whence the Indians came. It is supposed that the former were driven southward by the savage tribes from the north.

INDIAN CHARACTERISTICS

Arts and Inventions—The Indian has been well termed the "Red Man of the Forest." He built no cities, no ships, no churches, no schoolhouses. He constructed only temporary bark wigwams and canoes. He made neither roads nor bridges, but followed foot-paths through the forest, and swam the streams. His highest art was expanded in a simple bow and arrow.

Progress and Education—He made no advancement, but each son emulated the prowess of his father in the hunt and the fight. The hunting-ground and the battlefield embraced every thing of real honor or value. So the son was educated to throw the tomahawk, shoot the arrow, and catch fish with the spear. He knew nothing of books, paper, writing, or history.

Domestic Life—The Indian had neither cow, nor beast of burden. He regarded all labor as degrading, and fit only for women. His squaw, therefore, built his wigwam, cut his wood, and carried his burdens when he journeyed. While he hunted or fished, she cleared the land for his corn by burning down the trees, scratched the ground with a crooked stick or dug it with a clam-shell, and dressed skins for his clothing. She cooked his food by dropping hot stones into a tight willow basket containing materials for soup. The leavings of her lord's feast sufficed for her, and the coldest place in the wigwam was for her.

Disposition—In war, the Indian was brave and alert, but cruel and revengeful, preferring treachery and cunning to open battle. At home, he was lazy, improvident, and an inveterate gambler. He delighted in finery and trinkets, and decked his unclean person with paint and feathers. His grave and haughty demeanor repelled the stranger; but he was grateful for favors, and his wigwam always stood hospitably open to the poorest and meanest of his tribe.

Endurance—He could endure great fatigue, and in his expeditions often lay without shelter in the severest weather. It was his glory to bear the most horrible tortures without a sign of suffering.

Religion—If he had any ideas of a Supreme Being they were vague and degraded. His dream of a Heaven was of happy hunting-grounds or of gay feast, where his dog should join in the dance. He worshiped no idols, but peopled all nature with spirits, which dwelt not only in birds, beasts, and reptiles, but also in lakes, rivers, and waterfalls. As he believed these had power to help or harm men, he lived in constant fear of offending them.

He apologized therefore, to the animals he killed, and made solemn promises to fishes that their bones should be respected. He placed great stress on dreams, and his camp swarmed with sorcerers and fortune-tellers.

THE INDIAN OF THE PRESENT

Such was the Indian two hundred years ago, and such he is to-day. He opposes the encroachments of the settler, and the building of railroads. But he can not stop the tide of immigration. Unless he can be induced to give up his roving habits and cultivate the soil, he is doomed to destruction. It is to be earnestly hoped that the red man may yet be Christianized, and taught the arts of industry and peace.[4]

1899

Nearly a decade after the Wounded Knee Massacre and with the Plains Indian Wars having come to an end, students still read about the savagery of Native Americans.

Accordingly, when Europeans began coming to America in 1492, they supposed it was Asia, and as they found the country peopled by red men, they called these red men "Indians." Europeans at that time knew very little about the inhabitants of Asia or India, else they would not have made such a mistake. The natives of America are not especially like Asiatics. They are a race by themselves. They have lived in America for many thousand years; just how long nobody knows. One thing is sure, however. Before ever white men came here, the red men had for long ages been spread all over North and South America, from Hudson Bay to Cape Horn, and differences of race had grown up among them. All alike had skins of a cinnamon color, high cheek bones, and intensely black eyes and hair, with little or no beard. But in respect of size, as of general appearance and manners, there were differences between different tribes as marked as the difference between an Englishman and an Arab.

THE SAVAGE INDIANS

Some of these Indians were much more savage than others. There were three principal divisions among them: (1) savage, (2) barbarous, and (3)

half-civilized. In North America the savage Indians lived to the west of
Hudson Bay, and southwardly between the Rocky Mountains and the Pacific coast, as far as the northern parts of Mexico. The Athabaskans, the
Bannocks, and the Apaches were, and are, specimens of savage Indians.
They had little or no agriculture, but lived by catching fish or shooting
birds or such game as antelopes and buffaloes. They were not settled in villages, but moved about from place to place with very rude tent-like wigwams. They wove excellent baskets, but did not bake pottery.

MORE ABOUT THE BARBAROUS INDIANS

The religion of these Indians was the worship of their dead ancestors,
curiously mingled with the worship of the Sun, the Winds, the Lightning,
and other powers of nature, usually personified as animals. For example,
lightning was regarded as a snake, and snakes were held more or less sacred. Religious rites were a kind of incantation performed by men especially instructed in such things, and called "medicine-men." In most
religious ceremonies dancing played a great part.

The Indians had dogs (of a poor sort) which helped them in the chase
and served also as food: but they had neither horses, asses, cows, goats,
sheep, nor pigs—no domesticated farm animals of any sort. Without the
help of such animals it is very difficult to rise out of barbarism into civilized
life. The Indian's supply of food was too scanty to support a dense population. The people lived in scattered tribes, without any government higher
than the tribe; and hence they were almost always at war. Fighting was the
chief business of life, and a young man was not considered fit to be married until he had shown his prowess by killing enemies and bringing away
their scalps. Such a kind of life tended to make men cruel and revengeful,
and the Indians were unsurpassed for cruelty. It was their cherished custom to put captives to death with lingering tortures.[5]

1912

*By 1912, the "Indian problem" had become a thing of the past, since Native Ameri-
cans had, for the most part, been removed to the reservations. This textbook re-
flects the new situation by portraying Native Americans less as a physical threat to
whites and more as "inferior" individuals who need to improve their ways. It also*

shows a change in how students read about Native Americans: for the first time, the history of these people and events are reported in a more detached way.

The earliest settlers in the English colonies were indebted to the Indians in several ways. They learned the Indians' methods of hunting, fishing, and trapping; also, the value of maize and how to produce it upon new land. Thus colonization was assisted by a more available food supply. The Indians' canoe and their methods of travel and fighting were also adopted by the settlers.

On the other hand, the natives soon acquired from the whites tools and utensils, especially guns; these, together with cloth and horses, changed in many ways the character of their daily life. They learned few virtues, but acquired destructive vices, especially the use of intoxicants. Some efforts were made by the English to convert the Indians, but they were conducted, on the whole, without enthusiasm or persistence. The loud profession of missionary zeal with which the English colonization began was not made good.

The history of Indian relations in colonial times is one of continual strife. This was inevitable at that period in the contact between a superior and an inferior race. Of incidental causes for these troubles there was a large variety; the vicious and the drunken, whether whites or Indians, were especially numerous on the frontier, and they were ever ready to commit outrages and to begin quarrels. But the fundamental cause for this condition was the land question. The character of Indian industry, which was mainly hunting and fishing, with comparatively slight attention to agriculture, and the frequent movements of most tribes from one locality to another, made the Indians occupants rather than owners of the land in the true sense. In their simplicity and short-sightedness they were ever ready to part with their right of occupancy; but they did not comprehend the white man's idea of permanent transfer and possession. The purchase of Indian lands was a universal practice in colonial times. The different colonial governments undertook to regulate this subject by law, prohibiting the settlers from occupying lands until the Indian title was extinguished. The laws enjoined in many ways the fair treatment of the Indians in other transactions; for instance, the sale of fire-arms and liquors was quite generally prohibited. These laws, however, were little obeyed.

Trouble arose as soon as the natives realized the slow but sure advance of the whites into the country and the permanency of this process. Hunting grounds were destroyed, and the strip between the frontier of settlement, and the Allegheny Mountains became gradually narrower. The Indians were able to make but spasmodic, and on the whole, feeble, resistance to the advance of settlement because they did not present a united front; and this in turn was owing to their lack of political organization.

Under these circumstances the result was inevitable: civilization triumphed over savagery, doubtless through the commission of innumerable wrongs, in our judgment of which we must remember the ethical standards of that time and the failure of each race to comprehend the other's point of view.[6]

1916

This textbook story is a perfect example of the stereotype of the Native American as a noble savage.

Traits of Character

Living an outdoor life, and depending for daily food not so much on the maize they raised as on the fish they caught and the animals they killed, the Indians were most expert woodsmen. They were swift of foot, quick-witted, keen-sighted, and most patient of hunger, fatigue, and cold. White men were amazed at the rapidity with which the Indian followed the most obscure trail over the most difficult ground, at the perfection with which he imitated the bark of the wolf, the hoot of the owl, the call of the moose, and at the catlike tread with which he walked over beds of autumn leaves to the side of the grazing deer.

Courage and fortitude he possessed in the highest degree. Yet with his bravery were associated all the vices, all the dark and crooked ways, which are the resort of the cowardly and the weak. He was treacherous, revengeful, and cruel beyond description. Much as he loved war (and war was his chief occupation), the fair and open fight had no charm for him. To his mind it was madness to take the scalp of an enemy at the risk of his own, when he might waylay him in an ambush or shoot him with an arrow from behind a tree. He was never so happy as when, at the dead of night, he roused his sleeping victims with an unearthly yell and massacred them by the light of their burning home.[7]

1920

Reinforcing the stereotype of the noble savage, this story from the 1920s does suggest a change in the way that the original encounters between the Native American and the white settler were being perceived in the classroom.

Character and Fate of the Indians

In character the Indian showed the most astonishing extremes, now immovable as a rock, now capricious as the April breeze. Around the council fire he was taciturn, dignified, thoughtful, but in the dance he broke into unrestrained and uncontrollable ecstasies. He bore with stoical fortitude the most horrible tortures at the stake, but howled in his wigwam over an injured finger. His powers of smell, sight, and hearing were incredibly keen on the hunt or the warpath, but at the same time he showed a stolid stupidity that no white man could match. The Indian seems to have been generally friendly to the European on their first meeting, and it was chiefly the fault of the white man's cruelty and treachery that the friendly curiosity of the red man was turned so often into malignant hatred instead of firm alliance.[8]

1927

Rather then just discussing ambushes, savagery, and the brutality that used to be associated with Native Americans, twentieth-century history textbooks began to take a more balanced view of their culture and society. This period also saw a change in how the Native American woman was portrayed: she was no longer a virtual slave to her "lazy warrior husband" but rather an important member of her society—although this 1927 passage still refers to her using the derogatory term "squaw."

Columbus Finds a Strange People in America

The people Columbus found in America were very different from the Europeans with whom he was familiar. As we have said, he called them Indians, and they have always been known by that name. Since they were to play a considerable part in the history of our country, it is desirable we should know what kind of people they were.

THEIR DIVISION OF WORK

Although the Indian was a true child of nature, with a wild love of freedom, his life was not, as some have supposed, an idle one. Hunting and fishing were his chief occupations, these being the necessary means by which he obtained his food. But the Indian brave was first of all a warrior. He had to defend his hunting-grounds and ward off attacks of hostile tribes; and sometimes he took the war-path for his own gain. When not following the war-path or the chase, he had to make his weapons. They were mainly the bow and arrow, the war-club, and the tomahawk. He also required canoes and snowshoes for covering distances, and these, with other necessary conveniences or tools, he made with his own hands.

The squaw, too, led a busy life. Digging with shells and pointed sticks, she cultivated the soil and gathered the crops. These were more varied in the South than in regions farther north, for the climate was warmer and more attention was paid to a rude kind of agriculture. Indian corn was the chief crop, but tomatoes, beans, pumpkins, squashes, and tobacco were also raised. Besides cultivating the soil, the squaw dried the meat brought home from the chase and dressed the skins, making from them moccasins and other wearing apparel, for the hunt supplied clothing as well as food. She also rudely fashioned the simple household utensils, gathered wood, made fires, cooked the food, and set up the wigwam when on the trail, for the brave was supposed to be busy providing game or guarding against the enemy.

THEIR CHARACTERISTICS WERE PRIMITIVE

The instincts of the Indian were untrained, but he could be kind and generous. In the midst of famine he would cheerfully share his last morsel with a fellow sufferer, and in the hour of danger would lay down his life for a friend. He was also capable of lofty ideas of right and duty, and frequently gave proof of them in making and keeping treaties and in the beautiful and poetic expression of his thoughts.

THEIR BELIEF IN THE AFTER-LIFE

The Indian had faith in good and bad spirits, but had no clear idea of one God over all. He believed that Indians, good and bad, would after this life go to the happy hunting-grounds. This was his name for heaven, where life, he believed, would continue with the same occupations as in this world. It is thought that the practice of scalping enemies killed in battle was associated with the belief that the loss of the scalp prevented the spirit from entering the happy hunting-grounds. The Indian would, therefore, take almost any risk to save the dead body of his chief or his friend from being scalped by the enemy. It was common practice to bury arms with the "brave," so that he might have them in the happy hunting-grounds. That he might lack no means of comfort other articles of common use also were buried with him.[9]

1961

By the 1960s, Americans had become much more conscious of the multicultural makeup of their country, due in part to the Civil Rights Movement that began in the 1950s. Many U.S. history textbooks started to inform their students that Native Americans were actually a diverse group of people who had a different way of life, rather then a backward or savage one. Students were told that some Native American tribes not only had "fairly advanced cultures" but also may have helped the new Europeans instead of just acting as barriers to American progress.

Ancestors of the Indians Come from Asia to Settle in the New World

The American Indian is the most truly "native American." Between 20,000 and 40,000 years ago, people from northern Asia—the ancestors of the American Indians—began crossing the Bering Strait from Siberia to settle in Alaska. Over a period of thousands of years, they pushed down from Alaska and spread through-out the length and breadth of North and South America. In time, they lost all contact with Asia and began to develop various cultures of their own. By the time of Columbus, there were millions of Indians spread thinly throughout the vast areas of the New World. They were divided into hundreds of tribes, with different languages and customs, and were isolated from one another by great distances.

Some of these tribes lived by hunting and fishing. Others learned to support themselves by agriculture. Most of them were in a primitive stage of development when Columbus reached the Caribbean. Some of them, however, like the Incas of Peru and the Aztecs of Mexico, had developed fairly advanced cultures. But, on the whole, the American Indians were at a great disadvantage when confronted by fifteenth- and sixteenth-century Europeans. Even the most advanced Indian tribes lacked the wheel, the plow, iron implements, and livestock. Nor did any of them possess ships or gunpowder.

THE EUROPEAN SETTLERS RECEIVE MUCH FROM THE INDIANS

Nevertheless, the Indians had much to teach the white man. From the Indian, European settlers learned of many new products: maize (Indian corn), white potatoes and sweet potatoes, tobacco, pineapples, peanuts, maple sugar, various kinds of beans, tomatoes, squash, pumpkins, chocolate, quinine, vanilla, and rubber. It is estimated that one-third of our agricultural products came originally from the Indians.

The ability of the early white explorers and fur traders to survive in the wilderness was due, in part, to the forest lore they learned from the Indians. Like the Indians, the European pioneers wore deerskin clothing, used canoes and snowshoes, and learned to move in Indian file and fight in open formation for greater safety. The European settlers also borrowed many Indian names for villages, cities, lakes, rivers, and mountains throughout America. The names of 26 of our 50 states are taken from Indian names. Thus, the heritage of the United States is Indian as well as European. The Indian was to play an important part in the white man's exploration and colonization of America. He was to prove valuable as a friend and dangerous as an enemy.[10]

1986

By the 1980s, the story of Native Americans in U.S. history textbooks changed a great deal. One can see the impact politics has played on the publishing of textbooks simply by noting that terms such as "Indian," "squaw," and "savage" are no longer a part of the textbooks' vocabulary. Students also read more about anthropological research rather then the historical hearsay they were given in textbooks written one hundred years earlier. Finally, women in Native American society are given a vastly different set of societal roles as compared to earlier textbooks.

What did it feel like to be among the first humans to reach this great, empty land? We know what the first astronauts experienced when they set foot on the moon. They were aware that they were doing something no one had ever done before. We do not know exactly what the first Americans experienced. They did not know that they were exploring a new continent. Understanding the difference calls for an act of historical imagination. Having a good historical imagination means being able to look at past events from the outside, keeping in mind what the people of the day knew, but at the same time remembering what they did not know.

Once in North America, the wanderers moved slowly southward and to the east, following the life-giving game and grasses. The distances they covered were enormous. It is 15,000 miles (24,000 kilometers) from their homeland in Asia to the southern tip of South America and 6,000 miles (9,600 kilometers) to what is now New England. Many thousand years passed before they had spread over all of North and South America.

As they advanced and multiplied, the first Americans gradually changed their ways of life. Some made their homes in fertile valleys, others in tropical jungles. Some settled in mountainous regions or in deserts. Each group had different problems, and each learned to see the world in different ways. As a result each society created its own culture.

A society is a group of families who live and work together and who have common values and patterns of behavior. The culture of a society consists of the special characteristics of the people who make it up: the language they speak, their government, how they make a living, their family relationships, how they educate their children. Some sense of how many different cultures these first Americans and their descendants created comes from the fact that the peoples of North and South America spoke between 1,000 and 2,000 languages.

EARLY AMERICAN CULTURES

About 500 years ago there were more than 25 million people living in North and South America. Only about 1 million of these inhabited what is now the United States and Canada. Partly because they were so few in number and spread over such a huge area, these people had developed a number of distinct cultures. But they had many things in common. Most did not rely entirely on hunting and living off berries, fruits, and other wild plants. Many were farmers. Seed corn 4,000 years old has been found in caves in the Southwest. Those who planted seeds and cultivated the land instead of merely hunting and gathering food were more secure and comfortable. People who had mastered farming, or agriculture, could settle in one place instead of roaming in constant search of food. They built permanent houses. Their societies grew to include more members.

These agricultural people were mostly peaceful, though they could fight fiercely to protect their fields. The hunters and wanderers, on the other hand, were quite warlike because their need to move about brought them frequently into conflict with other groups. Some early American cultures were matrilinear, which means that family relationships were controlled by the female side. When a man and woman married in such a society, the man became a member of his wife's social group, or clan. A typical household might consist of an older woman, her daughters, and her granddaughters. Of course, the woman's husband, her sons-in-law, and her grandsons would also live in the household group. But only the female members were truly permanent members of the clan.[11]

2

The Vikings

The presence of the Vikings in U.S. history textbooks has become less and less important over the years. In the 1800s, textbooks gave a great deal of space to these seafaring adventurers. By the end of the twentieth century, the Vikings seem to have become more of a historical anecdote rather than crucial historical story for America's young to study.

1844

Most of the information we have about the Vikings' travels to North America comes from the Icelandic Sagas and archaeological findings. Today, while most Viking historians would agree that the Sagas are of immense historical importance, they are also quick to point out that there is a great deal of legend and myth interwoven into these tales—as opposed to this author's claim that the authenticity of the Sagas "seems indisputable."

The remarkable fact that in the tenth century the continent of America was visited by Europeans, who founded settlements on the shores of New England, seems to be fully substantiated by the Icelandic histories which have been brought to light within the last few years. According to these documents, the authenticity of which seems indisputable, the Northmen, who settled Iceland and Greenland, pushed their discoveries south as far as the coast of Massachusetts and Rhode Island; to which countries they gave the name of Vinland, from the wild grapes which they found growing there.

The first discoverer was Biarne, a young Icelander, who, on returning home from a voyage at the end of the summer of 986, found that his father had gone to Greenland. He sailed in pursuit of him, although he had never voyaged in that quarter, and was unacquainted with the route. For three days his voyage was prosperous; but then the sky became overcast, a strong wind blew from the north, and he was tossed about for several days, driving he knew not whither. At length, the sky grew clear, and after a day's sail, they descried an unknown land covered with woods and hills. Biarne sailed for several days along the coast, after which the wind shifted to the south, and he made his way north to Greenland.

This adventure was no sooner reported to Leif, the son of Eric the Red, a bold and enterprising young chief, than he determined upon an expedition to this newly-discovered region. He set sail, with thirty-five men, and, following the direction pointed out by Biarne, arrived in view of the unknown land. It was rude and rocky, with mountains covered with snow and ice. He named it Helluland, or the land of rocks. He next came to a flat region covered with forests, which he called Markland, or the woody land. Sailing still farther onward, and favored by a north-wind, he reached a delightful island near the continent. The soil was fertile, the ground was covered with bushes which bore sweet berries, and there were a river and lake, amply stored with salmon and other fish. The grass was covered with dew, sweet as honey. A German, named Tyrker, penetrated into the country, and came back in great exultation, announcing that he had discovered grapes. He showed them the fruit and they gathered large quantities; with which, and the timber they felled, they loaded their vessel, and returned home, naming the country Vinland.

The next adventurer was Thorwald Ericson, who sailed for Vinland in 1002. He arrived at a spot where Leif had built some huts, and to which he had given the name of Leifsbooths, spent the winter there, and caught fish. The next spring, he sent a party in his longboat to make discoveries to the southward. They found the country beautiful and well wooded, the trees growing nearly down to the water's edge. There were also extensive ranges of white sand. In 1004, Thorwald sailed eastward and then northward, passing a remarkable headland enclosing a bay; opposite to which was another headland. He called it Kialarnes, or Keel Cape. He then proceeded along the eastern coast to a promontory overgrown with trees, where he landed with all his crew. He was so well pleased with this place that he exclaimed, "This is beautiful; here I should like well to fix my dwelling." On the beach they found three canoes, and a number of Indians, whom the Northmen call *Skraellings*. They came to blows with them, and killed all but one, who escaped in his canoe. Afterwards a countless multitude came out of the interior of the bay against them. They endeavored to protect themselves by raising battle-screens on the ship's side. The *Skraellings* continued shooting arrows at them for a while, and then retreated. Thorwald was mortally wounded, and gave orders that they should bury him on the promontory, and plant crosses at his head and feet. From this circumstance the place was named Krossanes, or Cross Cape. The following year his men returned to Greenland.

Thorfinn, the brother of Leif and Thorwald, not discouraged by the fate of his kinsmen, fitted out another expedition in 1007. It consisted of three vessels, and one hundred and sixty men. They took with them various kinds of livestock, being determined to form a settlement if possible. In Helluland and Markland, they found much wild game. Sailing a great distance southwesterly, they arrived at Kialarnes, where they found long beaches and hills of sand, called by them *Furthurstrandir*. The land now began to be indented by inlets, and they found grapes and wild grain. They continued their course till they came to a bay penetrating far up into the country. At the mouth of it was an island, where the current ran very swiftly. Here the eider-ducks were so numerous, that it was scarcely possible to walk without treading on their eggs. They called the island *Straumey*, or Stream Island, and the bay *Straumfiord,* or Stream Firth. They landed on the shore of this bay, and made preparations for their winter residence. The company afterwards separated, and one party sailed further south to a place where a river falls into the sea from a lake. Opposite the mouth of the river were large islands. They steered into the lake, and called the place *Hop* (Hope). Grapes and wild grain were growing on the low grounds. Here they erected houses and spent the winter. No snow fell, and the cattle pastured in the open fields.

These voyages, and many others which the Northmen made to Vin-land, and of which the narratives are so minute and authentic as to place their truth beyond a doubt, render it an indisputable fact, that a consider-able part of the coast of America was known to these navigators. By a dili-gent examination of the routes pursued by them, and a comparison of the same with the coasts of Nova Scotia and New England, it appears that their excursions extended as far as Rhode Island. The bearings, distances and general description of the territories seen by the Northmen, corre-spond remarkably with the actual situation of the country. Hellerland is Newfoundland; Markland is Nova Scotia; Kialarnes is Cape Cod, and Furthurstrandir is the long sandy beach of that peninsula; Straumfiord is Buzzard's Bay; Straumey is Martha's Vineyard, and Hop is Mount Hope Bay, in Rhode Island; Krossanes is either Point Alderton at the entrance of Boston harbor, or the Garnet at Plymouth. The heights seen in the interior are Milton Hills.[12]

1881

Published three years after the end of Reconstruction, this textbook introduces the idea of race to the earliest period of European exploration. It is also notable that this story is absent from pre–Civil War textbooks.

"White-man's land." Subsequent parties of Icelanders are supposed to have visited the shores of what are now South Carolina and Georgia. The northern natives had told them of a "white-man's land" to the south-ward, where fair-faced processions marched in white robes, with banners at their heads, to the music of hymns. Though they never found this abode of pale-faces, the Northmen named it by anticipation, *Great Ireland;* and some wise men believe that Irish fishermen had indeed arrived on this con-tinent.

Thorfinn Karlsefne, a famous sea-king, reconnoitered the bays and harbors of the New England coast. Icelandic settlements were made, and a brisk trade was carried on with the natives, who were glad to exchange their furs for bright-colored cloth, knives, and trinkets. At least one little Northman was born on the American continent. His name was Snorri, and from him, in our day, the great sculptor, Thorwaldsen, and the learned philologist, Finn Magnusson, traced their descent.

In time, however, the people of Iceland ceased to hear from their brethren in America. The settlers, if any remained alive, became so mingled with the previous inhabitants that, when white men came again, their descendents were not to be distinguished from other barbarians on the coast.[13]

1914

In the early 1900s, history textbooks were no longer as certain about the Viking story as they once were. Starting in the late 1800s, the study of history became more of a science, and therefore mythical narratives were not going to be relied on as historical fact and included in history textbooks as much as before.

Long before any attempts were made to cross the Atlantic Ocean, the people who lived in Norway, Sweden, and Denmark had become daring and skillful sailors. They were called Northmen, or Norsemen, because they lived in the northern part of Europe. Their ships were long, carrying oars and sails, and having carved images on the bow. They sailed to Iceland and settled there, and afterwards sailed as far as Greenland. On the southwestern coast of Greenland, near Cape Farewell, these bold seamen founded a colony which lasted five hundred years, some ruins of which may be seen at the present day.

Soon after the Greenland colony was founded, one of the Norse leaders named Leif sailed westward with one ship and thirty-five men to see what he could find. Some sailors who had been blown off their course had told him there was land in that direction. After many days sailing he came to land somewhere in a strange country which he called Vinland or Vineland on account of the delicious grapes which grew there in abundance. We do not know where Vinland was or what shores the brave Norsemen saw, but we suppose they landed somewhere in Labrador, and then continued their voyage down the coast.

When they went back to the colony in Greenland they told strange stories of the fruits and timber they had found, and the wild people they had seen on those distant shores. The stories were written out afterwards, and are kept to this day. It is from them that we know of these early visitors to our country.

For a number of years ships went back and forth from Greenland to the new country. The sailors carried home fruit and timber, and told many stories of the wild natives they had seen.

All attempts of the Norsemen to found a colony in these strange lands failed. The natives were not friendly. They slew some of the settlers, and made so much trouble that the Norsemen gave up the effort to establish a colony. Their ships ceased to go back and forth, all records of their houses were destroyed, and the wild men of the West were left undisturbed by the wanderers from across the sea.

After all, we know very little of what the Norsemen did or what they saw in America. They may have come as far south as Rhode Island or Connecticut, but they left no houses or monuments to mark their paths. Their story is told in their old writings called the "Norse Sagas," from which we learn what kind of men they were, and we wonder where on our coasts their rude ships dropped anchor and what land their brave sailors explored.[14]

1954

By midcentury, the once-lengthy tale of Viking exploration to the New World had been reduced to a few concise paragraphs roughly reflecting the extent of historical knowledge about the Vikings at that point.

Expeditions of the Norsemen

The existence of lands to the west of Europe had been established long before the time of Columbus. The peoples of Norway, Sweden, and Denmark, who were called Vikings, lived in an area that encouraged turning to the sea for a livelihood. Beginning about the eight century, they began pillaging settlements at various points throughout western Europe. Some invaded England. Others established kingdoms in Normandy and in southern Italy and Sicily. Still others discovered Iceland and Greenland.

About the year 1000 an expedition under the leadership of Leif Ericson sailed still farther westward and stumbled upon the continent of North America. The heroic sagas of the Vikings describe a settlement on the mainland at a place called Vinland, probably somewhere along the coast of New England. News of the discovery seems to have had no effect on later exploration activities.[15]

1995

In the 1960s, Helge Ingstad, a Norwegian writer and explorer, came across the re-mains of a Viking settlement at L'anse aux Meadows, Newfoundland. Since then, al-though still influenced by the Icelandic Sagas, the history of the Vikings now primarily relies on archaeological evidence. Thus, with few historical facts and even less infor-mation in terms of a historical narrative to back up the story of the Vikings' discovery of the New World, by the end of the twentieth century the Viking story has dwindled to a brief passage in most U.S. history textbooks.

Viking Voyages

The Vikings were a bold, seafaring people from Scandinavia. In 1001, they settled briefly in North America, in a flat, wooded country they called Vinland. Today, archaeologists believe that the Viking settlement was lo-cated in present day Newfoundland, in Canada.

The Vikings did not stay in Vinland for long. No one is sure why they left. Viking stories, however, describe fierce battles with Skraelings, the Viking name for the Inuits.[16]

3

Columbus's Landing in the New World

Columbus, and his voyage to the New World, is one of those historical stories that makes it into every single U.S. history textbook. Up until the 1990s, Columbus was depicted as a great and brave man, and his story was used to teach young Americans that if they hold on to their convictions and ignore the naysayers, great things will come their way. Since Columbus shows up so often and usually has large sections of text dedicated to him, this section looks specifically at how textbooks dealt with the first contact made between Europeans and Native Americans.

1794

Originally published in the 1780s, Noah Webster's An American Selection of Lessons in Reading and Speaking *was used to improve students' grammatical and oral speaking skills, and therefore it would not be considered a "historical textbook" today. But by its third edition in 1787, approximately half of the entire book was dedicated to historical content, arguably making this textbook one of the first to record the historical events that led to the founding of the new nation.**

* In most printed material done before 1820, book publishers and newspaper editors did not use the letter "f" instead of the letter "s" within their text. Rather, they were using something called the "long S," which was actually a separate printed letter.

He [Columbus] therefore propofed that they fhould* obey his orders for three days longer and, fhould they not difcover land in that time, he would then direct his course for Spain.

They complied with his propofal; and, happily for mankind, in three days they difcovered land. This was a fmall ifland, to which Columbus gave the name of San Salvador. Their firft interview with the natives was a fcene of amufement and compaffion on the one part, and of aftonifhment and adoration on the other.

The natives were entirely naked, fimple and timorous; and they viewed the Spaniards as a fuperior order of beings, defcended from the Sun, which, in their ifland, and in moft parts of America, was worfhipped as a Deity. By this it was eafy for Columbus to perceive the line of conduct proper to be obferved toward that fimple and inoffenfive people.[17]

1830

The author of this textbook gives students an idealized view of Columbus and the Native Americans he seemed to have enchanted with his dress and behavior. Although highly overstated and lacking any real historical research, passages such as this must have given students in the 1830s a definite sense of being superior to these "simple" people.

At sunrise, Columbus, in a rich and splendid dress, landed, and, with a drawn sword in his hand, and displaying the royal standard, took possession of the island for the crown of Spain, all his followers kneeling on the shore and kissing the ground with tears of joy. The natives who had assembled in great numbers on the first appearance of the ships, stood around the Spaniards, gazing in speechless astonishment.

The Europeans were hardly less amazed at the scene before them. Every herb, and shrub, and tree was different from those which flourished in Europe. The inhabitants appeared in the simple innocence of nature, entirely naked. Their black hair, long and uncurled, floated upon their shoulders or was bound in tresses around their heads. Though not tall, they were well shaped and active. They were shy at first, through fear, but soon became familiar with the Spaniards; from whom, with transports of joy, they received

---

* An approximation of the "long S" (see the footnote on the previous page).

various trinkets, for which in return they gave such provisions as they had, and some cotton yarn, the only commodity of value they could produce.[18]

1880

Starting in the late 1800s, an interesting twist took place in the historiography of the Columbus story—Native Americans disappear completely. Now, Columbus and his men take over a new, completely uninhabited land.

On landing, he threw himself on his knees, kissed the earth, and returned thanks to God with tears of joy. His example was followed by the rest, whose hearts, indeed, overflowed with the same feelings of gratitude. Columbus then rising, drew his sword, displayed the royal standard, and assembling round him all who had landed, took solemn possession in the name of the Castilian sovereigns, giving the island the name of San Salvador. Having complied with the requisite forms and ceremonies, he called upon all present to take the oath of obedience to him as admiral and viceroy, representing the persons of the sovereigns.

The feelings of the crew now burst forth in the most extravagant transports. They had recently considered themselves devoted men hurrying forward to destruction; they now looked upon themselves as favorites of fortune, and gave themselves up to the most unbounded joy. They thronged around the admiral with overflowing zeal, some embracing him, others kissing his hands. Those who had been most mutinous and turbulent during the voyage were now most devoted and enthusiastic. Some begged favors of him as if he had already wealth and honors in his gift. Many abject spirits, who had outraged him by their insolence, now crouched at his feet, begging pardon for all the trouble they had caused him, and promising the blindest obedience for the future.[19]

1946

Columbus's taking the land and its people are justified in this 1946 except due to the fact that he did it for "their Highnesses." It is interesting to note that U.S. history textbooks written after 1945 would unanimously condemn Germany, Japan, and Italy for their aggressive acts of basically doing the exact same thing.

Setting out under the Spanish flag from the little harbor of Palos, in August, 1492, Columbus and his badly frightened crew reached one of the Bahama Islands the following October. "After a passage of seventy-three days," he wrote, ". . . I discovered very many islands inhabited by people without number: and of them all I took possession for their Highnesses with proclamation and the royal banner unfurled, no one offering any contradiction."[20]

1995

By the 1990s—amid widespread historical controversies surrounding the Columbus quincentennial—U.S. history textbooks began to question whether Columbus should be a celebrated hero or, as the following text suggests, regarded as a villain.

Columbus: Hero or Villain?

For years, Columbus has been remembered as the bold sea captain who "discovered America." In one sense, he deserves that honor. Europeans knew nothing of the Americas before Columbus brought them news of this "new world." Today, we recognize that other people "discovered" America long before Columbus. Still, his daring journey brought the peoples of Europe, Africa, and the Americas into lasting contact for the first time in history.

Native Americans, however, paid heavily for Columbus's voyage. Columbus and the Europeans who came after him forced native peoples to work in mines or on farms raising sugar cane and cotton. Over the next 50 years, hundreds of thousands of Caribbean Indians died from harsh working conditions and European diseases.

"Discovery" also cost Native Americans their lands. Starting with Columbus, Europeans justified seizing Indian lands. Some believed they had the right to take the lands because Indians were not Christians.

For better or worse, the rise of powerful nations in Europe signaled a new era for the Americas. Curious Europeans wanted to know more about the lands across the Atlantic. They saw the Americas as a place where they could trade and grow rich. Once Columbus reached the Americas, nothing could stop the flood of explorers and settlers who followed him.[21]

4

St. Augustine: America's First City

In the nineteenth century, U.S. history textbooks devoted considerable space to a series of stories about explorers from Portugal, Spain, and France. As the years went by, though, these stories started to fade. This trend is especially true of the French in America. The deeds of such men as Jacques Cartier, Samuel de Champlain, La Sieur de Salle, Jacques Marquette, and Louis Joliet were, up until the 1950s, a mainstay of U.S. history textbooks. Today, most of these early explorers are either glossed over quickly or completely ignored. Evidence of this French disappearing act from textbooks is portrayed in this section with the story of the Huguenots in St. Augustine.

1 8 4 2

By the mid-1830s John Frost's textbook, History of the United States *(1842), was condensed into a smaller, pocket-size book that he had subtitled "For the Use of Common Schools." This is significant because Frost's work was one of the more commonly used textbooks in the early 1800s; therefore, the story of the French and their colonizing efforts probably would have been heard by many U.S. students, giving them a more international perspective on American history.*

Thus far the Spaniards, although they claimed the whole coast of the United States under the name of Florida, had not effected a single settlement on the soil. For some years after Soto's failure the design seems to have been abandoned; until an attempt of the French to establish a colony in Florida awakened the jealousy of the Spaniards, and brought them forward once more, to revive and make good their claim to the land which had cost them so much blood and treasure.

Gaspar de Coligny, admiral of France, conceived the design of establishing a colony of French Protestants in America, which should afford a refuge to those who were persecuted for their religious opinions, during the civil wars with which his country was disturbed in the reign of Charles IX. He obtained a commission for this purpose from the king; and intrusted [sic] the expedition to John Ribault, who sailed with a squadron in February, 1562.

Having arrived on the coast of Florida in the latitude of St. Augustine, Ribault explored the coast, discovered the river St. Johns, which he called the river of May, and visited Port Royal entrance, near Beaufort, and having left a colony of 26 persons at a fort which he named Carolina in honour of Charles IX, he returned to France. The civil wars in that kingdom being revived, no reinforcements were sent out to the colony, and it was speedily abandoned.

On the return of peace (1564) Coligny was enabled to send out a new expedition under Laudonniere, an able and intelligent commander, who arrived on the coast of Florida in June, began a settlement on the river May, and erected a new Fort Carolina, many leagues to the south of its predecessor. Here they had to encounter the usual hardships and privations of settlers in a new country, till December of the same year, when a part of the colonists, under pretence of escaping from famine, obtained permission from Laudonniere to equip two vessels and sail for Mexico. But instead of doing so, they began to capture Spanish vessels. They were taken and punished, as pirates.

When the colony was nearly exhausted by the scarcity of food, relief was brought by the fleet of Sir John Hawkins, who furnished a supply of provisions, and made the offer of one of his vessels to convey the French to their own country. Just as they were preparing to embark, Ribault arrived with a reinforcement and ample supplies of every kind.

The colony had now a fair prospect of ultimate success. But it had been planted in a territory to which the Spanish had a prior claim, which, although dormant, was by no means extinct. An expedition was soon fitted out for the occupation of Florida; and its departure from Spain was hastened by the report that the country was already in possession of a company of settlers doubly obnoxious to the Spaniards on account of their nation and their religion. They were not only Frenchmen, but Protestants.

This expedition, commanded by Pedro Melendez, came in sight of the Florida shore in August, 1565. A few days afterwards Melendez discovered and named the harbour of St. Augustine, and learned the position of the French. Before attacking them, he landed at St. Augustine and took possession of the continent in the name of the King of Spain, and laid the foundation of the town. This interesting event took place on the 8th of September, 1565, more than forty years before the settlement of Jamestown in Virginia. St. Augustine can, therefore, boast a higher antiquity than the Ancient Dominion.

Meanwhile the French, having learned the arrival of the enemies, nearly all abandoned the settlement on the river May, embarked in their fleet, and were shipwrecked on the coast. The remnant were attacked and massacred by the Spaniards, who, in honour of the saint on whose festival the victory had been obtained, gave the river May the name of St. Matheo, or St. Matthew. Those Frenchmen who had survived the shipwreck of the fleet, surrendered to Melendez on a promise of safety; but they were nearly all put to death, many of them were hung on gibbets with the inscription over their heads, 'Not as French-men but as Protestants.' A few Catholics were saved from the massacre. After thus extirpating the French colony, the Spaniards sailed for their native country, leaving a force in possession of the settlement.

As the French government took no measures for punishing this aggression, Dominic de Gourgues, a French officer of some distinction, fitted out an expedition of three ships and one hundred and fifty men at his own cost, (1568) for the express purpose of avenging his murdered countrymen. He surprised the forts on the river St. Matheo, and captured a considerable number of prisoners, who were forthwith hanged upon trees with the inscription over their heads, 'I do not this as unto Spaniards or mariners, but as unto traitors, robbers, and murderers.' He then embarked without attempting to keep possession of his conquest. His acts were disavowed by the French government, and the Spaniards continued to hold the colony.

Thus it appears, that up to the year 1568, the Spaniards were the only nation holding possessions within the territory at present belonging to the United States. It was nearly forty years after this that England began the settlement of Virginia.[22]

1855

Forty years before the English settlement at Jamestown was founded, the French could not only lay claim to St. Augustine but also a failed colony in South Carolina. A historian might ask the counterfactual questions: What if the French had established the early colonies in America and not the English? How would that have changed U.S. history?

As early as the year 1562, a colony of Huguenots or French Protestants had been sent out by Admiral Coligny to found a home, free from persecution, in the New World. Reaching the southern coast of our country, they landed on a little island near the southern boundary of the present State of South Carolina, and raising a monument engraved with the lilies of France, they took possession of the country, and named it Carolina, in honor of Charles or Carolus IX king of France.

This feeble colony of twenty-six souls, receiving no supplies from France, soon became unhappy, and determined to return their native country. They built a small vessel, but neglected to take with them sufficient food. At sea, they endured all the horrors of famine; they were captured by an English vessel, a few landed on the coast of France, and the remainder were carried to England. Thus ended the French settlement of Carolina.[23]

1874

A consistent theme in this story over the years is the brutality of the Spanish Catholics toward the French Protestants. One has to wonder what impact these stories had on U.S. students who were Protestant, especially with the new influx of Catholic immigrants coming from Europe in the latter half of the 1800s.

The Huguenots

The celebrated Coligny obtained from King Charles IX permission to establish in America a settlement for French Protestants—Huguenots, as they were called. John Ribault led the expedition. In 1562 he reached Port Royal entrance, and built a fort, which, in honor of his king, he named *Carolina*—a name afterwards applied to the neighboring territory. Leaving a garrison of twenty-five men, he returned to France for supplies and reinforcements. But France was distracted by civil wars. Aid could not be obtained, and the colonists soon abandoned Carolina.

Two years later, a second colony of Huguenots came over, under Laudonniere, who had sailed with Ribault on the former voyage. This colony established itself on the banks of the St. John's in Florida. A second Fort Carolina was built. The next year Ribault arrived, bringing emigrants with their families, and abundant supplies. Spain, however, would not consent that land claimed by her should harbor Protestants and Melendez was commissioned to "root out the heretics." He took the settlement by surprise, and put most of the inhabitants to death with inhuman atrocity, "Not as Frenchmen, but as heretics," as he declared.

The French government made no attempt to avenge the destruction of the colony, but French Protestants were aroused to the highest pitch of indignation. Dominic de Gourgues sold his property, collected contributions from his friends, and fitted out an armament to retaliate upon the Spaniards. In 1568, he surprised the Spanish forts erected near the ruins of Fort Carolina, and hanged the garrisons, placing over them the inscription, "Not as Spaniards and mariners, but as traitors, robbers and murderers." De Gourgues, having accomplished his purpose of revenge, embarked for France. His king disowned the expedition, and Florida returned to the possession of Spain.[24]

1899

Published less then one year after the onset of the Spanish-American War, this textbook tells U.S. students about a long history of Spanish cruelty and barbarism.

The Huguenots in Florida

During this period, however, there was one memorable attempt at colonization which grew directly out of the wars of religion. The illustrious Protestant leader, Coligny, conceived the plan of founding a Huguenot state in America, and, in 1562–65, such a settlement was begun under the lead of Jean Ribault; but in the autumn of the latter year it was wiped out in blood by Pedro Menendez. That Spanish captain landed in Florida and built the fortress which was the beginning of the town of St. Augustine. Then he attacked the French colony, overcame it by surprise combined with treachery, and butchered everybody, men, women, and children, some seven hundred in all; a very few escaped to the woods, and after strange adventures made their way back to France.

According to the Spanish government, which laid claim to the whole of North America as lying west of the Line of Demarcation, these Frenchmen were trespassers or invaders, and deserved their fate. The government of France at that moment was too subservient to Spain to call her to account; but a private gentleman, named Dominique de Gourgues, took it upon himself to avenge his slaughtered countrymen. Having fitted out a secret expedition at his own expense, he sailed for Florida, surprised three Spanish forts, slew every man of their garrisons, and returned in grim triumph to France. This was early in 1568. Menendez was at that time in Spain, but he returned two years later, and the Spaniards kept possession of Florida.[25]

1933

Several decades later, this story was far less prominent in textbooks and had been greatly watered down. In this excerpt, the author claimed that the French were "wiped out," with no mention of any massacres, bloodthirsty ambushes, or hangings.

Florida Occupied

The success of the Spaniards and their great power in Europe awakened the jealousy of the French and English. The French attempted to found colonies in the New World and finally succeeded in planting a settlement on the east coast of Spanish Florida. The Spaniards had made several attempts to occupy Florida, but each expedition had met with disaster. When they heard of the French settlement, an expedition under Menendez was fitted out. In September, 1565, Menendez reached Florida and founded St. Augustine. He then proceeded to wipe out the French settlement. Several Spanish forts, towns, and missions were established along the coast, the most northern being a temporary mission on the James River, near the spot where about forty years later the English were to found their first settlement in the New World.[26]

1995

And then there were none. Most U.S. history textbooks today refer to the city of St. Augustine to let students know that Spain actually built the first city in the New World. The French settlements have become a historiographical casualty.

During their first hundred years in the Americas, the Spanish did not build settlements in the borderlands. The only exception was at *St. Augustine,* Florida, where a presidio was erected in 1565.[27]

5

Captain John Smith and Pocahontas

The story of the Jamestown colony, Captain Smith, and Pocahontas are staples of almost every U.S. history textbook. For over two hundred years, Smith's story has been repeated time and again to intrigue young students—from tales of his swashbuckling throughout Europe, to his bravery and cunning in the face of danger from Native Americans. The story of Pocahontas is equally prominent, but has changed more over time then Smith's. Pocahontas's role in the following stories says a great deal more about the time period in which each text was written then the actual historical character herself. Of particular interest is how often the textbook authors themselves question the story's validity. If they doubted much of its historical content, why did they then feel the need to incorporate it in their text?

1805

A public relations firm today probably could not give Smith more of a glorified spin then the passage below. Pocahontas, on the other hand, runs into a historical problem. By informing the English of her father's plans is she, as this text claimed, an "angel of peace" or, from the Native American viewpoint, a traitor to her people?

History of Pocahontas

Perhaps they who are not particularly acquainted with the hiftory of Virginia may be ignorant that Pocahontas was the protectrefs of the Englifh, and often fcreened them from the cruelty of her father.

She was but twelve years old, when Captain Smith, the braveft, the moft intelligent and the moft humane of the firft colonifts, fell into the hands of the Savages. He already underftood their language, had traded with them feveral times, and often appeafed the quarrels between the Europeans and them. Often had he been obliged alfo to fight them, and to punifh their perfidy.

At length, however, under the pretext of commerce he was drawn into an ambufh, and the only two companions who accompanied him fell before his eyes but though alone, by his dexterity he extricated himfelf from the troop which furrounded him; until, unfortunately imaging he could fave himfelf, by croffing a morafs, he ftuck faft, fo that the favages, againft whom he had no means of defending himfelf, at laft took and bound him, and conducted him to Powhatan.

The king was fo proud of having Captain Smith in his power, that he fent him in triumph to all the tributary princes, and ordered that he fhould be fplendidly treated, till he returned to fuffer that death which was prepared for him.

The fatal moment at laft arrived. Captain Smith was laid upon the hearth of the favage king, and his head placed upon a large ftone to receive the ftroke of death; when Pocahontas, the youngeft and darling daughter of Powhatan, threw herfelf upon his body, clafped him in her arms, and declared that if the cruel fentence was executed, the firft blow fhould fall on her.

All favages (abfolute fovereigns and tyrants not excepted) are invariably more affected by the tears of infancy, than the voice of humanity. Powhatan could not refift the tears and prayers of his daughter.

Captain Smith obtained his life, on condition of paying for his ranfom a certain quantity of mufkets, powder, and iron utenfils; but how were they to be obtained? They would neither permit him to return to James-Town, nor let the Englifh know where he was, left they fhould demand him fword in hand.

Captain Smith, who was as fenfible as courageous, faid, that if

Powhatan would permit one of his fubjects to carry to James-Town a leaf which he took from his pocket book, he fhould find under a tree, at the day and hour appointed, all the articles demanded for his ranfom.

Powhatan confented; but without having much faith in his promifes, believing it to be only an artifice of the Captain to prolong his life. But he had written on a leaf of few lines, fufficient to give an account of his fitua-tion. The meffenger returned. The king fent to the place fixed upon, and was greatly aftonifhed to find every thing which had been demanded.

Powhatan could not conceive this mode of tranfmitting thought; and Captain Smith was henceforth looked upon as a great magician, to whom they could not fhow too much refpect. He left the favages in this opinion, and haftened to return home.

Two or three years after, fome frefh differences arifing amidft them and the Englifh, Powhatan, who no longer thought them forcerers but ftill feared their power, laid a horrid plan to get rid of them altogether. His project was to attack them in profound peace, and cut the throats of the whole colony.

The night of this intended confpiracy, Pocahontas took advantage of the obfcurity; and, in a terrible ftorm which kept the favages in their tents, efcaped from her father's houfe, advifed the Englifh to be on the guard, but conjured them to fparc her family; to appear ignorant of the intelli-gence fhe had given, and to terminate all their differences by a new treaty.

It would be tedious to relate all the fervice which this angel of peace rendered to both nations. We fhall only add, that the Englifh, I know not from which motives, but certainly againft all faith and equity thought proper to carry her off. Long and bitterly did fhe deplore her fate; and the only confolation fhe had was Captain Smith, in whom fhe found a fecond father.[28]

1842

The relationship the very young Pocahontas had with an older white European male has been a controversial historical story that textbook authors have struggled with for two hundred years. In 1842, though, the issue was made quite clear.

While she [Pocahontas] was detained at Jamestown, Mr. John Rolfe, a young Englishman, gained the favour of the princess, and desired her in marriage. Powhaton consented; and with his daughter, the noble-spirited prince gave his heart. He was ever after the firm and sincere friend of the colony. The powerful tribe of the Chickahominies also 'sought the friendship of the English, and demanded to be called Englishmen.'

Though the marriage of Pocahontas was hailed as an auspicious event at the time, and has always been celebrated in the annals of the colony, it never operated as an example. The English and Indians would not intermarry, and the races have always remained distinct.[29]

1 8 6 6

Here is an example of historical storytelling in full flower, replete with vivid (mainly fictitious) detail and a clearly conveyed moral.

Two large stones were brought in, and laid at the feet of the savage king, and Smith's head was placed on one of them, while the savages gathered around to witness the execution. At length the club of the destroyer was raised, and every one was waiting in silent suspense to see it fall on the victim.

At this critical instant, Pocahontas, the eldest of the king's daughters, now scarcely twelve years of age, rushed forward with a shriek, and threw herself between the unhappy stranger and the executioner. Her hair was loose, and her eyes were wild and streaming with tears. She raised her hands to her father, and besought him, with all her power of eloquence, to spare his captive.

Powhatan, though little used to pity, could not resist her entreaties and tears. He paused, and looked round upon his warriors, as if to gather their opinion of what was proper to be done. They too were touched with pity, though they were savages. At last he raised his daughter, and promised her to spare the prisoner's life.

He was accordingly saved, and the very next day conducted by a guard of twelve men to Jamestown. He had been a prisoner about seven weeks. Before his departure he made a treaty with the king, by which he was to send back two cannon and a grindstone, for which Powhatan was to let him have a large tract of country, and forever regard him as his son.

He reached Jamestown in safety, but not wishing to send guns to the savages, he determined to frighten them. However, he brought forward the two cannon and a grindstone, but they thought them too heavy to carry. He then discharged the cannon, loaded with stones among the trees, which so terrified them that they were glad to return to Powhatan with a quantity of toys and trinkets in their stead.

Powhatan was greatly pleased with the presents, but Indian friendships are not always permanent. Some time afterward, his savage feelings became again excited against the English, and a plan was laid for cutting them all off at a blow, which, but for the interference of Pocahontas, would probably have succeeded. The day and the hour were set, and Pocahontas was informed of both.

The very night before the deed was to be done, in the midst of a terrible storm, which, with the thick darkness, kept the savages in their huts, Pocahontas proceeded to Jamestown, and revealed the plot. The colonists were, therefore, on their guard, and a part of them saved. This first Indian plot to massacre the English took place in 1609.

It does not appear that the savages ever found out who revealed their plan, for Pocahontas remained at her father's house for some time afterward. In the meanwhile, with the aid of Captain Smith, peace was once more established between the two nations.

Pocahontas, having now become the warm friend of the English, came every few days to the fort at Jamestown, with her basket of corn for the garrison, which proved of great service to them. At length, however, she was stolen by a foraging party of the white people, and a large sum was demanded of her father for her ransom.

Powhatan was unwilling to comply with the terms proposed, and began to prepare for a war with the English; and had it not been for an event as singular as it was unforeseen, a most fatal conflict would doubtless have arisen. A young Englishman, by the name of Rolfe, proposed to marry Pocahontas, and the proposal met with approbation of the king.

She accordingly professed the faith of the Christian religion, and was baptized from a font hewn from the trunk of a tree, in the little rugged church at Jamestown. Soon after she was married. She became a faithful wife and an exemplary and pious mother. Some of the principal families in Virginia are descended from this union of a young planter with an Indian princess.

In 1616, Pocahontas went with her husband to England, but she was unhappy there. Captain Smith, who was in London at the time of her arrival, called to her, but he was a little reserved in his manners toward her. This added to the intensity of her feelings, and she wept like a child.

Captain Smith inquired the cause of her grief. "Did I not save thy life," said she, "in America? When I was torn from the arms of my father, and conducted among they friends, didst thou not promise to be a father to me? Didst thou not say that if I went into thy county, thou wouldst be my father, and I should be thy daughter? Thou hast deceived me and behold me here, now, a stranger and an orphan!"

Captain Smith could not resist such eloquence. He introduced her to many families of respectability, and did all he could, while she remained in England, to make her happy; he never, however, ventured to bring her before the king. She fell a victim to the united influence of grief and the climate, and died at the age of twenty-two, as she was about to re-embark for America.[30]

1872

Even though the author of this textbook clearly questioned the validity of the historical story he was writing about, he nevertheless decided that it was such an important part of the study of American history that it must be kept in the narrative.

Accordingly he was bound, and his head placed upon a stone; but, just as the savages were raising their clubs to dash out his brains, Pocahontas, a daughter of Powhatan, rushed forward, clasped the captive's head in her arms, and begged that his life might be saved. It is further related that the conduct of Pocahontas touched her father's heart, and the sentence was revoked. Recent investigations, however, render it nearly certain that no such event ever took place.[31]

1897

This textbook discussed the story of the Rolfe-Pocahontas marriage in terms of international relations. Historical writing and teaching had become increasingly "professionalized" by the late 1800s, which is reflected in the sober tone and direct reference to historical sources.

In the course of the exploration Smith was captured by the Indians, and taken to their chief, Powhatan. The chief was "a tall, sour-looking old man"; he ordered his warriors to knock Smith's brains out. According to the valiant captain's account, he was saved by Pocahontas, the chief's youthful daughter, who ran up, just as the club was raised, and put her arms round the prisoner's head.(1)*

Some years afterward, John Rolfe, a colonist who had come over to Virginia at a later period, became interested in Pocahontas. He labored for the conversion of the tender-hearted heathen, and labored so effectually [*sic*] that she not only embraced Christianity, but took Rolfe for her husband besides. The marriage was a fortunate one, since it made Powhatan the firm friend of the colony at a time when it needed all the friends it could get. King James, however, shook his head over the matter, and questioned whether Rolfe, being a man without rank, had not committed treason in presuming to marry a native American princess![32]

1936

One has to question why this author felt the need to explain the story of Smith's near-death situation and then add the caveat that it is likely not true. Considering that history was seen as a science by a great many academicians in the 1930s, allowing a historical story with no fact into a textbook seems to be an odd choice.

A Born Leader—John Smith

The whole colony was in danger of extinction when John Smith took charge. He was a young man thirty years of age, but he had traveled much and had experienced many thrilling adventures. He was a strong character and a born leader. Under his direction the food supply was replenished by bartering with the Indians and the colony was saved.

Smith's explorations along the Virginian rivers and his experiences with the Indians make an interesting story. He made many journeys throughout the country to the west of Chesapeake Bay. On one of these voyages up the Chicahominy River he was captured by the Indians and taken before their chief, Powhatan, who controlled at least thirty-four tribes of the Algonquin race. His dominion extended from the Roanoke River to the head

---

* [Original footnote] (1)Certain inconsistencies in Smith's account of the affair have caused most recent historians to question the truth of his story; otherwise it is not at all improbable.

of Chesapeake Bay. Powhatan, according to an account by Smith, would have put him to death had it not been for Pocahontas, the chief's daughter, who, when Smith was about to be killed, threw herself between him and the executioner and saved his life. Some historians doubt the story. But everyone who has read about Virginia knows how John Rolfe, an English planter, fell in love with and married Pocahontas. To this day, Americans are proud to trace ancestry back to this couple.[33]

1978

By the latter half of the twentieth century, the heroism of Smith disappeared along with Pocahontas from the Jamestown story. Rather than a mythical story of these two characters, students begin to receive a more sophisticated understanding of the colony's history and its impact on the development of the United States.

Smith Becomes the Leader

Very likely the little settlement would have perished completely in those early years but for the efforts of one man, Captain John Smith. It was Captain Smith who saw to it that defenses were built against the Indians. He was firm in his dealings with the Indians and forced them to be cautious about attacking the new colony. Smith also insisted that the men work, that they plant corn for food and not spend their time digging for gold. He established the policy of "no work, no food." Even a lazy man will work rather than starve! In September, 1609, however, Captain Smith was badly burned by an explosion of gunpowder. He went back to England to receive treatment for his burns and to escape some violent quarrels with other colonists. He never returned to Virginia.

One of the early settlers, named John Rolfe, learned from the Indians how to produce fine tobacco. This plant was unknown to Europeans until they learned about it from the American Indians. Smoking soon became popular in England, so the Jamestown colonists found it easy to sell all the tobacco they could grow. The colony at last began to prosper. Workers were needed to grow tobacco, and many white indentured servants were imported. About this time, also, a Dutch ship brought 20 Negroes from Africa to Jamestown. The first of these blacks, who were indentured servants rather than slaves, proved very helpful as workers in the tobacco fields. Small farms gave way to large plantations. The colony now spread far beyond the limits of Jamestown and became known as Virginia.[34]

1995

As this excerpt reveals, Smith's story is simply too alluring to keep on the historical sidelines, despite the wealth of new knowledge about the Virginia colony and its development. There is perhaps no better example of the role of mythical stories in the teaching and learning of American history.

The Indomitable Captain John Smith

Virginia might have gone the way of Roanoke had it not been for Captain John Smith. By any standard, he was a resourceful man. Before coming to Jamestown, he had traveled throughout Europe, fought with the Hungarian army against the Turks, and if Smith is to be believed, was saved from certain death by various beautiful women. Because of his reputation for boasting, historians have discounted Smith's account of life in early Virginia. Recent scholarship, however, has reaffirmed the truthfulness of his story. In Virginia, Smith brought order out of anarchy. While members of the council in Jamestown debated petty topics, he traded with the local Indians for food, mapped the Chesapeake Bay, and may even have been rescued from execution by a young Indian girl, Pocahontas. In the fall of 1608, he seized control of the ruling council and instituted a tough military discipline. Under Smith, no one enjoyed special privilege. Individuals whom he forced to work came to hate him. But he managed to keep them alive, no small achievement in such a deadly environment.[35]

6

The Pilgrims Land in the New World

The Pilgrims' landing on the shores of modern-day Massachusetts has gone down in our textbooks (as well as our historical consciousness) as a major turning point in American history. This section looks at how U.S. history textbooks have taught generations of American students what life was like when the Pilgrims first landed and the months that followed.

It should be noted that these early settlers to the shores of North America were not the first true settlers of the continent. They were actually preceded by the Native Americans, the Vikings, the Spanish, and the Dutch, as well as other English colonists in Roanoke and Jamestown.

1794

This early piece laid the groundwork for the common belief expressed in most textbooks that a strong conviction and hard work were the keys to the Pilgrims' success. This image was a common theme in the historical narrative about the Pilgrims throughout nearly two centuries of history textbooks.

The same year in which this grant was made, a number of Puritans, who had experienced fome feverities from the intolerant fpirit of James and archbifhop Laud, fought a retreat in the wilds of America.

They, to the number of one hundred and one, arrived in the month of November, and feated themfelves at Plymouth, in Maffachufetts Bay. Here they fuffered all the inconveniences of cold, poverty, and ficknefs.

Many of them died, during the winter; but the free enjoyment of their religion, reconciled the furvivors to their new fituation. They bore their hardfhips with unexampled patience; and, by their induftry, foon procured a comfortable fubfiftence. Within eight years from the firft planting of Plymouth, the colony had become refpectable, by new emigrations from England.[36]

1838

Well into the 1900s, Christianity played an explicit role in U.S. history textbooks. God, in many of these earlier textbooks, was vital to the outcome of historical events, and Christianity is taken for granted as a commonly held belief system.

In the year 1620, a ship called the Mayflower arrived on the coast of New England. On board of this vessel were a number of ministers, and pious men and women. They had brought their children with them, for they never expected to return to their native land.

They had been driven from England by persecution, and they had come to this dreary wilderness, in order to worship God according to their own consciences. It was in the cold wintry month of December, when the Mayflower anchored in the harbour of Plymouth. The people went on shore, and the rock on which they landed has ever since been considered sacred.

They went to work and built themselves some poor huts. At first, they met with great difficulties and hardships. Many of them fell sick and died. The survivors were often in want of food, and were forced to dig for shellfish on the sea-shore.

In addition to their other troubles, the wild Indians sometimes threatened to attack them. But the Pilgrims were as brave and patient as they were pious. They put their trust in God, and steadily pursued their design of making a permanent settlement in the country.[37]

1844

The author of this book gave his students two unique stories about the Puritans—
ones not usually heard in the historiography of this event.

Their original purpose was to establish themselves on the Hudson; but
the Dutch, having designs of their own in that quarter, had bribed the captain of the Mayflower to mislead them, and, after a passage of sixty-three
days, they made the land at Cape Cod, on the ninth of November. But
"what could they see," says Morton, in his Memorial, "but a hideous and
desolate wilderness, full of wild beasts and wild men and what multitudes
there might be of them, they knew not. Neither could they, as it were, go
up to the top of Pisgah, to view from this wilderness a more goodly country, to feed their hopes. For which way soever they turned their eyes, save
upward to the heavens, they could have little solace or content in respect
of any outward objects. For summer being gone, all things stood for them
to look upon with a weather-beaten face; and the whole country, being full
of woods and thickets, represented a wild and savage hue. If they looked
behind them, there was the mighty ocean which they had passed, and
which was now as a main bar and gulf to separate them from all the civil
parts of the world." . . .

No Indians were seen, and the land was completely covered with a forest of oaks, pines, junipers, sassafras, "and other sweet wood." A party of
sixteen men, under Captain Miles Standish, each individual equipped
with a match-lock, sword and corslet, set out to explore the country. They
marched in single file along the shore, and at the end of a mile discovered
five or six Indians with a dog, who, on espying the English, ran into the
woods. Standish and his men tracked them through the forest for ten
miles, and got sight of them running up a hill as night was approaching.
They encamped in the woods, and recommenced their pursuit of the Indians the next morning, hoping to discover their dwellings. The thick wood
shattered their armor, and they were distressed with thirst. About the middle of the forenoon they came to a deep valley, full of bushes and long
grass, where they saw a deer, and found springs of fresh water, "of which
they were heartily glad; and sat down and drank their first New England
water with as much delight as ever they drunk drink in all their lives." Further onward, they saw signs of cultivation, and, digging into a heap of

sand, they found a basket of Indian corn containing three or four bushels, "with some six and thirty ears, some yellow and some red, and others mixed with blue, which was a very goodly sight." . . .

On the same day, they made a discovery somewhat curious. We shall transcribe the narrative of one of the party. "When we had marched five or six miles into the woods, and could find no signs of people, we returned another way; and as we came into the plain ground, we found a place like a grave, but it was much bigger and longer than any we had yet seen. It was also covered with boards, so as we mused what it might be, and resolved to dig it up. We found first a mat, and under that a fair bow, and under that another mat, and under that a board about three-quarters [of a yard] long, finely carved and painted, with three tines or broaches on the top, like a crown. Also, between the mats we found bowls, trays, dishes, and such like trinkets. At length we came to a fair new mat, and under that two bundles, the one bigger, and the other less. We opened the greater, and found in it a great quantity of fine and perfect red powder, and in it the bone and skull of a man. The skull had fine yellow hair still on it; and some of the flesh unconsumed. There were bound up with it a knife, a packneedle and two or three old iron things. It was bound up in a sailor's canvass cassock and a pair of cloth breeches. The red powder was a kind of embalmment, and yielded a strong, but not offensive smell; it was as fine as any flour. We opened the less bundle likewise, and found of the same powder in it, and the bones and head of a little child. About the legs and other parts of it were bound strings and bracelets of fine white beads. There was also by it a little bow, about three quarters long, and some other odd knacks. We brought sundry of the prettiest things away with us, and covered the corpse up again. There was a variety of opinions amongst us about the embalmed person. Some thought it was an Indian lord and king. Others said the Indians have all black hair, and never any was seen with brown or yellow hair. Some thought it was a Christian of some special note who had died amongst them, and they thus buried him to honor him. Others thought they had killed him, and did it in triumph over him."[38]*

*[Original footnote] The particulars of this account have induced the belief that this was a Northman who, as we have seen, landed on Cape Cod, and were involved in hostilities with the natives.

1855

Thus commenced, in faith and hope, this first New England Colony. It was named Plymouth from the last place parted from in England. Severe trials surrounded them in their new home. Disease and famine did their fearful work among them. Governor Carver, his wife and child, died during the winter; and by spring only forty-six of the one hundred passengers who came in the May Flower [*sic*] were living.

But although exposed to these trials, they were mercifully preserved from the murderous tomahawk of the Indian, a pestilence having the previous year carried off the more dangerous of these savage neighbors. The first Indian they saw, met them with the cheering salutation, "Welcome Englishmen! Welcome Englishmen!" His name was Samoset: he came from what is now Maine, and had learned to speak English from the captain of a fishing vessel on the coast. He gave the information that Massasoit, the great Indian chief of that region, was approaching with sixty men. The Governor engaged Samoset as an interpreter, and by means of a few kindly presents, the Sachem's good will was secured, and a treaty made, which was faithfully kept for more than fifty years. Through Massasoit's influence, ninety less powerful chiefs were brought into treaty with the English; and the only hostile one, Canonicus, was awed when the Governor returned the arms and rattlesnake skin, which the savage chieftain had sent in token of defiance, stuffing the latter with powder and ball.[39]

1936

The Plymouth Company's Attempt Fails

The Plymouth Company was first in securing emigrants for a trial voyage with a view to making a settlement. It was not difficult to procure men for such an experiment because there were many unemployed in England due to the fact that great tracts of arable land had been converted into sheep pasture for the wool trade which was then flourishing. Many returned soldiers of the war with Spain were without work and eager for any chance that might lead to a happy home and perhaps wealth beyond the sea.

In 1606, and again in 1607, expeditions set out from Plymouth, but both ended in failure. During the second attempt, however, forty-five men braved the hardships of the winter of 1606–1607 and remained at the mouth of the Kennebec River until a ship arrived in the spring. All returned to their homes discouraged with the country of which they had expected so much. . . .

STOUT HEARTS WIN SUCCESS

It was discouraging to attempt home-making in a new land in the midst of winter and it was not long before nearly half the newcomers were in their graves. They were a determined people, however, and when the Mayflower sailed for England in the spring, none of them wished to return. John Carver, the governor, died during the first winter. He was succeeded by William Bradford. Miles Standish was the military leader and Elder Brewster, the minister.

The relations between the Pilgrims and the Indians were much more fortunate than in the case of Virginia. Many Indians died from a severe sickness that had recently visited that country. Those who remained were not unfriendly to the white men. Massasoit, chief of the Wampanoags, visited Governor Bradford in 1621 and a treaty of peace was agreed upon that lasted fifty years.[40]

1986

By the 1980s, U.S. history textbooks began to spend a great deal of time focusing on the various cultures and ethnic groups that make up the United States. In this passage, we learn that the people who met the Pilgrims were not just "Indians" but specific groups who aided the new settlers in their quest to establish a colony. Textbooks from the 1960s on also began to include the story of Squanto and how he helped the European settlers during those first few months.

The Plymouth colony was a success, although the Pilgrims suffered terribly from disease at first. In fact only 44 of them lived through the winter of 1620–1621. At one time only seven in the whole colony were well enough to bury their dead in frosty graves. . . .

In addition to their own courage and hard work, the men and women of Plymouth owed some of their success to the Indians.

When the spring arrived, neighboring Indians appeared. Two of them, Samoset and Squanto, could even speak English! Samoset and Abnaki had learned the language from fisherman along the coast of Maine. Squanto had once visited Europe with English fisherman and spent several years there. On his return he joined the Wampanoag tribe.

The Indians helped the settlers. They showed them how to plant crops by fertilizing the land with dead fish. The Pilgrims made a treaty of friendship with Massassoit, the neighboring Indian chief. For many years there was no war.[41]

7

New Sweden

One major trend over the past two hundred years is that the number of pages in U.S. history textbooks has continued to increase. One obvious reason is that the United States today has a great deal more history then it did in the early 1800s; one not-so-obvious reason is that textbooks have grown as more and more groups demand fair representation. What has been left out of textbooks over the centuries is often more interesting than what has changed within them. The case of New Sweden is an example of one of those events that history seems to have forgotten.

1794

From the very beginning, the story of New Sweden was important enough for students to learn about, although without much detail.

The Swedes and Dutch were among the firft fettlers in North America. They had planted themfelves on the banks of the Delaware, many years before William Penn obtained his grant, and their defcendants remain there to this day.

Their fettlements were comprehended in the grant to the Duke of York; and when William Penn came to take poffeffion of his lands in America, he purchafed the three counties, now ftate of Delaware, of the Duke, and united them to his government.[42]

1821

This passage not only mentions the Swedes who were living in that area but also gives credit to a number of Finns who had helped establish this new colony. It is interesting to note that in a number of early nineteenth-century U.S. history textbooks the Dutch are often portrayed in a negative light.

Gustavus Adolphus, king of Sweden, having listened to the representations of William Usselin, with respect to the country around New-Netherlands, urged his subjects to associate and form a settlement there. A number of Swedes and Fins [sic] landed at Cape Henlopen (1627), which they called Paradise Point: the Delaware they called Swedeland stream.

They purchased lands of the Indians, and began a settlement. Four years after, they laid out a town near Wilmington, which was destroyed by the Dutch. They had, however, a fort lower down the bay, near Lewistown.

The Dutch laying claim to the territory as included in their grant, built a fortification in 1651 near where Newcastle now stands, and made a purchase of considerable tracts of land from the natives. The Swedes remonstrated, but without effect, till the next year when the Swedish governor took the place by force, and called it fort Casimer.

Four years after, the Dutch governor at Manhattan, having received a sufficient force from Amsterdam, attacked fort Casimer, which soon surrendered. Fort Christina, near Lewistown, commanded by the Swedish Governor, surrendered a few days after. Most of the Swedes returned to Sweden, about thirty only submitting to Dutch jurisdiction.[43]

1855

While the Puritans were trying to escape religious prosecution, and the Jamestown colony was organized as a business venture, textbooks rarely ever explained why the Swedes decided to establish a colony in the New World.

Between the years 1623 and 1631, the Dutch visited Delaware Bay, and during the latter year, a feeble settlement was planted near the present site of Lewistown. The Dutch, however, were not to be the settlers of this little colony. In the year 1626, the brave Gustavus Adolphus, King of Sweden, determined to send some of his subjects from the wars and tumults of their own country, to found a peaceful colony in America. He fell on the battle-field of Lutzen, before his plan could be carried out. When his little daughter Christiana succeeded to the throne, her wise and good minister, Oxenstiern, accomplished the noble purpose which Gustavus had formed. In 1638, he sent out a little colony of fifty men to Delaware Bay. They built Christiana, and named it after their young queen. Delaware belonged to the Swedes for nearly twenty years, when, in 1654, Stuyvesant, the Dutch governor of New York, became jealous of this Swedish colony, and claimed the country as a part of New Netherlands. He seized upon it, and for a few years, Delaware became a Dutch province, although its inhabitants were Swedes. The Swedish settlements extended along the banks of the Delaware river and bay, as high up as Trenton.

In 1664, it shared the fortune of the rest of New Netherlands, and became, with New York and New Jersey, an English province. In 1681, when King Charles II granted to Penn his Colony of Pennsylvania, the Duke of York still claimed the "three lower counties," now forming the State of Delaware. To prevent disturbances, William Penn purchased these counties, and Delaware was united to Pennsylvania. In 1703, it became a separate province.[44]

1880

In the 1800s, Americans began to see a tidal wave of new immigrants, primarily from southern and eastern Europe, bringing with them their Catholic religion. Notice in this textbook selection how the author makes the point that Gustavus Adolphus wanted to create a site that would be "open to the whole Protestant world."

Previous to this—more than forty years before—Gustavus Adolphus, the brave king of Sweden, proposed to found in America "a free state, where the laborer should reap the fruit of his toil, where the rights of conscience should be inviolate, and which should be open to the whole Protestant world." A Hollander presented himself to the king, and laid before him a proposition for a trading company, to be established in Sweden, its operations to extend to Asia, Africa, and America. Full power was accordingly given to carry out this project, but before the necessary arrangements could be made, the German war and the king's death occurred, which caused the work to be laid aside, and the whole project seemed about to die with the king. But just as it appeared to be at its end, it received new life.

Another Hollander, by the name of Peter Minuit, made his appearance in Sweden. He had been in the service of Holland, in America, but had been recalled home and dismissed from service. He was not, however, discouraged by this, and went over to Sweden, where he renewed the representations in regard to the excellence of the new country, and the advantages that Sweden might derive from it. Queen Christina, then a child of only eleven years of age, who had succeeded her royal father in the government, was glad to have the project thus renewed.

As a good beginning, the first colony was sent off, and Minuit was placed over it, as being best acquainted in those regions. They set sail in a ship-of-war, followed by a smaller vessel, both laden with people, provisions, ammunition, and merchandise suitable for traffic and gifts to the Indians. The ships reached their places of destination; and the high expectations which the emigrants had formed of that new land were well met by the first views which they enjoyed of it. They made their first landing on the bay or entrance to the river Poutaxat, which they called the river of New Sweden. A purchase of land was immediately made from the Indians. Posts were driven into the ground as landmarks; and a deed was drawn up for the land thus purchased. This was written in Dutch, because no Swede was yet able to interpret the language of the heathen. The Indians subscribed their marks; and the writing was sent home to Sweden, to be preserved in the royal archives (1638).[45]

1914

This selection comes from a textbook titled The Essential Facts of American History, *which is exactly how the author portrays this story: brief and to the point. By the turn of the century, the story of New Sweden becomes hard to find in U.S. history textbooks, and it virtually disappears by the 1960s. In its place now are stories of how William Penn and the Quakers organized this colony.*

Let us now see how Delaware was also made out of some of the terri-tory that had been acquired from the Dutch. Peter Minuit, who had been governor in New Netherlands, entered the service of Sweden, and was en-gaged to bring over a body of Swedes to America and find them a place to live. In 1638 he brought them over and settled at a place he named Christina, in honor of the young queen of Sweden.

When Stuyvesant became governor of New Amsterdam, as New York was first called, he came down the coast with a big force of men, captured the Swedish fort, took the officers off to New Amsterdam, and made all the Swedes swear fidelity to Holland. This broke up the Swedish colony, and the Dutch remained in possession of the territory.[46]

8

Anne Hutchinson

It is interesting to see how U.S. history textbooks have portrayed early colonial women throughout much of the nineteenth and early twentieth centuries: as if they did not exist. The single exception was Anne Hutchinson. She came to the New World with her husband and eight children. The daughter of a Puritan minister, Hutchison was knowledgeable about the Bible. After a while she gained a small following in the Puritan colony, but was later banished due to some of her personal beliefs and her questioning of the clergy.

1830

This early text offers a surprisingly evenhanded summary of the Hutchinson affair— one that uniquely acknowledges her strengths. This view of Hutchinson is even more unusual when you consider the fact that the only students allowed to read this passage in the 1830s would have been the sons of wealthy white Americans.

In 1635, Massachusetts received from England a large number of inhabitants, and among them came two who afterwards acted conspicuous parts in the affairs of their native country. One was Hugh Peters, who was subsequently a chaplain of Oliver Cromwell; the other was Mr. Vane, afterwards Sir Henry Vane. The latter was but twenty-five years of age; but by his show of great humility, his grave and solemn deportment, and his ardent professions of attachment to liberty, he stole the hearts of the puritans, and, the year after his arrival, was made governor of the colony.

His popularity, however, was transient. During his administration, the celebrated Mrs. Hutchinson, a woman who was distinguished for her eloquence, and had imbibed the enthusiasm of the age, instituted weekly meetings for persons of her own sex, in which she commented on the sermons of the preceding Sunday, and advanced certain mystical and extravagant doctrines. These spread rapidly among the people, and many became converts.

Governor Vane, with Mr. Cotton and Mr. Wheelwright, two distinguished clergymen, embraced them with ardor; but lieutenant governor Winthrop, and a majority of the churches, deemed them heretical and seditious. Great excitement was produced among the people; many conferences were held; public fasts were appointed; a general synod was summoned; and after much intemperate discussion, her opinions were determined to be erroneous, and she and some of her adherents were banished from the colony.[47]

1855

U.S. history textbooks from the 1800s were split over the issue of whether or not the Puritans went too far with their exclusionary policies. This textbook took a swipe at Hutchinson's beliefs, calling them "strange and unscriptural doctrines," but also questioned the Puritans' reaction to this whole situation.

Between the years 1630 and 1636, we find the settlements belonging to the Massachusetts Bay company rapidly increasing. Persecution in England was sending many wise and able men to the Colonies. Among them came Sir Henry Vane, a friend of the poet Milton. He so won the hearts of the people, that at one time they made him governor. But though an earnest and good man, he was not a very safe one, and becoming the supporter of the party of Mrs. Anne Hutchinson, he led himself and the Colonies into serious difficulties. This Mrs. Hutchinson held many strange and unscriptural [sic] doctrines. She believed, for instance, that equally with "holy men of old," she and her followers were favored with special divine revelations. This party, opposing the ministers and magistrates of the Colony, created great disturbances. At length, Sir Henry Vane returned to England, and Mrs. Hutchinson and her followers were banished from Massachusetts.

The Puritans were too earnest in their faith to live in peace with those who differed from them. Not only were the followers of Mrs. Hutchinson persecuted and banished, but the Quakers and Baptists also were cruelly treated, four of the former being put to death on account of their opinions.[48]

1874

Two themes run through this passage: first, that Hutchinson was just another in a series of people who began to question the doctrine of the Puritans in America, and second, that there may have been a political argument going on. Rather than just being persecuted for their religious beliefs, Hutchinson and her followers may have also been caught in between the Vane-Winthrop fight over who should be the governor of the colony.

The Puritans did not escape religious dissensions in New England. In 1635, Roger Williams was banished from the colony for publishing opinions which were deemed seditious and heretical by the ministers and magistrates. Banishing Williams did not end the trouble. A year later, Mrs. Ann [*sic*] Hutchinson began to teach doctrines at variance with those generally received. She was declared to be "like Roger Williams, or worse." This trouble assumed a more formidable aspect from the fact that Henry Vane, a young man of twenty-three, whose popular talents and winning manners had caused him to be elected governor that year, became one of her supporters. The next year, however, Winthrop was again made governor, and Mrs. Hutchinson, with the most prominent of her followers, was exiled from the colony.[49]

1914

By the 1900s, Hutchinson's story shifted away from that of political intrigue to one of a woman not knowing her place in society. With the Women's Suffrage Movement fully under way in 1914, it would have been interesting to know if this story added to the current dialogue about whether women should have the right to vote.

Another member of the Puritan church in Boston was Mrs. Anne Hutchinson. She declared that the preachers did not preach sound doctrine. The preachers replied that a woman had no business mixing in public affairs, and should not hold meetings in her own house to discuss religious matters. The preachers then banished her from Boston.

With a few friends she went to Providence where Roger Williams was, and by his advice and help bought some land from Canonicus, the Indian chief. The first settlement was called Portsmouth, and the second was called Newport. After a while the towns of Providence, Portsmouth, and Newport were united under one government, and were called Rhode Island and Providence Plantations. These settlements were the beginning of the present State of Rhode Island.⁵⁰

1944

Students reading this textbook during the World War II era were informed that Williams and Hutchinson granted America an idea of religious liberty, a cornerstone of this country's value system.

In the case of the Massachusetts Bay Colony, religious affairs took a course unlike that in Virginia or Maryland. Although, like Virginians, the Puritans who settled on the bay were members of the Church of England when they arrived, they had wanted to alter some of its practices and soon they separated from it entirely in their new home. After the separation each town set up a church of its own, called Congregational, and taxpayers were required by law to support it. For a long time every voter in Massachusetts had to be a member of a Congregational church.

Strenuous efforts were made to bar immigrants belonging to other religious denominations. Dissenters and critics who appeared among the Puritans were frowned upon and sometimes severely punished, executed, or exiled into the wilderness. In short Puritans came to Massachusetts to develop, among other things, religious liberty for themselves, not to establish an ideal of toleration for all religions—a liberty utterly unknown as practice in the England they had left.

The first English colony in America to grant general religious liberty as
a matter of law and principle was an offshoot from Massachusetts, at first
called the Rhode Island and Providence Plantations. It was not founded
by settlers coming directly from England but by inhabitants of Massachusetts who rebelled against the teachings and practices of Puritan preachers
and magistrates. In 1636 Roger William's, ordered to conform or get out,
fled with a few friends into the wilderness and founded the town of Providence at the head of Narragansett Bay. Two years afterward Anne
Hutchinson, also outlawed by the Puritan clergy of Boston for her religious and general independence, took refuge with her companions for a
while at Portsmouth on Rhode Island.

Both Roger Williams and Anne Hutchinson believed that the government should not force any form of religion by law on anybody; that every
person should be free to worship God according to his conscience. This
rule of broad tolerance, extended to Quakers and Jews, was retained in the
Providence and Rhode Island plantations after all the townships were
united in an independent colony—by a charter from Charles II granted in
1663. It made Rhode Island unique among the colonies.[51]

1995

More recently, many U.S. history textbooks have begun to elaborate more fully on
the Hutchinson story. Now portrayed as a strong, intelligent woman, Hutchinson
seems to be making a stand against the theocratic church and state found in Mass-
achusetts Bay Colony as well as for women's rights.

The magistrates of Massachusetts Bay believed Anne Hutchinson
posed an even graver threat to the peace of the commonwealth. This extremely intelligent woman, her husband William, and her children followed John Cotton to the New World in 1634. Even contemporaries
found her religious ideas, usually termed Antinomianism, somewhat
confusing. Whatever her thoughts, Hutchinson shared them with other
Bostonians, many of them women. Her outspoken views scandalized orthodox leaders of church and state. She suggested that all but two ministers in the colony had lost touch with the "Holy Spirit" and were preaching
a doctrine in the Congregational churches that was little better than that
of Archbishop Laud. When authorities demanded she explain her unusual

opinions, she announced she experienced divine inspiration independently of either the Bible or the clergy. In other words, Hutchinson's teachings could not be tested by Scripture, a position that seemed dangerously subjective. . . .

When this woman described Congregational ministers—some of them the leading divines of Boston—as unconverted men, the General Court intervened. For two very tense days in 1637, the ministers and magistrates of Massachusetts Bay cross-examined Hutchinson; in this intense theological debate, she more than held her own. She knew as much about the Bible as did her inquisitors, and no doubt her brilliance at that moment provoked the Court's misogyny.

Hutchinson defied the ministers and magistrates to demonstrate exactly where she had gone wrong. Just when it appeared Hutchinson had outmaneuvered—indeed, thoroughly embarrassing—her opponents, she let down her guard, declaring forcefully that what she knew of God came "by an immediate revelation. . . . By the voice of his own spirit and my soul." Here was what her accusers had suspected all along but could not prove. She had confessed in open court that the Spirit can live without the Moral Law. This Antinomian statement challenged the authority of the Bay rulers, and they were relieved to exile Hutchinson and her followers to Rhode Island.[52]

9

Witchcraft in the Colonies

Witchcraft in colonial America—and the Salem Witch Trials especially—have aroused historical controversy for nearly three centuries. While no known textbook ever endorsed the treatment of the accused "witches," the reasons put forth for the episode have varied sharply over time.

1823

This early passage suggested that a physical illness might have caused the outbreak of the witch hunts.

We should be willing, in silence and sorrow, to pass all notice of an infatuation, which prevailed generally for a long time, and the consequences of which were the imprisonment and other sufferings of a great number, and the death of a less; but truth and impartiality compel us, most reluctantly, to give a very brief account of what has usually been called the Salem Witchcraft.

Early in the year [1692], two children of the family of a clergyman in Salem village, the one eleven, the other nine years of age, having been for some time indisposed, and no relief being obtained from medical aid, the attending physician suggested the probability of their being bewitched. The children, informed of their supposed situation, complained of an Indian woman, and declared they were "pinched, pricked, and, tormented" by her.

Other persons, soon after, afflicted with various complaints, attributed their sickness to the same cause; and several of the imagined witches were put in prison. In the month of June eleven persons were tried, condemned, and executed.

The awful mania increased. In September, nine more received sentence of death. Each became suspicious of his neighbour. The charges of witchcraft, commencing with the lower part of society, extended to all ranks; even a clergyman, among others, having been executed. A confession of guilt became the only security for life; such not being condemned. In October, the number of persons accused was so great, and their standing in society so respectable, that by general consent, all persons were released, and all prosecutions dropped.[33]

1855

In this pre–Civil War text, students were informed that the problems in Salem were not unique to that city alone but had also transpired in Europe. What makes this passage different from others is that it portrayed a theological reason for what occurred in Salem.

We hear so much about Salem witchcraft, that we are apt to imagine this little town is the only one in the world that was ever troubled by such a calamity. This is a great mistake. Many years before, and many years after the twenty persons were put to death in Salem for witchcraft, more than one hundred and thirty thousand were executed in England, Scotland, France, and Germany, upon the same pretext.

The belief in witchcraft was this: it was supposed that if the devil could persuade any human being to help him, he could do a great deal to tempt and destroy mankind. It was thought that the devil appeared to some persons, and persuaded them to enter into a league with him, and become his servants. Some went so far as to say, that he caused such to sign their names in blood in a little red book, and that they promised to do his bidding, and he, in return, promised to give them power to distress or persecute any whom they chose. This league between the devil and a witch (as such a person, whether man or woman, was called) was believed to give more power for evil to both, than either would have alone.[54]

1866

Coming on the heels of the Civil War, this text offered a psychosocial interpretation of the Salem episode.

It was during the long period of peace which has been alluded to in the foregoing chapters that the troubles arose in Massachusetts about witchcraft, of which so much has been said in history, and on account of which such heavy charges have been made against our forefathers.

The first case of the kind occurred in Springfield, in 1645. In June, 1648, the charge of witchcraft was brought against Margaret Jones, of Charlestown, and she was executed. Ann Hibbins, of Boston, came next—she was executed in 1656. Here the subject rested for about thirty years, when it was again revived; and there was one more execution in Boston.

Four years afterward, viz., in 1692, the supposed witchcraft broke out in Salem and Danvers. Here the first subjects of it were children. The disorder, whatever its character may have been, spread to the neighboring country towns, particularly Andover, Ipswich, and Gloucester. At first it affected the lower classes only; but at length it pervaded all ranks and conditions.

Two daughters of a minister, in Salem, were strangely affected. Before this they had been quiet, happy children but now they began to look wild, shriek, tell strange stories, sit barefoot among the ashes, or go abroad with their clothes and hair in great disorder, looking like insane people. Sometimes they were dumb; at others they would complain of being pricked severely with pins.

The madness continuing to spread, the charge of witchcraft was at length brought against one poor minister himself. All sorts of strange stories were told about him. It was especially said that he had intercourse with the devil; and the fact that he was an uncommonly athletic and strong man, may have favored this idea. He would not confess guilt, and was hanged. Those who confessed the crime of witchcraft, however, were not executed.

It was indeed a fearful time. Multitudes were suspected and accused, and at one period no less than one hundred and fifty were in prison for witchcraft. What number were actually executed, while "the fever lasted," is not quite certain. It is generally said that two hundred were accused, one hundred and fifty imprisoned, twenty-eight condemned, nineteen hanged, and one pressed to death.

But the excitement at length passed away; and the more rapidly in proportion as the criminals were treated with clemency. Multitudes owned, at length, that they confessed their guilt to save their lives! For a century past little has been said of witchcraft in the United States, and few believe in its existence. The events we have narrated are supposed to have been the result of delusion.[55]

1912

In the early 1900s, students in some history classes were reading that the Puritans were actually a rather sane group due to how they handled this situation.

The severely religious trend of thought, the barrenness of life, and the dangers from Indian attacks that impended about the year 1691, account for the occurrence in Massachusetts of the witchcraft troubles. The theory of Satanic manifestations was commonly held in European countries, and there claimed its thousands of victims. In Salem and surrounding towns, two or three hundred persons, some of them being of the highest character, were accused of having allowed themselves to become possessed by the devil. Of these, nineteen were judicially condemned and were put to death. The comparative brevity and mildness of this outburst of religious fanaticism testifies to the real saneness of the Puritan mind. Nowhere in the world at this time was life more pure or thought more elevated.[56]

1936

By the 1930s, textbook authors had started to point the finger at a societal belief in superstition as a cause for the witchcraft craze.

Superstition and Witchcraft

Many superstitious beliefs based upon the forces of nature are to be found among primitive people, but, in civilized conditions, it is only among the unlearned that foolish practices and beliefs without any foundation arise. In colonial times there were many people who thought that evil spirits sometimes entered the bodies of persons and caused them to work harm on anyone whom they might select. In most cases those who were said to be possessed of the evil spirit were friendless old women. This superstition led men to preach and write about the evils of witchcraft. Cotton Mather, a leading Boston minister, wrote a long treatise dealing with witchcraft.

The result of such teaching was a real calamity. In 1692 some children of Salem complained that they had been bewitched. Many accused persons were seized and brought before the court for trial. On the testimony of a few girls, apparently suffering from hysterical fits caused, as they declared, by being bitten and pinched by persons in league with the devil, many people were convicted and nineteen were hanged. After the excitement was over many of the leaders in the persecution realized how foolish all of them had been and were sincerely repentant. There has been no execution for witchcraft in America since the Salem affair.[57]

1982

For nearly two hundred years, history textbooks had argued that the Salem witch hunt was caused by either mental illness, society's belief in superstition, and/or intervention by the devil. By the end of the twentieth century, textbooks had begun to add more socioeconomic issues to this ever-changing historiography.

The extreme stress New England was undergoing as a result of upheavals in its religious life, social organization, and economic system gave rise in 1692 to accusations of witchcraft in Salem Village (now Danvers), Massachusetts. Like their contemporaries elsewhere, seventeenth-century New Englanders believed in and greatly feared witches, who appeared human but whose power, they thought, came from the devil. If New Englanders could not find rational explanations for their troubles, they tended to suspect they were being bewitched. Although such accusations occurred elsewhere, the tensions resulting from New England's commercialization and secularization exploded most dramatically in a little rural community adjoining the bustling port of Salem.

The crisis began when a group of adolescent girls accused a number of older women—mostly outsiders of one sort or another—of having bewitched them. Before the hysteria spent itself ten months later, nineteen people (including several men, most of them related to accused female witches) had been hanged, another pressed to death by heavy stones, and more than one hundred others jailed. Historians have puzzled ever since about the origins of the witchcraft episode. It has been variously attributed to tension between mothers and daughters (with the witches serving as surrogate mothers), persistent antagonisms among the town's leading families, and even hallucinations arising from a form of food poisoning.

But the most plausible explanation may lie in the uncertainty of life in late seventeenth-century New England. Salem Village, a farming town on the edge of a commercial center, was torn between old and new styles of life. Some families were abandoning agriculture for trade, while others were struggling to maintain traditional ways. The villagers who exploited the new economic opportunities were improving their status relative to their neighbors. Most people were uncertain about their destiny, but none more so than adolescent girls. As children their fate lay in the hands of their parents, yet their ultimate destiny would depend on their husbands. But would their husbands be farmers or artisans or merchants? What would their future lives be like? No one knew. By lashing out and in effect seizing command of the entire town, the girls gave their lives a certainty previously lacking. At the same time, they afforded their fellow townspeople an opportunity to vent their frustrations at the unsettling changes in their lives. The accused witches were scapegoats for the shattered dream of an isolated Bible Commonwealth.[58]

PART II

The American Revolution

IO

George Washington and Fort Duquesne

The debate over what is written in U.S. history textbooks has been ongoing throughout American history. Over the past thirty years, numerous groups have waged battles over whether U.S. history textbooks spend too much or not enough time on what is known as "Great White Man" history. Some make the argument that we need to understand these great men to truly understand what makes our nation great, while others contend that the overglorification of single individuals does not do American history justice. With this debate in mind, this section looks at George Washington, whose story permeates every single U.S. history textbook. Rather than focusing on his entire career, however, this section looks at the first time his name appears in most accounts—in connection to the events at Fort Duquesne. While what happened at Fort Duquesne and Fort Necessity would have been considered a defeat for almost any other American, for Washington this was simply not the case.

1821

"Honorable capitulation?" Some might call it a surrender. But when discussing Washington, textbooks in the nineteenth century did not use any kind of negative connotation.

Dinwiddie laid the subject before the assembly who determined to de-mand, in the name of the king that the French should desist. George Washington, then in his twenty-second year, was dispatched with a letter to the commandant on the Ohio, who said he acted according to orders; and transmitted the letter to the Governor. After receiving a written an-swer, Washington returned to Virginia; but not before he had carefully sur-veyed the fort.

The British ministry being informed of the determination of the French to claim and hold by force the country, and make prisoners of every Englishman found there, directed the Virginians, and an independent company arrived from South Carolina. Two other companies were ordered from New York.

Washington was raised to a Colonel, and commanded the troop. With-out waiting for the New York companies, he began his march. On his route he learned from a friendly Indian that the English, who had been erecting a fort at the confluence of the Alleghany and Monongahela, had been at-tacked and defeated by the French, who were then finishing the fort for themselves; and that a party of French were encamped at a short distance, being on their march to the Great Meadows.

This party he surprised and wholly defeated. Here he erected a small stockade fort, and proceeded towards the French fort Du Quesne (now Pittsburgh). But, learning that the French commander was approaching with nine hundred men, besides Indians; having himself not four hundred; he returned to his fort at Great Meadows. Here he and his little party de-fended themselves so well, that an honorable capitulation was the result, and he returned with his troops to Virginia.[1]

1855

In this passage, students were not only told of Washington's cunning and bravery but also that he was assisted by divine intervention.

The French continued their encroachments year by year, and at length planned a chain of forts extending through the western parts of Pennsylva-nia and Virginia to the Ohio, and down that river and the Mississippi to New Orleans. To oppose these, on the part of the English, there were only a few traders' homes west of the Alleghanies [*sic*] in Virginia, and a feeble settlement at Laurel Hill, in the western part of Pennsylvania. The governor of Virginia now resolved to send a remonstrance to the French on the Ohio, warning them against intrusions on English colonies. The mission was a difficult one, but the messenger was well chosen. George Washington, then twenty-one years of age, an heroic, noble youth, whose early self-denials gave promise of what his future life would be, was sent by Governor Dinwiddie on this long and perilous journey.

Leaving Williamsburg on the last day of October, Washington, with four attendants, a guide, and an interpreter, started for the West. Their route lay through the gloomy autumn woods, across swollen streams, and over rugged mountains; an unbroken wilderness, with no path but the trail of the Indian to guide them. In nine days they reached the spot where the city of Pittsburgh now stands. Washington's quick eye saw the advantages of the position for a fortress to defend the Ohio, and determining to advise it, pushed on to the northern part of Pennsylvania, where he met the French commander, and presented the English governor's remonstrance. The answer which Washington received was not very satisfactory, and he hastened his return to Virginia. The horses which they had brought on the journey had given out, and they were obliged to return on foot. "The cold increased very fast; the paths grew worse by a deep snow continually freezing," but Washington, wrapping himself in an Indian dress, with gun in hand, and pack on his back, the day after Christmas quitted the usual path, and with but one companion, hurried the nearest way to the Forks of the Ohio. In passing through the forest, an Indian, lying in wait for him, shot at him but missed his aim. On reaching the Alleghany, with one poor hatchet and a whole day's work, a raft was constructed and launched. But before they were half over the river, they were caught in the running ice, expecting every moment to be crushed, unable to reach either shore. Putting out a pole to stop the raft, Washington was jerked into the deep water, and saved himself only by grasping at the raft-logs. They were obliged to make for an island. There they remained all night; in the morning the ice had frozen, and they crossed upon it. Amid all these perils, the goodness of God conducted Washington in safety.

The refusal of the French to give up their claim to western Pennsylvania and Virginia, caused great alarm in the colonies, and preparations were made for war. An attempt was made by the colonists to establish themselves at the point where the three rivers meet, as Washington had recommended; but they were driven away by the French, who built a strong fort at this advantageous spot, and named it Du Quesne.

In May of 1751, Washington was sent against the enemy, and his first battle was fought at a place called the Great Meadows.

He was victorious, and in the engagement the French commander was killed. The advantage thus gained was soon lost, for want of a sufficient number of men to keep up the struggle; and by the end of the year, the French again held possession of the valley of the Ohio.[2]

1866

By the mid-nineteenth century, the narrative of Washington and the mythology surrounding him had become even more elaborate.

The messenger intrusted [*sic*] with this important errand was George Washington, then scarcely twenty-one years of age. He was a Virginian by birth, and had received no other education than that of the family and the common school. His mind, as it appears, had taken quite a mathematical turn, and he had early become a surveyor.

But he was most distinguished for his excellent moral character. In this respect few young men of his time stood higher. His passions were indeed strong, but he strove to govern and subdue them. At the age of nineteen he had been made an adjutant-general of some troops, raised for the defence of the country against the Indians, and held the rank of major; but he had never been called into service.

Such was the person selected by Governor Dinwiddie for an expedition at once difficult and dangerous. Several young men, to whom the commission had been offered, refused it, for want of courage to engage in the undertaking. But Washington was born to save his country, and not solely to seek his own ease and comfort.

He set out on his journey from Williamsburg, the capital of Virginia, October 31, 1753. He had with him an Indian interpreter, a French interpreter, a guide, and four other persons, two of whom were Indian traders; making, in all, a company of eight men, with their horses, tents, baggage, and provisions.

The distance from Williamsburg to the principal fort of the French was about five hundred and fifty miles. They were to pass high and rugged mountains and cross deep rivers. Half the distance, moreover, was through a pathless wilderness, where no traces of civilization had yet appeared, and where, perhaps, none but savages and wild beasts had ever trodden.

But danger did not move Washington where duty was concerned. He pursued his way, and delivered his letter to St. Pierre, the French commander, whom he found at a fort on French Creek, sixty-five miles north of Fort du Quesne. He obtained a reply from the French officer, and returned, having, however, secretly taken the dimensions of the French fort, and collected much useful information.

His mission did not prevent a war from breaking out, but it was at least satisfactory to him to know that he had done what he could. He received the thanks of the governor and council of Virginia for his services.

Some few anecdotes of this journey are worth relating. On their return homeward, Washington was shot at by a French Indian, but, though the savage was not fifteen paces off, according to Washington's own statement, and probably meant to kill him, not the slightest injury was done him.

Again, as they were obliged to cross the rivers on rafts, and in such other ways as they could, and as it was winter, they sometimes narrowly escaped being drowned. In one instance they were wrecked on an island, and obliged to remain there all night; the cold, in the meantime, being so intense that the hands and feet of the guide were frozen.

In another instance, while descending a river in a canoe, perplexed by rocks, shallows, drifting trees and currents, they came to a place where the ice had lodged, which made it impassable by water. They were, consequently, obliged to land and carry their canoe across a neck of land for a quarter of a mile or more.[3]

1899

At the close of the nineteenth century, students were given yet another positive spin on Washington's defeat at Fort Necessity—framed as a precursor to his later role as a Revolutionary War hero.

In 1753, the French, taking the alarm, crossed Lake Erie, and began to fortify themselves at Presque Isle, at Le Boeuf, and at Venango on the Allegheny River. The governor of Virginia, Robert Dinwiddie, was much annoyed at this, and sent a messenger to warn the French not to advance any further. It was a delicate business, requiring firmness and discretion. The governor intrusted [sic] it to a young land surveyor, only twenty-one years of age, but already familiar with Indians and with woodcraft, and already noted for courage and sound judgment. The name of this young man was George Washington. His task involved a winter journey of a thousand miles through the wilderness, with seven companions, negotiations with Indian chiefs as well as French officers, and the gathering of information regarding the enemy's plans.

This difficult task was splendidly performed, though, of course, the Frenchmen did not heed Washington's warnings. The most important point on all that long frontier was the spot where Pittsburgh now stands. It was the main entrance to the valley of the Ohio, and for a long time was called the Gateway of the West. It was the object of the French to keep the English colonists from ever getting through this gateway, or across the Allegheny Mountains. They wished to keep all the interior of the continent for themselves. So, in the spring of 1754, while a party of English were beginning to build a fort at this gateway, a stronger party of French came and drove them off, and built a fortress of their own there, which they called Fort Duquesne. A regiment of Virginia troops was already on its way to the place, and upon the death of its commanding officer, George Washington, the lieutenant-colonel, took command. In a skirmish with the French (May 28, 1754), Washington fired the first shot in one of the greatest wars of modern times. This skirmish brought the enemy upon him in overwhelming numbers, and at a stockaded place, called Fort Necessity, the young commander was obliged (July 4) to surrender his little army. Thus early was he taught to endure adverse fortune.[4]

1936

Written during the Great Depression, this excerpt emphasized Washington's patriotic duty to his country—an interesting message to students during a trying time in U.S. history.

The governor of Virginia at that time was Rober Dinwiddie. He was intensely patriotic and very zealous where the rights of Englishmen were concerned. As soon as he heard of the operations of the French, he determined to send a written protest against such actions together with a request that they retire from the Ohio valley. For his messenger he selected George Washington, a young man but twenty-one years of age.

GEORGE WASHINGTON ENTERS THE SERVICE OF HIS COUNTRY

No other character in history measures up more completely to our expectations than Washington. He was always equal to any task required of him. His early training as a surveyor made him familiar with the wilderness ways and the habits of the Indians. His military education fitted him for leadership in the years of strife through which his country passed, and his good judgment, fair-mindedness, and knowledge of men and affairs of state made him a recognized leader among statesmen.

The young surveyor was accompanied on his mission by Christopher Gist and six other white men. The journey was filled with hardships and adventures. It is not easy at any season to travel through an unknown country, but this trip was made during the winter months when the snow and ice added to the burden of the travelers. Fort Le Boeuf finally was reached, and the French governor's reply to Governor Dinwiddie was given to Washington. The reply was an absolute refusal to leave the country. It also asserted that the king of France owned all the land west of the Allegheny mountains [sic].[5]

1950

In this U.S. history textbook, a new twist was added to Washington's journey to the French fort. While his greatness was rarely in question, how Washington got to and from Fort Duquesne seems debatable.

The French begin to fortify the disputed territory. When the governor of New France learned of this grant in 1749, he sent an expedition to the Ohio country. As the expedition traveled down the Allegheny River and a portion of the Ohio River, it planted plates of lead which stated that this land belonged to France. The Indians were warned to have nothing to do with the English. Shortly afterward, the French began to build forts on Lake Erie and at points southward toward the Ohio River.

The English attempt to drive out the French. England, in turn, became alarmed at the advances of the French in the Ohio region. In the autumn of 1753 a messenger was sent through the wilderness to the forts which the French had built in the disputed region. The messenger was George Washington, who at that time was just twenty-one years old. He carried a letter from the governor of Virginia to the French commander of the forts. This letter warned the French to leave the territory because it belonged to England. Over difficult trails, through snow and rain, young Washington made his way to deliver his message. But the French commander refused to heed the warning, and Washington started back. On his return trip he barely escaped death when he slipped off a raft and nearly drowned.

The next year Washington returned to the Ohio country, this time with a small group of soldiers. They had been sent out to seize Fort Duquesne, a French fort at the fork where two streams join to form the Ohio River. But Washington and his men were outnumbered. They not only failed to capture Fort Duquesne but were forced to surrender and return to Virginia. With this clash the French and Indian War began.[6]

1966

In this textbook, students learned that there may have been financial incentives to send Washington to Fort Duquesne. This passage also showed that Washington and the events at the fort were beginning to be de-emphasized.

The First Clash

A group of wealthy Virginians were responsible for the first of a series of events that led to the French and Indian War. For business reasons and with no thought of the fateful consequences, these men formed a company and secured from the British king a huge grant of land in the upper Ohio Valley. They intended to make a profit from this land by dividing it into small farms, and then selling these farms to settlers.

The French, alarmed at these real estate activities on what they considered to be French territory, sent an expedition to strengthen France's claim to the land. In 1753 the French started constructing a chain of forts connecting Lake Erie with the Ohio River. George Washington, a twenty-one-year-old surveyor from Virginia whose brother had invested in the Ohio real estate venture, was sent by the governor of Virginia to warn the French that the land belonged to the British. (The land had been originally granted to the colony of Virginia by the charter of 1609.) The French ignored the warnings of George Washington.

The following year Washington, this time a major at the head of a force of militia, returned to the frontier and constructed Fort Necessity, a few miles south of the French Fort Duquesne. Fort Duquesne itself was situated at the strategic point where the Monongahela and Allegheny Rivers join to form the Ohio River—the present site of Pittsburgh. A small force of French and Indians defeated Washington in a battle which was fought at Fort Necessity on July 4, 1754.[7]

1982

This textbook, written in the early 1980s, began to question Washington's role as well that of other "Great White Men" found in the annals of American history. New adjectives such as "foolhardy and inexperienced" crept into the once-heroic narrative.

The delegates to the Congress did not know that, while they deliberated, the war they sought to prepare for was already beginning. Governor Robert Dinwiddie of Virginia had sent a small militia force westward to counter the French moves. Virginia claimed ownership of the region that is now western Pennsylvania, and Dinwiddie was eager to prevent the French from establishing a permanent post there. But the Virginia militiamen arrived too late. The French had already taken possession of the strategic point—now Pittsburgh—where the Allegheny and Monongahela rivers meet to form the Ohio, and they were busily engaged in constructing Fort Duquesne. The foolhardy and inexperienced young colonel who commanded the Virginians allowed himself to be trapped by the French in his crudely built Fort Necessity at Great Meadows, Pennsylvania. After a day-long battle in which more than one-third of his men were killed or wounded, the twenty-two-year-old George Washington surrendered. He signed a document of capitulation, and he and his men were allowed to return to Virginia.

Washington had blundered grievously. He had started a war that would eventually encompass nearly the entire world. He had also ensured that the Indians of the Ohio Valley would for the most part support France in the coming conflict. The Indians took Washington's mistakes as an indication of Britain's inability to win the war, and nothing that occurred in the next four years made them change their minds. In 1755 a combined force of French and Indians ambushed General Edward Braddock, two regiments of British regulars, and some colonial troops a few miles south of Fort Duquesne. Braddock was killed and his men demoralized by their complete defeat. For three more years one disaster followed another for Great Britain. Everywhere the two sides clashed, the French were consistently victorious.[8]

11

The Boston Massacre

Certain historical events consistently appear in U.S. history textbooks over time. The Boston Massacre is one of these. The massacre has become part of our national historical narrative, and helps provide moral justification for the war against the British. It is interesting to note, then, that the textbooks reviewed here offer such different perspectives on this well-known event.

1823

The Boston Massacre today is seen as one of those great patriotic moments in our history where everyday American colonists stood up to the tyranny of the British government. Ironically, rather then heralding the cause of the Bostonians, this textbook seemed to blame them for egging on an unnecessary fight.

On the fifth of March, while some of the British troops in Boston were under arms, they were insulted and pelted by a mob having clubs, snow balls, stones, &c. The soldiers were dared to fire. One, who had received a blow, fired. Six others discharged their pieces; by which three of the citizens were killed, and five wounded. The town was immediately in an uproar; and nothing but an engagement to remove the troops, saved them from falling a sacrifice to the indignation of the people.

The captain, Preston, who commanded, and eight soldiers, were tried, and acquitted; two soldiers excepted, who were brought in guilty of manslaughter. This affray was represented in its worst light, and had no small influence in increasing the general indignation against the British.[9]

1855

By the mid-nineteenth century, American schoolchildren were still learning that the Boston Massacre was caused by the Bostonians' reaction to the British soldiers. In this antebellum textbook, the author further pointed an accusatory finger at Boston's children and the "negro who had excited the disturbance." This "negro" was Crispus Attucks, who was part African American and likely part Native American. Attucks, throughout much of the 1800s and 1900s, was often either completely ignored or blamed for what transpired that evening. By the end of the twentieth century, Attucks would again cause controversy by being used as an example for what was wrong with modern-day textbooks.

In Boston, the presence of the British soldiers caused constant affrays. In one of these, the soldiers fired upon the populace and killed three men: one of these men was the negro who had excited the disturbance. This deed was called the Boston Massacre, and caused high indignation among the people: they were, however, much in fault, having aroused the attack which ended so fatally.

In the course of a few months, the captain who had ordered the soldiers to fire was tried in Boston for murder: notwithstanding the strong feeling of the excited Bostonians against him, two distinguished citizens, John Adams and Josiah Quincy, undertook his defence, and he was acquitted.

Even the children of the town were greatly disturbed by the presence of British troops among them.

In the winter, the boys were in the habit of building little hills of snow, and sliding down them to the pond on the Common, for amusement. The English soldiers, to provoke them, would often beat down these hills. On one occasion, having rebuilt them, and finding, on their return from school, that they were again demolished, several of the boys determined to wait upon the captain and complain of his soldiers. The officer made light of it, and the soldiers became more troublesome than ever. At last, a meeting of the larger boys was held, and a deputation was sent to General Gage, the commander-in-chief. He asked why so many children had called upon him. "We come, Sir," said the tallest boy, "to demand satisfaction." "What!" said the General, "have your fathers been teaching you rebellion, and sent you to exhibit it here?" "Nobody sent us, Sir," replied the boy, while his eyes flashed and his cheek reddened at being accused of rebellion; "we have never injured nor insulted your troops, but they have trodden down our snow-hills, and broken the ice on our skating-grounds. We complained, and they called us young rebels, and told us to help ourselves if we could. We told the captain of this, and he laughed at us. Yesterday our works were destroyed the third time, and we will bear it no longer." The nobler feelings of the general's heart were awakened, and, after gazing upon them in silent admiration for a moment, he turned to an officer by his side, and said, "The very children here draw in a love of liberty with the air they breathe. You may go, my brave boys, and be assured, if my troops trouble you again, they shall be punished." [10]

1856

Textbooks in the early 1800s seemed to emphasize stories in which young boys showed their bravery and patriotism to the United States. Considering that the country was about to plunge into the Civil War, one has to wonder how the concept of patriotism was taught between the North and the South. This selection was unique due to the story about the boy being killed as a cause of the Boston Massacre. Interestingly, this young lad's name was not important enough for the author to recount.

Give an Account of the Shooting of the Boy in Boston

At one time the boys became involved in an affray with one of the men who was thus obnoxious to them, and followed him to his house. The man went in, and thus escaped out of their hands. The boys then began to throw snowballs and pieces of ice at the house. The man became exasperated with them, and, thinking that he had a right to protect his dwelling from such an attack, brought a gun to the window and fired, and killed one of the boys.

WHAT EFFECT DID THIS OCCURRENCE PRODUCE?

This occurrence produced an intense excitement throughout the town. The funeral of the boy was attended by an immense concourse of people. For some days nothing else was talked of and everywhere were heard the most violent denunciations and threats of vengeance.

GIVE AN ACCOUNT OF THE SOLDIERS SHOOTING INTO THE CROWD IN STATE STREET, BOSTON

After this, disputes and collisions between the people on the one hand, and the soldiers, and the government officers, and all who were supposed to favor the British side, on the other, grew more and more frequent and alarming. When blood begins to be shed in such contentions, the effect is always to exasperate the parties more and more against each other, instead of intimidating them. At length, on one occasion, a very serious collision took place in Boston between the troops and the citizens, which increased the general excitement to a higher degree than ever. One night—it was in the evening of the fifth of March, 1770—some young men threw snowballs at a sentinel who was on guard at the Customhouse. He probably repelled the assault somewhat rudely, and this led to a disturbance. Soon a crowd collected, and there were indications of a riot. The captain of the guard, hearing of this difficulty, sent a sergeant and six men to the spot. He thought the appearance of the soldiers would intimidate the crowd and drive them away, but it seemed only to increase their excitement and exasperation. At last the command was given to fire. The soldiers obeyed. Three of the crowd were killed on the spot, and two more were mortally wounded. This occurrence produced a prodigious sensation, and aroused the people almost to phrensy [sic]. They called it a massacre.[11]

1866

It is interesting to note that throughout much of the nineteenth century, U.S. history textbooks blamed the mob in Boston for this tragic event. This selection was different from the rest because it not only brought in a rope maker as a cause for the hostilities but also, for the first time, gave a name to Crispus Attucks, a "gigantic negro," as a hero.

Samuel G. Goodrich (aka Peter Parley), the author of this textbook, was known for both his writing style, which bordered on pure fiction, and for having taken a stand against slavery, which would explain Attucks's portrait as a hero in this selection.

During the session of the British parliament in the spring of 1770, an act was passed for repealing all the duties which caused so much complaint, except that on tea. This was continued, to show that they had not yielded the right to impose taxes, if they chose to exercise it. As might have been expected, however, the colonists were still dissatisfied.

The British troops remained in Boston, and seemed determined to remain there, notwithstanding the known disgust of the citizens at the idea of having a foreign force stationed among them. There was, it is true, for some time, no open quarrel, but the citizens and soldiers were continually insulting each other.

Things could not long remain thus. On the 2d of March, 1770, as a soldier was going by the shop of a rope-maker, he was attacked and severely beaten. He ran off, but soon returned with a number of his comrades, and attacked and beat some of the rope-makers.

The people were now excited to the highest pitch. Between seven and eight o'clock in the evening of March 5, a mob collected armed with clubs, and proceeded toward King-street, now State-street, crying, "Let us drive out these rascals—they have no business here—drive them out! Drive out the rascals!" Meanwhile, there was a cry that the town had been set on fire.

The bells rang, and the throng became still greater, and more tumultuous. They rushed furiously to the custom-house, and seeing an English sentinel there, shouted, "Kill him! Kill him!"—at the same time attacking him with pieces of ice and whatever they could find. The sentinel called for the rest of the guard, and a few of them came forward.

The guard now marched out with their guns loaded. They met a great crowd of people, led on by a gigantic negro, named Attucks. They brandished their clubs and pelted the soldiers with snowballs, abusing them with harsh words, shouting in their faces, and even challenging them to fire. They even rushed close upon the very points of their bayonets.

The soldiers stood awhile like statues, the bells ringing and the mob pressing upon them. At last, Attucks with twelve of his men, began to strike upon their muskets with clubs, and to cry out to the mob, "Don't be afraid—they dare not fire—the miserable cowards—kill the rascals—crush them underfoot!"

Attucks now lifted his arm against the captain of the guard, and seized hold of a bayonet. "They dare not fire!" shouted the mob again. At this instant the firing began. Attucks dropped dead immediately. The soldiers fired twice more, and two others were killed and others still wounded. The mob dispersed, but soon returned to carry off the bodies.

The whole town was now in an uproar. Thousands of men, women, and children rushed through the streets. The sound of drums, and cries of "To arms! to arms!" were heard from all quarters. The soldiers who had fired on the people were arrested, and the governor at last persuaded the mob to disperse and go quietly to their homes.

The next morning, the troops in the city were ordered off to Castle William, one of the city fortifications. On the 8th of March, the three slain citizens were buried. The shops were all closed during the ceremony, and the bells in Boston and the adjoining towns were all the while tolling. An immense procession followed to the churchyard. . . .

There is no doubt that in most of these transactions the mob were in the wrong; the source of the mischief lay, however, in the fact that the British government insisted upon keeping an army among a people outraged by a series of unjust and irritating laws. This conduct showed that the king and parliament of Great Britain intended to compel the colonists to submission by force of arms, and not to govern them by fair and proper legislation.[12]

1880

Toward the end of the nineteenth century, a romanticized patriotic narrative of this story had emerged in full bloom.

As the people of Boston showed the most decided opposition to the tax, a body of the king's soldiers were sent to keep them in subjection. The presence of these "redcoats," or "lobsterbacks," as they were called by the boys in the streets, caused constant affrays, in one of which, known as the "Boston Massacre," the soldiers fired on the people. A gush of smoke overspread the scene. It rose heavily, as if it were loath to reveal the dreadful spectacle beneath it. Eleven of the sons of New England lay stretched upon the street. Some, sorely wounded, were struggling to rise again. Others stirred not nor groaned; for they were past all pain. Blood was streaming upon the snow; and though that purple stain melted away in the next day's sun, it was never forgotten nor forgiven by the people (1770).[13]

1936

By the early to mid-twentieth century, the story of the Boston Massacre had been assigned its pivotal, historical role in American history books.

The Boston Massacre: An Excited Country

The king and his followers were determined to enforce the unpopular laws. In order to show their determination in the matter, troops were sent to Boston to help enforce the trade laws. These troops were looked upon by the colonists as intruders. There were many street quarrels between soldiers and citizens. The soldiers gambled, held horse races, and indulged in other sports, all of which annoyed the church-going Bostonians. Finally the fatal clash came. On March 5, 1770, as the result of a street quarrel the soldiers fired into a crowd of men and boys who had been calling them names and pelting them with snowballs. This event, afterwards known as the "Boston Massacre," stirred the whole country against Great Britain and helped to fan the fire of hatred.[14]

1996

While every textbook tells the story of the Boston Massacre, it was not until later in the twentieth century that some began to argue that this event was probably used as a public relations ploy to get the colonists fired up about breaking ties with England.

One of the ablest organizers of colonial rebellion was Sam Adams of Boston. . . . He was clever at creating a sensation out of every incident and blaming it all on the British. Two regiments of British troops sent to Boston in 1768 had been taunted for months by people there. Then late one March night in 1770 a small group of redcoats was jeered at and pelted with snowballs by a few restless unemployed workers. In their confusion, the British troops fired and killed five colonists. The first to die was Crispus Attucks, a black man of giant stature who was the leader of the throng.

Sam Adams advertised this event as the "Boston Massacre" where bloodthirsty British soldiers slaughtered innocent Americans. Later, Sam's cousin, John Adams, defended the soldiers in court and was able to get them acquitted of murder. But most Americans still believed Sam Adam's portrayal of the event.[15]

12

Lexington and Concord

Over the past two hundred years, the story of the American Revolution has not changed a great deal in how it has been taught to U.S. students. Therefore, rather than observing a grand shift in the narrative, it is usually the smaller changes in this story that makes its historiography so interesting. Yet even small adjustments, such as differing accounts as to who warned the Minutemen that "the British are coming" or who took the first shot on Lexington Greene, can strongly influence how we understand this story and our historical past.

1794

The acts that this section alluded to were the Stamp, Tea, and other British Parliament Acts placed on the colonists in the years before the Revolutionary War. Unique to the more modern versions of this story was the addition of the town of Salem and the nonexistence of any midnight rides.

Preparations began to be made, to oppofe by force, the execution of thefe acts, of parliament. The militia of the country were trained to the ufe of arms, great encouragement was given for the manufacture of gunpowder, and meafures were taken to obtain all kinds of military ftores.

In February, Colonel Leflie was fent with a detachment of troops from Bofton, to take poffeffion of fome cannon at Salem. But the people had intelligence of the defign; took up the drawbridge in that town, and prevented the troops from paffing, until the cannon were fecured; fo that the expedition failed.

In April, Colonel Smith, and Major Pitcairn, were fent with a body of troops, to deftroy the military stores which had been collected at Concord, about twenty miles from Bofton. At Lexington, the militia were collected on a green, to oppofe the incurfion of the Britifh forces. Thefe were fired upon by the British troops, and eight men killed on the fpot.

The militia were difperfed, and the troops proceeded to Concord; where they deftroyed a few ftores. But on their return, they were inceffantly harraffed by the Americans, who, inflamed with just refentment, fired upon them from houfes and fences, and purfued them to Bofton.

Here was fpilt the first blood in the late war; a war which fevered America from the Britifh empire. Lexington opened the firft fcene of the great drama, which, in its progrefs, exhibited the moft illuftrious characters and events, and clofed with a revolution, equally glorious for the actors and important in its confequences to the human race.

This battle roufed all America. The militia collected from all quarters, and Bofton was in a few days befieged by twenty thoufand men. A ftop was put to all intercourfe between the town and country, and the inhabitants were reduced to great want of provifions.[16]

1830

Students today are taught that Paul Revere made the infamous midnight ride and that the identity of whoever took the first shot that day in Lexington remains a historical mystery. In the 1830s, students were taught that a series of bells warned the Minutemen; they were also given the exact name of the culprit who fired the first shot of the American Revolution.

On the evening of the 18th of April, general [*sic*] Gage dispatched from Boston a body of eight hundred troops, to destroy a quantity of provisions and military stores deposited, by the committee of supplies, at Concord. Intelligence of this movement was sent to Lexington and Concord a few hours before the troops embarked. The ringing of bells and the firing of signal guns brought the minute-men together. Early the next morning, those of Lexington assembled on the green near the meeting-house. A few minutes afterwards, the advanced body of the regulars approached within musket shot. Major Pitcairn, riding forward, exclaimed, "Disperse, you rebels, throw down your arms and disperse." Not being instantly obeyed, he discharged his pistol and ordered his men to fire. They fired and killed several. The militia dispersed; but the firing continued. In the whole, eight were killed, some of whom were shot in their concealment behind the fences.[17]

1844

By the 1840s, this story emerged fully as the stuff of legend. This selection also finally introduced the idea of the midnight ride, but not that of Paul Revere's.

The rashness of General Gage, the British commander in Boston, precipitated this event, and plunged at once the two countries into a war the most disastrous to Great Britain that she ever experienced. That officer, having learned that the provincials had collected a quantity of provisions and military stores at Concord, fourteen miles from Boston, resolved upon sending a party of troops to destroy them. He hoped also to seize John Hancock and Samuel Adams, two persons of high distinction and great influence in the colony, who had ardently espoused the cause of liberty. He made his preparations with the utmost secrecy and caution. On the 18th of April, a number of British officers were sent to dine at Cambridge; after which, towards evening, they scattered themselves on the road toward Concord, and took their stations so as to intercept any expresses which might be sent from Boston to alarm the country. Gage hoped to manage the affair so skillfully, that the Americans would be completely taken by surprise. The grenadier and light infantry companies were taken off duty on the pretext of learning a new exercise, and at eleven o'clock at night, eight hundred picked men embarked from the west side of Boston common, landed near Lechmere Point, and marched rapidly towards Concord.

But it was impossible to evade the jealous vigilance of the Bostonians. Every movement of the troops had been watched, and no sooner had they entered the boats, than a beacon light blazed from the tower of the north church, and spread the alarm into the country. On all the roads leading from Boston, the inhabitants were roused, took to their arms, and collected at different points, not knowing in what direction the enemies were proceeding. The inhabitants of Lexington received intelligence from Dr. Warren, a little after midnight, that the British were on their march to that town. The militia immediately assembled, and as the day began to dawn, the royal troops, on entering the town, were met by a body of about sixty Americans, drawn up on the green. The British advanced upon them with loud shouts, and Major Pitcairn, their commander, cried out, "Disperse, you rebels; throw down your arms, and disperse!" He then fired his pistol, and this was followed by a heavy volley from his men. No resistance could be offered by the provincials against so superior a force, and they immediately scattered, leaving eight of their number dead on the ground, and having ten wounded.

Such is the history of the encounter in which the first blood was shed in that memorable war which put an end to the British empire within the present territory of the United States. The royal troops gave three cheers, and pursued their march to Concord. A guard of about one hundred militia was posted at the outskirts of the town. Early in the morning, the British were discovered advancing by the Lexington road. The sun shone with uncommon splendor, and the arms of eight hundred men, glittering in his bright beams, formed a novel, imposing, and alarming sight to this small band of undisciplined rustics. At first, they determined to face the enemy, and abide the consequences; in this they were encouraged by the clergyman of the town, Mr. Emerson, who had turned out at the first alarm to animate the people by his counsel and example. "Let us stand our ground!" said he; "if we die, let us die here." "No," said another, "it will not do for us to begin the war." They did not then know what had taken place at Lexington. Finally, it was decided to retire and wait for reinforcements. The British marched in, and took possession of the town. The greater part of the stores had been secreted, so that the main object of the expedition was frustrated. The British staved about sixty barrels of flour, knocked off the trunnions of three iron cannon, burnt four carriage-wheels, and threw five hundred pounds of ball into the millpond and wells; but before their work of destruction was completed, the sounds of the alarm bell and the sight of numbers of people gathering on the surrounding hills, warned the

British commander that he was in danger of having his retreat cut off, and he hastily took up his march for Boston.[18]

1899

In 1860, Henry Wadsworth Longfellow wrote his now-famous poem "Paul Revere's Ride." Published in 1863, it told of the story of one man, Paul Revere, and his clandestine mission to warn the people of Lexington and Concord of the oncoming British, thereby eclipsing the large network of Minutemen historians now credit with that effort.

Lexington and Concord

It was a formal defiance to the king, and was so accepted. In spite of earnest opposition, the king managed to get retaliatory acts passed by Parliament, in April, 1774. One of these acts shut up the port of Boston until the people should be starved and frightened into paying for the tea that had been thrown overboard. By another act, the charter of Massachusetts was annulled, and a military governor appointed with despotic power like Andros. This new governor, Thomas Gage, had for some years been commander of the regular troops in America. He assumed command over Massachusetts on the 1st of June, 1774, but his authority was never recognized. Courts were prevented from sitting, no money was paid into Gage's treasury, and he was in every way ignored.

The other colonies all showed sympathy with Massachusetts, and a Continental Congress met at Philadelphia, in September. This Congress drew up a Declaration of Rights, and sent it to the king. The people of Massachusetts formed a Provincial Congress, with John Hancock for its president, and began organizing provincial troops, and collecting military stores at Concord and other inland towns. In April, 1775, Gage received orders to arrest John Hancock and Samuel Adams, and send them over to England to be tried for treason. On the 18th of April, these gentlemen were staying at a friend's house in Lexington; and Gage that evening sent out from Boston a force of 800 men to seize the military stores at Concord, with instructions to stop on the way at Lexington and arrest Adams and Hancock. But his plan was detected, and Paul Revere galloped on far in advance of the soldiers, shouting the news at every house that he passed. At sunrise, the soldiers found a party of armed yeomanry drawn up in military array on Lexington Common. One of the British officers, Major Pitcairn, ordered them to disperse, and as they remained motionless, the soldiers fired, killing seven men. This event was the beginning of the Revolutionary War.

Before sunset, there was more fighting than the British had bargained for. By the time they reached Concord most of the stores had been removed. In a sharp skirmish the troops were defeated, and as they marched back toward Boston, hundreds of farmers came swarming upon them, firing from behind walls and trees after the Indian fashion. Militia from twenty-three townships joined in the pursuit. The British lost nearly 300 men, and though heavily reinforced, narrowly escaped capture. The alarm spread like wildfire through New England. Within three days, Israel Putnam and Benedict Arnold had come from Connecticut, and John Stark from New Hampshire, and Governor Gage was besieged in Boston by 16,000 yeomanry.[19]

1944

Somewhere during the first half of the twentieth century, history textbooks seemed to have lost the historical information about who took the first shot of the American Revolutionary War. What was once common historical knowledge has since become a historical mystery. Also, considering that students would have been reading this textbook while World War II raged around the world, U.S. students at home were still learning about America's past wars. In this passage, students had to read about their former enemy—or then current ally—Great Britain.

Meanwhile British officers—civil and military—in the colonies tightened, instead of relaxing, their efforts to compel obedience to British authority. It was in the fulfillment of this duty that General Gage, in Boston, dispatched a small force of soldiers toward Lexington and Concord in April 1775 for the purpose, among other things, of seizing some military supplies supposed to be stored in that neighborhood.

Warned by William Dawes and Paul Revere that British soldiers were on the march, a small number of American militiamen gathered on the green at Lexington early in the morning of April 19. With about thirty or forty onlookers the militiamen were standing there when the British forces arrived under the command of Major John Pitcairn. Seeing that armed resistance would be futile, the captain of the militiamen, John Parker, ordered his men to disperse. While they were slowly breaking ranks a shot was fired. By whom? British who were present at the time laid the blame for the first shot on Americans; and Americans put it on the British. Since that day the question of blame has been repeatedly debated without reaching any generally accepted conclusion. Whoever cares to weigh the evidence of contemporary witnesses who saw the fray with their own eyes may find the testimony admirably summarized in the pages of Allen French's *The Day of Concord and Lexington.*

Although the person who fired the first shot that nineteenth day of April 1775 must apparently remain forever unknown, it is certain that his shot was followed by firing all day, as militiamen poured in from the surrounding country and harassed British troops on their retreat to Boston. It is also certain that this shot, "heard around the world," heralded a war.[20]

1978

Two years after Americans celebrated the bicentennial, students read in this passage that brave colonists not only fought but also "went on to defend their rights and create a new nation."

A Shot Is "Heard Round the World"

When the British soldiers reached Lexington in the early morning of April 19, 1775, they found a band of determined minutemen barring their way. Shots were fired. Eight of the Patriots were killed and ten more were wounded. Then the British marched on to Concord six miles away. There they burned the courthouse and destroyed military supplies collected by the colonists. At a bridge on the edge of town, the British met another group of determined minutemen, and several volleys were fixed by each side. But the fighting was not over. As the British soldiers marched back to Boston, other Patriots seized guns and took their positions along the road. From behind stone walls and trees the Americans poured a withering fire upon the British. Before the redcoats reached Boston, nearly 300 were killed, wounded, or missing.

What would happen next? Blood had been shed on both sides. Possibly the colonists still could have gone back to resisting the laws they disliked with written protests and fiery speeches. But the colonists did not put down their arms. Instead, they went on to defend their rights and create a new nation.[21]

1999

In the early 1800s, many textbooks spoke in vague terms about a small group of people who belonged to the Boston network of spies. Then, later textbooks began to focus on specific names, and recently, it seems this story has come full circle in that we are now giving names to a small group of people who warned the colonists about the approaching Redcoats.

Meanwhile, every colony organized military forces. Fighting between the Americans and the British soon broke out near Boston, which had been occupied in 1774 by a British army. Early on April 19, 1775, a detachment of 700 British soldiers was secretly sent to destroy the military supplies colonists had collected at Concord, 21 miles from Boston.

Learning of the soldiers' destination, the Boston Sons of Liberty took action. The organization sent Paul Revere and William Dawes, later joined by Samuel Prescott, to alert the minutemen, or militia members so named because they could be ready for battle on a minute's notice, in the towns and villages along the way. When the British reached the town of Lexington, about 70 armed minutemen awaited them. In the skirmish eight colonists were killed. The British force pushed on to the neighboring town of Concord and burned what little gunpowder the colonists had not used for themselves.

By the time the British began their march toward Boston, the countryside was swarming with minutemen, who fired at the redcoats from behind trees, buildings, and stone walls. Only a brigade sent out from Boston saved the British from annihilation. About 270 British and 100 Americans were killed or wounded at Concord.[22]

13

Massacre at Wyoming

In U.S. history textbooks published before the 1860s, the American Revolution was presented as the most important event in the nation's history. Following the 1860s, textbooks began to incorporate other major events and therefore had to edit out the lengthy sections dealing solely with the Revolutionary War. One of those stories related to the events that transpired at Wyoming, Pennsylvania, in 1778.

1851

This selection mentions that the tragedy at Wyoming may not have been the only instance of this sort during the Revolutionary War.

The enemy spent the rest of the summer [1778] in plundering expeditions. At New-Bedford, Fair-Haven, Egg-harbor, and other places, a vast amount of public and private property was seized, and much wantonly destroyed. The inhabitants were sometimes left in a state of abject wretchedness.

Several instances of shocking barbarity occurred during the summer. A regiment of cavalry under the command of Colonel Taylor, called the Washington Light-Horse, while asleep in a barn at Tappan, were surprised by the British, and about half of them killed. General Grey, who commanded the enemy, ordered his men to give "the rebels" no quarter. They fell upon them with their bayonets, and notwithstanding their entreaties for mercy, pierced them through and through. About forty were saved by the compassion of the soldiers, contrary to the orders of the general.

But a tragedy still more horrid was acted at Wyoming. This was a delightful settlement in the northern part of Pennsylvania, which contained over 1000 families. A body of 1600 men, mostly Indians who had been excited by a party of more savage whites, fell upon the inhabitants, set fire to the houses, cut the men to pieces, and left women and children to perish in the flames. The crops were laid waste, and fruit trees were torn up by the roots. This horrid massacre was brought about through the influence of the English, and those who favored their cause.[23]

1866

It is difficult to distinguish who was actually viewed as the most evil in this story: the "savage" Indians or the "savage" Tories?

The savages on the western frontier, during the year 1778, were exceedingly troublesome. There was a beautiful settlement on the eastern branch of the Susquehanna River, comprising four townships, each five miles square, and so thickly peopled that, according to some statements, it had already furnished one thousand men to the continental army.

This district of Wyoming was settled by Connecticut people, who carried with them their industrious habits, and were very prosperous and happy. They lived in the shade of their own forest-trees in summer; and in winter, by their own bright and warm firesides. Their barns were filled with grain and corn, and their green pastures, by the river banks, were spotted with sheep.

Excited, as is supposed, by the tories [sic], the Indians fixed an evil eye on these settlers; but, to prevent suspicion, first sent messages of peace and friendship. Suspicion, however, was now raised, and the settlers applied to Washington for an armed force to protect them, but it was too late. Early in July, four hundred Indians, with more than twice that number of tories and half-blooded Englishmen, came upon the settlement and destroyed it.

They were headed by Brandt, a cruel half-breed Indian, and John Butler, a tory. The officers only were dressed in British uniforms; the rest were all painted and dressed like Indians. The colonists, in their apprehension of what might happen, had built a few small forts, and gathered their families and some of their effects into them.

The savages and savage-looking whites now appeared before one of the forts, which was commanded by a cousin of Butler, and demanded its surrender. They persuaded its commander to come out to a spot agreed upon, in the woods, for the purpose, as they said, of making peace. He accordingly marched to the spot with four hundred men; but not an Indian or a tory was to be found there.

They pressed on through the dark paths of the forest, but still no one was to be found. At last they saw themselves suddenly surrounded by the enemy. The savages were in every bush, and sprang out upon them with terrible yells. All but sixty of these four hundred men were murdered in the most cruel manner.

The enemy now went back to Kingston, the village, and, to strike the Americans in the forts with as much fear as possible, hurled over the gates to them the reeking scalps of their brothers, husbands, and fathers. The distressed people now inquired of Butler, the leader of the tories, what terms he would give them. He answered only—"the hatchet."

They fought as long as they were able, but the enemy soon enclosed the fort with dry wood, and set it on fire. The unhappy people within—men, women, and children—all perished in the fearful blaze. The whole country was then ravaged, and all the inhabitants who could be found were scalped; the houses, crops, and orchards were burned; and even the tongues of the domestic animals were cut out, and the poor creatures left to perish.

This was one of those bloody deeds which the Indians are so apt to perpetrate, especially when led on by designing white men. The same company of Wyoming murderers committed other acts of violence than those above related. They were, however, at length invaded and humbled, and made willing to remain at peace.[24]

1916

Following this brief passage from the early 1900s, the story of the Wyoming Massacre virtually disappeared from U.S. history textbooks.

While Washington's army was besieging New York, the Americans were not inactive elsewhere. Scarcely a week after Monmouth, the beautiful Wyoming Valley in the northern part of Pennsylvania, which had been settled by New Englanders from Connecticut, was the scene of a terrible British Indian massacre. The fourth of July, which came the day after the massacre, disclosed a scene such as the frontier had seldom witnessed, causing a shudder of sympathy from Maine to Georgia. Hundreds of settlers went to their death under the most exquisite torture that the Indian fiends could invent. The attacking party came out of New York State, where a few months later they fell upon more victims in Cherry Valley.

Washington determined to put a stop to these outrages. In the summer of 1779 he sent an army of five thousand men under General Sullivan to devastate the entire Iroquois country of western New York, and seldom have instructions been more faithfully carried out. After a battle on the present site of the city of Elmira, the lands of the Indians were laid waste for miles around, their crops destroyed, forty of their villages burned, and the inhabitants themselves put to flight.[25]

14

Women in the Revolutionary War

In U.S. history textbooks, individual women have long played prominent roles in the presentation of the American Revolution, arguably more so than for any other period in the nation's history. It is only in recent years, however, that women's history more generally has been woven into our revolutionary narrative.

1851

Here is a typical example of a heroic narrative of the American Revolution, in a case that highlighted the actions of individual women on behalf of the patriotic cause.

Another event is still more worthy of admiration; as proceeding from the patriotic feeling of the female sex, who are less enabled to recover, by future industry, from the devastations of civil war. The British having built some works around Mrs. Motte's dwelling, situated above the fork, on the south side of the Congaree, she aided the Americans in burning her own house; and was thus the means of compelling the garrison of nearly two hundred men to surrender at discretion. The manner of accomplishing this was singular. Opposite to the hill on which this lady's mansion stood, was another elevation, where she resided in the old farm-house. On this height, Colonel Lee was posted, while General Marion occupied the eastern declivity of the ridge on which the fort stood. Lee having imparted to Mrs. Motte his design of burning her mansion by means of combustible matter conveyed by arrows, this magnanimous woman cheerfully presented him with a bow and its apparatus imported from India. The first arrow struck, and kindled a flame: a second and a third were equally successful, and very soon the entire roof was in a blaze. . . .

An American soldier, flying from a party of the enemy, sought the protection of Mrs. Richard Shubrick. His pursuers pressing closely after him, insisted that he should be delivered up, and, in case of refusal, threatened immediate destruction to her house. But, this intrepid female placed herself before the chamber into which the unfortunate fugitive had been conducted, and resolutely said; "To men of honour, the chamber of a lady should be sacred. I will defend it, though I perish. You may succeed and enter it; but it shall be over my corpse." The officer was, for a moment, speechless. "If muskets," he exclaimed, "were placed in the hands of a few such women, our only safety would be in retreat. Your heroism, Madam, protects you; I relinquish the pursuit." So much, indeed, were the ladies of the south habituated to injuries; and so warmly were they interested in the contest, that misfortunes were a cause rather of jocularity, than regret. Mrs. Sabina Elliott having witnessed the activity of an officer who had ordered the plundering of her poultry-house, and finding an old Muscovy drake which had escaped the general search, had it caught, ordered a servant to follow, on horseback, and deliver the fowl to the officer; with her compliments, that she concluded, in the hurry of departure, it had been left behind, altogether by mistake.

An anecdote is related of Mrs. Charles Elliott. A British officer, noted for inhumanity and oppression, meeting this lady in a garden adorned with a great variety of flowers, asked the name of the chamomile, which seemed to flourish with remarkable luxuriance. "That is the rebel flower," she replied. "The rebel flower!" rejoined the officer, "Why did it receive that name?"—"Because," answered the lady, "it thrives most, when most trampled on."

Volumes would not record all the heroism of the American females. Shortly after the commencement of the war, the family of Dr. Charming, then residing in England, removed to France, and sailed thence in a well-armed vessel for America. They had proceeded only a short way, when they were attacked by a privateer. A fierce engagement ensued; during which, Mrs. Charming stayed on deck, handing cartridges, dressing the wounded, and exhorting the crew to resist till death. The colours of her vessel, were, however, struck; when, seizing the pistols and side-arms of her husband, she threw them into the sea; declaring, that she would rather die, than see them surrendered to the English.[26]

1878

Molly Pitcher—now understood to be a fictitious character—long held a prominent place in textbook accounts of the war. Even today, when historians widely consider her story to be a fabrication, she appears from time to time in history textbooks.

During the day an artillery man was shot at his post. His wife, Mary Pitcher—a "red-haired, freckled-faced young Irishwoman," who was already distinguished for having fired the last gun at Fort Clinton—while bringing water to her husband from a spring, saw him fall and heard the commander order the piece to be removed from the field. Instantly dropping the pail, she hastened to the cannon, seized the rammer, and with great skill and courage performed her husband's duty. The soldiers gave her the nickname of Captain Molly. On the day after the battle, she was presented to Washington, and received a sergeant's commission with half-pay through life. Her bravery made her a great favorite among the French officers, and she would sometimes pass along the lines holding out her cocked-hat, which they would nearly fill with crown pieces.[27]

1995

While the occasional textbook published in the nineteenth century told stories of female patriotic heroism, in the twentieth century these tales began to diminish. This is ironic due to the fact that in the twentieth century, girls were more commonly found in high school history classes as compared to the 1800s. Then, in the 1970s, with the advent of the modern feminist movement, the stories of women in the war started to reappear.

Women also helped in the struggle for independence. When men went off to war, women took on added work. They planted and harvested the crops that fed the Continental Army. They made guns and other weapons. One woman, known as "Handy Betsy the Blacksmith," was famous for supplying cannons and guns to the army.

Women made shoes and wove cloth for blankets and uniforms. Betsy Ross of Philadelphia sewed flags for Washington's army. Legend claims that Washington asked her to make the first American flag of stars and stripes. But the story cannot be proved. Many women also joined their soldier husbands at the front. There, they washed clothes, cooked, and cared for the wounded. Martha Washington joined her husband whenever she could.

A few women took part in battle. During the Battle of Monmouth in 1778, Mary Ludwig Hays carried water to her husband and other soldiers. The soldiers called her Moll of the Pitcher or Molly Pitcher. When her husband was wounded, she took his place, loading and firing a cannon. Deborah Sampson of Massachusetts dressed as a man and fought in several battles. Later, she wrote about her life in the army.

Most colonists saw little actual fighting. For them, daily life went on much as usual. But when armies marched through an area, no one escaped the effects of war. For 16-year-old Sally Wister of Philadelphia, the war brought both excitement and fear. In 1777, Sally and her family fled when the British approached Philadelphia. The Wisters were Quakers and opposed fighting. Still, they favored the Patriot cause. They settled behind American lines, in a country house outside Philadelphia.

A house full of officers. One autumn day, two Patriot officers rode up to the house to warn the Wisters of British troops nearby. "About seven o'clock we heard a great noise," Sally reported in her diary.

"To the door we all went. A large number of waggons [sic] with about three hundred of the Philadelphia Militia [were outside]. They begged for drink, and several pushed into the house."

Even though the men were Patriots, Sally rushed out the back door, "all in a shake with fear; but after a while, seeing the officers appear gentlemanly . . . my fears were in some measure dispelled, tho' my teeth rattled, and my hand shook like an aspen leaf." For a time, Patriot General William Smallwood and his officers made the Wister home their headquarters. "How new is our situation!" Sally wrote. "I feel in good spirits, though surrounded by an Army, the house full of officers, the yard alive with soldiers very peaceable sort of men, tho'."

Many Patriot officers came from other colonies. Sally "took great delight in teasing" two Virginians about their accents. They, in turn, told her about life at home and "how good turkey hash and fryed hominy is."

Handsome Major Stoddert. Sally's favorite soldier was 26-year-old Major Benjamin Stoddert. But the handsome young man from Maryland was "vastly bashful" at first. He said little to her except "Good morning," and "Your servant, madam." One night, Major Stoddert stood by the dining room table, holding a candle so that General Smallwood could read his newspaper. Sally managed to strike up a conversation. "We talked and laughed for an hour. He is very clever, amiable, and polite. He has the softest voice, never pronounces the R at all."

Before long, the militia—and Major Stoddert—had to move on. "Good-bye, Miss Sally," he said, in a voice so "very low" that Sally guessed he was sorry to leave her. A month later, Major Stoddert returned. He could "scarcely walk," reported Sally, and "looked pale, thin, and dejected." He had caught a fever. The Wisters looked after him until he recovered. Then he was off to war once more. Sally never saw him again.

Back home. Sally Wister's experience of war was like that of many Americans. At times, armies marched and drilled nearby while musket and cannon fire sounded in the distance. Then life returned to normal.

In mid-1778, the British left Philadelphia. Sally Wister returned to the city and "the rattling of carriages over the streets." By then, the fighting had shifted from the Middle States to the South.[28]

PART III

The New Nation

15

Andrew Jackson and the Battle of Horseshoe Bend

The War of 1812 is sometimes characterized as the second American War of Independence. While this is partly true, it is not an accurate portrayal of the fighting that took place during those years. In the War of 1812 Native American tribes, led by leaders such as Tecumseh, ended up involved in a great deal of the fighting, and therefore joined with the British in hopes that this would halt the constant migration westward of American settlers into their territories. Students reading these passages were also introduced to Andrew Jackson for the first time. Jackson, nearly as much as Washington, falls into the category of being one of the near-mythical historical figures that U.S. history textbooks loved to gush over.

1845

The Battle of Horseshoe Bend between Andrew Jackson's militia (along with some Native American allies) and the Creek Indians is today a little-known episode. At one time, however, it occupied a prominent place in America's historical imagination. As this textbook explained in sobering terms, after this battle the Creek peoples were an "unfortunate nation [that] was totally overthrown and subjected to the whites."

On the 30th of August, 1813, the Indians of Florida attacked Fort Mims, and, after a desperate conflict with the garrison, succeeded in setting the place on fire. A dreadful carnage ensued; and only seventeen, out of the whole number of three hundred men, women, and children, escaped to carry the dreadful intelligence to the neighbouring settlements. In order to chastise these Indians for this and other unprovoked attacks on the white settlers, General Jackson was dispatched with an army of 3,500 men. A detachment of this army, on the 2d of November, fell in with a large body of Indians at Tallushatchee, which, after a desperate and obstinate resistance, was at length overcome, with the loss of one hundred and eighty-six men. Of the detachment only five were killed and forty wounded.

On the 9th of December, General Jackson succeeded in relieving the fortress of Talladega, which was then closely besieged by the Indians. The enemy were totally defeated. From this time Jackson gained victory after victory over the Indians; until at last, on the 27th of March, 1814, the spirit of the Creeks was entirely broken, and that unfortunate nation was totally overthrown and subjected to the whites, by the battle of Tohopeka. Tohopeka was a strongly fortified Indian fortress at the Horse-shoe Bend, on the Tallapoosa River, and at the time of attack was garrisoned by one thousand men, who were aware of the approaching danger, and made every preparation in their power to meet it.

When General Jackson arrived in front of their breastwork, his troops advanced with unexampled gallantry, and were received with the greatest coolness. A most destructive contest was maintained at the port holes, until Major Montgomery, springing to the wall, called to his company to follow him. He was immediately killed, but his followers unrestrained by his fall, scaled the ramparts, and the remainder of the army following their example, soon succeeded in driving the enemy into the brush. The Indians, refusing to surrender, the brush was set on fire, and soon being exposed to the view of their enemies, their numbers were materially thinned. Darkness put a stop to the slaughter. Soon after this a treaty of peace was concluded with the Indians at the Hickory Ground.[1]

1874

Students were informed in this text that what happened at Tohopeka was "eye for an eye" justice, with the United States repaying the Creeks for an earlier massacre.

While the Creeks were often portrayed as evil aggressors in this story, students here were also introduced to the concept of the "friendly Indians," who helped Jackson defeat his enemies.

Events of 1814. On the 27th of March General Andrew Jackson, with an army of volunteers, completely broke the power of the Creeks, in a battle fought at Tohopeka, or Horse-shoe Bend, on the Tallapoosa River.

The fall of Tecumseh has already been noticed. That chieftain's influence was felt beyond the tribes of the north-west. He had stirred up the Creeks to war. The inhabitants of Southern Alabama took refuge in forts, one of which, Fort Mims, was surprised and captured, August 30, 1813. Nearly four hundred men, women, and children were consigned to death within the walls. Volunteers from all quarters flocked in to avenge this horrid massacre. The principal body of these was from Tennessee, under Jackson, whose standard was also joined by friendly Indians. In a series of conflicts, beginning with the early part of November and ending with the battle of Tohopeka, the Creeks were defeated, yet at a great sacrifice of life to the victors. The next August Jackson concluded a treaty with them, by which they surrendered a large part of their territory.[3]

1911

If it is true, as this textbook claims, that this historical event was one of the "bloodiest Indian battles that ever occurred on our country's soil," then it is interesting to note that it does not get near the attention in U.S. history textbooks as other battles with Native Americans.

One August day, in 1813, a thousand Indian warriors rushed upon the four hundred helpless men, women, and children at Fort Mims, in southern Alabama.

The news of this dreadful massacre reached Tennessee. "What can we do to avenge this awful deed?" the people asked. "We will march into this Indian country," said General Andrew Jackson, the commander of the Tennessee volunteers. And that is what they did.

After one successful encounter with the Indians, Jackson's men desired to return home. The general pleaded with them to remain until the Creeks were subdued. We cannot blame these men for desiring to go; supplies were scarce, and for several weeks they had almost nothing to eat. Now provisions arrived but, nevertheless, these volunteers were determined to return to Tennessee. Finally they arose in a body. General Jackson was as determined that they should finish the work of subduing the Indians. Riding in front of the moving column, he declared, "I will shoot the first man that moves to go." Not a soldier dared to stir, and they all agreed to remain.

But they were discontented, and later General Jackson saw that it was better to let them go. They were not regular soldiers, they had never been in war before, and they became tired of it.

His next army was much better, and at Horseshoe Bend, in March, 1814, they fought one of the bloodiest Indian battles that ever occurred on our country's soil. The conflict raged all day, and before the sun set, nearly a thousand Indians lay dead upon the field. The power of the Creek Indians was now entirely broken.

General Jackson offered to spare all the red men who would lay down their arms and promise to let the white settlers alone in the future. But he made one exception—the Indian chief, Wetherford, who had led the massacre at Fort Mims, Jackson desired to punish.[3]

1933

By the 1930s, and throughout the rest of the twentieth century, the story of Jackson and the war against the Creeks began to slowly disappear from history textbooks.

The Creek War. Early in the war the Creek Indians went on the warpath. Many settlers congregated at a fort on the Alabama River. The Indians massacred those who had taken refuge there. General Andrew Jackson of Tennessee was placed in command of forces to operate against the Creeks. He carried on an energetic campaign and in March, 1814, won a great victory. The Creeks signed a treaty by which they gave up most of their lands, about two-thirds of the modern state of Alabama.[4]

1974

While the narrative of Jackson and the battle at Horseshoe Bend began to fade, stories about Jackson's appeal to the "common man" as president seemed to get more coverage in textbooks.

It would have been difficult for Britain to have a complete victory, as military developments in the South proved. General Andrew Jackson, with the aid of the Cherokees, campaigned against Britain's Indian allies. In the Battle of Horseshoe Bend in March 1814, his troops defeated the Creek Confederacy, the most powerful group of Indians in the South. Under the treaty that followed, the Creeks surrendered large tracts of land in the Mississippi Territory, more than half their lands. This rich land later became the heart of the cotton country.[5]

1995

By the 1990s, U.S. history textbooks had edited the War of 1812 down to as few pages as possible. Lost in this historical editing was the story of the Creek War along with the tragedies that befell the people of both Fort Mims and Horseshoe Bend.

The battles of the Thames and Horseshoe Bend basically brought to an end the Native American resistance to American expansion east of the Mississippi River. These battles formed the final chapter in a long struggle dating back to the early 1790s, when many Miami, Delaware, Shawnee, and others had come together and created a sizeable opposition in this region.[6]

16

The Monroe Doctrine

Written in 1823, the Monroe Doctrine did not gain a prominent place in U.S. history textbooks until the end of the nineteenth century. One can clearly track how the country perceived its role in the world and the history of U.S. foreign involvement by the extent the Monroe Doctrine is treated in the following textbooks.

1878

This textbook is typical of most of the Monroe Doctrine coverage in the 1800s. The emphasis was less on America's role in world politics than it was on teaching students about the importance of freedom from colonization.

On the occasion of the recognition of the independence of Mexico and five provinces in South America, which had thrown off the yoke of Spain, the President enunciated a principle since famous as the MONROE DOCTRINE. In a message to Congress in 1823 upon this subject, he says: "The American continents, by the free and independent position which they have assumed and maintained, are henceforth not to be considered as subjects for future colonization by any European power."[7]

1900

In 1900, the United States had just established control over the Philippines, Guam, Hawaii, Wake Island, and Puerto Rico, and had made Cuba into a protectorate. Students in the U.S. would learn from reading this text that this was beneficial for all parties involved.

The Monroe Doctrine has its root in Washington's Farewell Address of a quarter of a century before the declaration by Monroe; and indeed the germs of it may be found in his Proclamation of Neutrality of a still earlier date. In the Farewell Address, Washington urged that America stand aloof from the political broils of Europe. A few years later, Jefferson, in his first inaugural address, warned against "entangling alliances" with foreign nations. This attitude of non-interference in matters wholly European expanded until it included a determination to oppose all European interference in affairs wholly American. This doctrine had become a settled policy in the public mind, and needed only an occasion to call forth a declaration of it from the highest authority. This occasion arose in 1823, when, in his annual message to Congress (December 2), President Monroe gave utterance to the "doctrine" that has since been called by his name.

It is generally asserted that the "Holy Alliance" was formed in Europe for the purpose of assisting Spain to reduce her rebellious South American colonies to submission; but the fact is, this alliance was simply a joint resolution of the sovereigns of Russia, Austria, and Prussia to rule their respective countries in strict accordance with the principles of the Christian religion. It was an outburst of religious enthusiasm occasioned by the fall of Napoleon at Waterloo, and there is no proof that any ulterior motives entered into the agreement.

It was these same three powers, however, that met in conference at Verona in October, 1822, to consider plans to put down an insurrection in Spain and to aid that country in reducing the South American Republics. They had met two years before for the purpose of crushing out the spirit of freedom in Naples, and an Austrian army had succeeded in doing this. Now they turned their attention to Spain. England was represented at this Verona conference, and she entered her earnest protest against any interference in South America. Two reasons may be given for this stand taken by England—first, she was beyond a doubt farther advanced in her ideas of liberty and of human rights than were the continental countries, and second, she had important commercial interests with the South American Republics which she desired should not be disturbed.

The power of Spain had been greatly reduced by Napoleon I, and she was no longer able to govern her colonies. These colonies in the Western World, except Cuba, had revolted against the mother country, and after a revolutionary war of more than ten years were in 1822 recognized as independent republics by our own country. Before the close of that year the Verona Congress met, and the three monarchs who had entered into the Holy Alliance, ever vigilant to uphold absolutism as against natural human rights and liberties, proposed to aid Spain in subjugating her western possessions.

In August, 1823, Mr. Canning, the English minister of foreign affairs, proposed to Mr. Richard Rush, our minister at the Court of St. James, that Great Britain and the United States issue a joint declaration in opposition to the designs of the allied powers. Mr. Rush fully agreed with Canning that something should be done to save the new republics from reenslavement, but he had no instructions to act. He wrote a full account of the whole matter to President Monroe, who, after careful deliberation, and after asking the opinions and receiving the written approval of both Jefferson and Madison, decided to embody the general public sentiment on the subject in his message to Congress, which was soon to meet. In his annual message, therefore, we find these words:

"In the wars of the European Powers in matters relating to themselves we have never taken any part, nor does it comport with our policy to do so. . . . We owe it, therefore, to candor, and to the amicable relations existing between the United States and those Powers, to declare that we should consider any attempt on their Part to extend their system to any portion of this hemisphere as dangerous to our peace and safety. With the existing colonies or dependencies of any European Power we have not interfered and shall not interfere; but with the Governments who have declared their independence and maintained it, and whose independence we have acknowledged, we could not view any interposition for the purpose of oppressing them, or controlling in any other manner their destiny, by any European Power, in any other light than as the manifestation of an unfriendly disposition toward the United States."

This is the famous Monroe Doctrine. Its secondary immediate object was to stop the colonizing of the Pacific coast by Russia, which had been going on for some time. John Quincy Adams had expressed the same thought in very similar language, some time before, in a letter to Mr. Rush; and it is generally believed that Adams wrote this part of Monroe's message. But be that as it may, the "doctrine" took the name of Monroe, and so it will ever be known in history.

When this message was promulgated, the English people rejoiced; but their joy was mild compared with that in South America. No more was heard of the unholy alliance in Europe. From that day to the present the free republics of South and Central America have basked in the favor, and lived under the protection from foreign conquest, of the Great Republic of the North; and but for that protection most or all of them would no doubt ere this have been reduced to the vassalage of some European Power.[8]

1920

Following World War I, a great many Americans felt that the United States should return to its previous isolationist stance in world affairs—a feeling clearly expressed in this excerpt.

Interpretations of the Doctrine

The Monroe Doctrine has been called "the cornerstone of American foreign policy." It goes back for its basal idea to George Washington's warning against "entangling our peace and prosperity in the toils of European ambitions and rivalries," in his Farewell Address of 1796; and it has been ardently defended whenever there is a question of settling a boundary or collecting a debt in the Spanish-American states. Our statesmen have gradually stretched the doctrine far beyond its original declaration of the protection of the territory and the government of the republics of Central and South America. It has even been invoked as a reason for annexing territory to the United States in order to prevent the seizure of the same territory by some European power. With the entrance of the United States into the great World War, in April, 1917, and the conspicuous participation of our President in the adjustment of complicated world problems at the Peace Conference at Paris (1918–1919), that part of the Monroe Doctrine which regards the world as divided into two separate and remote halves has been rendered obsolete. If we still maintain that our interests are "paramount" in the Western Hemisphere, we no longer refrain from interfering in the political and territorial questions of the Eastern Hemisphere.[9]

1944

This textbook would have been read at the end of World War II and in the immediate postwar era in which most Americans came to realize that the United States was now, like it or not, an official world power. No longer just a historical footnote, the Monroe Doctrine was a "momentous declaration of foreign policy for the United States."

Following Washington's example, President Monroe, in 1823, formulated a momentous declaration of foreign policy for the United States—the third notable measure of his administrations. Recently Spain's colonies in the New World had nearly all declared their independence, and President Monroe, like other Americans, was troubled in mind lest European monarchs help the Spanish King in his efforts to recover control over them. From such schemes Great Britain, however, held aloof. British merchants, winning a profitable trade in Latin America, were reluctant to see Spain's commercial monopoly restored. Fully appreciating their situation, the British government proposed to the minister of the United States in London that the two countries join in; upholding the independence of the Latin American republics.

On receipt of the news President Monroe turned to Jefferson, Madison, and John Quincy Adams, the Secretary of State, for advice. They all agreed on the desirability of backing up the freedom of the Latin American republics. Jefferson welcomed the assistance of Great Britain in such a project—one so clearly advantageous for the security of the United States in the Western Hemisphere. With the aid of Adams, Monroe framed a message on the question and sent it to Congress in December 1823.

In this message, which was to bear his name in coming times as the Monroe Doctrine, the President made four clear-cut assertions. First, the United States did not propose to interfere with any colonies still owned by European Powers in the New World. Second, any effort on the part of monarchs in Europe "to extend their system to any portion of this hemi-sphere" would be regarded as "dangerous to our peace and safety." Third, the attempt of a European government to oppress or control colonies that had declared their independence would be viewed as showing "an un-friendly disposition toward the United States."

With reference to a claim to a part of the Pacific coast which the Czar of Russia had lately put forward, Monroe made the fourth assertion: "The American continents . . . are henceforth not to be considered as subjects for future colonization by any European powers." While proclaiming free-dom for the Western Hemisphere, however, he informed European gov-ernments that in turn the United States would not interfere in European affairs.

Coupled with Washington's Farewell Address to the nation, the Mon-roe Doctrine was long a main "cornerstone" of American foreign policy. Thus the last, as well as the first, of the Presidents belonging to the Revo-lutionary generation fortified the independence of the United States and the security of the Republic.[10]

1961

Written in the midst of the Cold War, this textbook highlighted Russia's action as one of the main reasons for a doctrine to protect the United States and other freedom-loving nations in South America.

Adams Urges Monroe to Reject Canning's Proposal

Monroe liked Canning's proposal, but John Quincy Adams argued against a joint declaration. He thought that Cuba might want to join the United States eventually, and he objected to tying our hands in any way.

Adams had a further reason for opposing a joint declaration. He was concerned about Russian expansion on the Pacific coast. Canning's pro-posal referred only to an invasion of Spanish America by the Holy Al-liance. Adams wanted to take action to warn Russia as well.

From her colony of Alaska, established in the eighteenth century, Rus-sia had been moving down the coast toward San Francisco Bay. In Sep-tember, 1821, the czar issued a proclamation extending Alaska down to the 51st parallel. This was part of the Oregon region which was claimed jointly by Britain and the United States. Russia also warned all foreign vessels to stay away from the Russian-American coast. Adams quickly protested. New England merchants were engaged in the fur trade in the Oregon country. If Russia's claim went unchallenged, it might exclude Americans from this region.

MONROE DECIDES ON INDEPENDENT AMERICAN ACTION

By 1823, Adams was convinced that the United States should make it clear to European powers that all parts of the New World were closed to further colonization. He wanted to send direct warnings to the nations involved. Adams managed to win Monroe partially to his views. The President was persuaded to reject the idea of a joint declaration with England in favor of an independent statement. He also adopted Adams' view that the statement should apply the non-colonization principle to the entire New World. Monroe insisted, however, on making the declaration in a public document rather than in notes sent directly to the nations involved.

MONROE WARNS FOREIGN NATIONS AGAINST COLONIZATION AND INTERFERENCE

The Monroe Doctrine, as the declaration came to be called, appeared in the President's annual message to Congress on December 2, 1823. The declaration consisted of two sections. The first was a warning to Russia in the Pacific Northwest and contained Adams' non-colonization principle: "The American continents, by the free and independent condition which they have assumed and maintain, are henceforth not to be considered as subjects for future colonization by any European powers."

The second section was directed against those powers that might intervene in South America. It declared that the United States would not interfere with "existing colonies or dependencies of any European power" in the New World. However, any attempt to reconquer [sic] the independent republics of Latin America would be considered as "the manifestation of an unfriendly disposition toward the United States."

THE MONROE DOCTRINE BECOMES A PERMANENT
PART OF AMERICA'S FOREIGN POLICY

The Monroe Doctrine was greeted with enthusiasm by the American people. They welcomed a strong foreign policy. The Monroe Doctrine expressed the self-confident nationalism of the Era of Good Feeling. Few Americans doubted the ability of their government to enforce it.

The Monroe Doctrine became one of the cornerstones of American foreign policy. It expressed the determination of the United States not to permit a powerful foreign nation to secure a foothold in the Western Hemisphere. In the later nineteenth and twentieth centuries it was frequently invoked by the American government.[11]

| 999

Written at the end of the twentieth century, this excerpt focused on competing imperial objectives—including those of the United States.

In 1800, the United States was the only independent country in the Americas. European powers, such as Great Britain, France, the Netherlands, Portugal, and particularly Spain, ruled the rest of the hemisphere. Over the next two decades, however, many Latin American colonies revolted against Spain and declared their independence. In the early 1820s, Spain gave signs of trying to regain its colonial empire. In 1823, Great Britain suggested to the United States that the two nations oppose intervention in Latin America by any power and that neither nation would acquire any part of Latin America for itself.

At that time, the Monroe administration was wrestling with another foreign-policy concern. Russia already claimed Alaska and was making aggressive moves on the Pacific coast. Reflecting the strong nationalism of the period, Monroe and Adams decided that the United States would act on its own, without consulting the British. In an address to Congress late in 1823, President Monroe set forth the policy that is now called the Monroe Doctrine. He declared that the Americas "are henceforth not to be considered as subjects for future colonization by any European powers" and that "we should consider any attempt on their part to extend their system to any portion of this hemisphere as dangerous to our peace and safety."

Throughout the 1800s, the European powers made few interventions in the Americas; however, it was the British navy, not the Monroe Doctrine, that made them back down. The significance of the Monroe Doctrine is in later events. Its bold warnings gained meaning only when the United States became a major sea power—a development that took nearly a century. Nor did the Monroe Doctrine restrict the nationalism, expansion, and intervention of the United States itself over the next 150 years.[12]

17

The Caroline Affair

The story of the Caroline Affair is a good example of the power that textbooks can exert over our historical memory: In this case, by the power of selection (or selective inclusion). The affair appears in textbooks over the past two hundred years in an unpredictable fashion, with authors alternately telling the story as a minor historical footnote, an extremely lengthy detailed narrative, or most often, not at all.

1845

The first time the Caroline Affair began to appear in U.S. history textbooks was in the 1840s.

In December, 1836, the Canadian rebellion broke out, and an American steamboat was taken, by order of the commander of the Canadian militia, set on fire, and then suffered to drift, in flames, down the Falls of Niagara. Notwithstanding the excitement produced by this affair, the President and Congress succeeded in their endeavors to preserve the neutrality of the United States. The affair of the steamboat was soon after settled between the secretary of state and Mr. Fox, the British minister, at Washington.[13]

1900

This excerpt accorded far greater significance (and length) to the event than nearly any other U.S. history textbook. Its author also gave students a few hints as to why this story might be found sporadically in U.S. history textbooks.

The Caroline Affair

To show how an apparently trifling matter may disturb the friendly relations between two great nations, and bring them to the verge of war; to reveal a feature of weakness in our dual system of government, State and National, as regards to our foreign relations; and to illustrate that the public mind may be thoroughly agitated over a subject and forget all about it within a few years—no better example can be found than that known in our history as "The *Caroline* Affair." Few of our citizens to-day, if asked about the *Caroline* Affair, could give any intelligent account of it, and the majority could not even tell what it was; while during the year of 1838, and for several years following, it was one of the most prominent subjects before the American public. It was brought about by an insurrection in Canada, and the dispute it occasioned between the United States and Great Britain became quite serious, and extended over several years.

THE CANADIAN REBELLION

There had been for many years previous to 1837 serious differences in both Upper and Lower Canada, between the popular and loyalist parties. In the latter part of that year an open insurrection broke out against the Government, then in the hands of the loyalists, or British party, as they were called. The discontent had its origin in the concentration of the Government into the hands of a few great families, the misuse of public funds, and the setting apart of certain tracts of land for the benefit of the clergy. The immediate cause of the uprising was the refusal of the Assembly to appropriate money to pay the public officials, and the carrying through the

English House of Commons, by Lord John Russell, a series of resolutions, rejecting the demand for an elective legislative council.

The leader of the revolt in Upper Canada was William Lyon MacKenzie, a Scotchman, an editor of Toronto, and first mayor of that city after its name was changed from York. He was a man of much ability, but rash, and wanting in tact; he was an intense hater of toryism [sic] in every form. The leader in Lower Canada was Louis J. Papinau, a member of the Assembly from Montreal. Papinau was a man of energy and courage, nor could any one question his honesty. Neither of these men could be accused of sinister motives nor of selfish ambition. They fully believed that the only remedy for the evils in the Government was an appeal to arms. The insurgents called themselves "patriots," and their avowed object was to break away from English rule and to set up a republic in Canada.

The rebellion found many sympathizers in the United States. All along our northern border from Vermont to Michigan there was great excitement. Men assembled and formed themselves into companies and battalions, and chose officers, intending to march into Canada to aid the patriots.

When President Van Buren became aware of these proceedings, he issued a proclamation commanding all citizens to abstain from taking part in such illegal acts, and threatening the guilty with the utmost penalty of the law. He stated that, as the United States enjoyed the most friendly relations with Great Britain, our citizens must not disturb those relations by abetting or aiding an insurrection in her colony. The President did still more; he called upon the governors of the border States to assist in suppressing all illegal movements, which they did; he sent General Winfield Scott with a body of troops to the frontier, and he chartered several steamboats on Lake Erie, manned them with soldiers, and set them to guard against all offenders. Nevertheless, a considerable number of Americans succeeded in crossing into Canada and joining the insurgents.

The rebellion was not a great one, and in a few weeks after the first outbreak it was suppressed. Sir John Colborne with an army of regulars appeared against the rebels, and after a few sharp skirmishes in which something over a hundred were killed, succeeded in dispersing them. Many laid down their arms and gave up the struggle; others fled across the border into New York. The discontent in Canada was widespread, it is true, but the revolt failed for want of leadership, neither MacKenzie nor Papinau proving successful as military leaders. The movement would scarcely be remembered in history but for an occurrence that immediately gave it international importance, and was henceforth known as the *Caroline* Affair.

DESTRUCTION OF THE CAROLINE

The *Caroline* was a small steamboat on Lake Erie, and was owned by a citizen of the United States. She was employed in illegal traffic with the Canadian insurgents on Navy Island. This island, situated in the Niagara River above the falls, had become the rendezvous of a body of rebels to the number of about five hundred under the leadership of MacKenzie. They had been beaten and driven from the mainland by the regular troops, and had here taken refuge with a view of collecting materials for another attack upon the enemy. Opposite Navy Island, near Chippewa, Ontario, several thousand Canadian troops were stationed under the command of Colonel MacNab. When it became known to MacNab and his soldiers that the *Caroline* was carrying men and supplies to the rebels on the island, they determined to destroy the vessel.

The night of December 29, 1837, was chosen for the exploit. Colonel MacNab sent Captain Drew with a flotilla of five boats to destroy her. They approached silently under cover of darkness to the shore of Navy Island, where the *Caroline* had been seen during the afternoon; but the boat was not there. Captain Drew was unwilling to give up the project so readily, and without authority from his chief proceeded to cross into American waters in search of the offending steamer. About the hour of midnight the searching party found the little steamer moored to the shore at Fort Schlosser, Grand Island, which is a part of the territory of New York. The officers and crew of the *Caroline* consisted of but ten men, but on that night twenty-three other men, who could not be accommodated at the neighboring inn, had found lodging on board the vessel. Nearly all these were American citizens.

About fifty of the British party, well armed, boarded her without warning to the occupants, most of whom were asleep at the time. The Americans sprung from their berths and grappled with the foe; but the contest was an unequal one, and in a very few minutes the British party had possession of the boat, after having killed one man and wounding several others. The victors now put the Americans ashore, cut the vessel from her moorings, set her on fire and sent her burning over the Falls of Niagara. Several of the men who had gone aboard to spend the night were afterward missing, and it was believed that they were still on board the burning steamer when she leaped over the cataract, and that they found a watery grave in the depths of the dashing river.

The news of the destruction of the *Caroline,* an American boat in American waters manned by American sailors, spread with great rapidity. The feelings of the people in the border States were inflamed to the highest degree. Retaliatory expeditions were immediately planned, but the President took measures to repress them. At the same time he sent a message to Congress stating that a hostile invasion had been made into our territory, and an outrage of the most aggravated character had been committed against our citizens. He also informed them that an immediate demand for reparation would be made upon the Government of Great Britain.

The feeling in Congress was scarcely less intense than along the northern border. An act was immediately passed placing large military supplies in the hands of the President, for the protection of the frontier; while his decision to demand redress was unanimously approved.

Scarcely a week had passed after the unfortunate occurrence, when Mr. John Forsyth, the secretary of state, addressed a letter to Mr. Fox, the English minister at Washington, in which he referred to the invasion of our territory, destruction of our property, and the assassination of American citizens at a time when it was well known that the President was doing all in his power to prevent our people from giving aid and comfort to the insurgents. The British Government made no reply to President Van Buren's demand.

The destroyers of the *Caroline* disclaimed all intention to invade American soil; they fully expected to find the vessel at Navy Island, which belonged to Canadian territory, where she had been seen a few hours before. The boat being engaged in furnishing supplies to the rebels, was, according to the rules of war, subject to seizure by the British. It was, therefore, not the act itself, but the place in which it was done, that caused all the trouble. On this ground the English ministry justified the act without assuming the responsibility. Every effort of our minister at London to bring about a settlement was treated, not perhaps with contempt, but with a dignified silence. So matters continued for three years, when, near the close of Van Buren's administration, another event occurred that changed the relative position of the two countries—the United States was put on the defensive, and Great Britain became the aggressor.

ARREST AND TRIAL OF MCLEOD

Alexander McLeod was a British subject, a resident of Ontario, a blustering braggart of no importance in his own neighborhood nor elsewhere; yet this man became the cause of the most serious disturbance between two great nations—the United States of America and the British Empire.

Three years had passed since the burning of the *Caroline*. The British Government had made no reparation for the offence and it was still a subject of general discussion among the people; but no one believed that war was likely to result, however the ministry might decide. Alexander McLeod had boasted that he was of the party that had destroyed the *Caroline,* and that he had himself killed one of the "Yankees." He appeared on the American side, and repeated his foolish boast, whereupon he was instantly arrested and clapped into prison on a charge of murder and arson.

The excitement again rose to the highest pitch. The English minister at Washington addressed a letter to the President, calling upon him to take steps for the immediate release of McLeod, taking the ground that the latter if guilty was only acting under authority, and was not personally responsible for what had been done. Mr. Forsyth in a very able paper stated that the crime had been committed on the soil of New York in time of peace between the two countries, that the whole matter of personal responsibility of the perpetrators came under the jurisdiction of that State, nor had our National Government, under our dual system, any power to interfere in the matter. He further stated that if the British Government had assumed the responsibility of destroying the *Caroline,* the United States had not been officially informed of the fact.

This answer of Forsyth plainly exhibits the weak point in our system. Here was a subject of a foreign power indicted for violating the laws of a State in the American Union, and the State has no foreign relations whatever. Great Britain could not, therefore, treat with the State of New York; she must deal with the United States Government alone. But the United

States Government has no power, under our Constitution, to take a case at common law out of the hands of a State, nor to interfere in any way with constitutional State laws.

The affair had assumed a serious aspect, and thus it remained in an unsettled condition during the winter of 1840–1841. The official term of Martin Van Buren now drew to a close, and William Henry Harrison became President.

No sooner had the United States Government changed hands, than the English ministry assumed a bolder and more menacing tone. The followers of Van Buren were prompt to assert that England had avoided showing her true colors until the party she feared had gone out of power, but she felt that she could bully the new administration as she chose. Whether the change of administration had anything to do with the matter we are unable to say, but it is a fact that the change of attitude in the British ministry began at about the same time.

On the day of Mr. Harrison's inauguration a rumor gained currency through the capital city that the British Government had assumed the destruction of the *Caroline*. One week later the English minister addressed a communication to Daniel Webster, the new secretary of state, demanding in the name of her Majesty's Government, and in a threatening manner, the immediate release of McLeod. It was learned soon after that English ships were being sent to Halifax, troops were landing in Canada, and that Lord Palmerston had openly stated in Parliament that the ministry had assumed the act of destroying the *Caroline*. The London newspapers were aflame with threats of war.

The wisdom of the British ministry in waiting for the new administration to come in before assuming its threatening attitude seemed now to be confirmed; for Mr. Webster, in answering Mr. Fox, stated that "the Government of the United States entertains no doubt of the asserted British principle," but that McLeod, being in the hands of the State of New York, was beyond the authority of the General Government. This was practically conceding the whole matter. After such a concession from such an authority, the only logical thing for the administration to do was to take the British side, and to use its efforts to effect the release of the prisoner—and that is precisely what it did.

Meantime the trial of McLeod approached. The administration requested the New York authorities to release him without a trial, for the sake of national peace; but this they refused to do. Every means was now employed by the Washington Government to secure the release of the now famous prisoner. It is said that Mr. Webster exacted a secret promise from Mr. Seward, New York's governor, to pardon McLeod if convicted. Mr. Crittenden, the attorney-general of the United States, was sent by the President to the scene of the trial at Lockport to use his efforts for acquittal.

The trial was conducted with the utmost fairness before an impartial judge and jury—and how ludicrous it all turned out! It was proved at the trial that McLeod had no part in the destruction of the *Caroline*. His boast was an idle and false one. It was shown that he had slept that night at Chippewa; that, on hearing of the exploit next morning, he expressed the wish that he had been with the party. This wish had been changed to the assertion that he had been one of them, and had killed one of the Yankees! Thus the idle boast of a brainless braggart brought about international disturbance of the most serious nature. Of course McLeod was acquitted, and the war attitude of Great Britain soon subsided. The claims of the United States against the English Government for indemnity on account of the destruction of the little steamboat were eventually abandoned, and the *Caroline* Affair, which fills a curious page in American history, was soon dropped from the public mind.[14]

1982

At the beginning of the twentieth century, the Caroline Affair was given a great deal of detail and explanation as to its historical significance. Then, the story nearly disappeared from U.S. history textbooks until the end of the century, when textbooks randomly included the story, usually as an interesting historical tidbit.

Virtually expelled from the Whig party and at war with them over domestic policy, Tyler turned his attention to territorial questions. During the late 1830s, Anglo-American relations, which had been friendly since the War of 1812, had again become tense. Southern alarm over West Indian emancipation; northern commercial rivalry with Britain; the default of state governments and corporations on British-held debts during the Panic of 1837; rebellion in Canada; boundary disputes; and American expansionism all fueled Anglo-American tensions.

Among the most troublesome of these disputes was the quarrel resulting from the *Caroline* affair, in which a United States citizen, Amos Durfee, had been killed when Canadian militia set the privately owned
steamer *Caroline* afire in the Niagara River. (The *Caroline* had supported
an unsuccessful uprising against Great Britain in Upper Canada in 1837.)
Britain refused to apologize for its revenge, and patriotic Americans
seethed with rage. Fearing that popular support for the Canadian rebels
would ignite war, President Van Buren posted troops at the border to dis-
courage border raids. Tensions subsided in November 1840 when Alexander McLeod, a Canadian deputy sheriff, was arrested in New York for the
murder of Durfee. Fortunately McLeod was eventually acquitted; had he
been found guilty and executed, Lord Palmerston, the British foreign minister, would surely have sought vengeance in war.[15]

18

The Trail of Tears

In these accounts of the notorious Trail of Tears—the forced removal of the so-called Five Civilized Tribes from the Southeast—one can see an unexpected historical narrative. While U.S. history textbooks—especially in the nineteenth century—went out of their way to criticize Native Americans and accuse them of savagery and being uncivilized, the Trail of Tears was the great exception to this trend.

1849

Written at a time when most other textbooks described Native Americans as "savages" (which the author of this particular textbook actually does in an earlier passage), this selection was surprising for the way it discussed how "civilized" the Cherokee were and how wrong the U.S. government had been in this situation.

A few events concerning the Cherokees require notice in this portion of our history. These Indians had long been involved in the same difficulties as those which had troubled their Creek neighbors. They were the most civilized of all the Indian tribes, had an established government, a national legislature, and written laws. During the administration of Mr.

Adams, they were protected in their rights against the claims of the state of Georgia, but in the following administration, the legislature of Georgia extended the laws of the state over the Indian territory, annulling the laws which had been previously established, and among other things, declaring that "no Indian or descendant of an Indian, residing within the Creek or Cherokee nations of Indians, should be deemed a competent witness or party to any suit in any court where a white man is a defendant."

Although the supreme court of the United States declared the acts of the legislature of Georgia to be unconstitutional, yet the decision of that tribunal was disregarded, and the president of the United States informed the Cherokees that he had no power to oppose the exercise of the sovereignty of any state over all who may be within its limits; "and he therefore advised them to abide the issue of such new relations without any hope that he will interfere." Thus the remnant of the Cherokees, once a great and powerful people, were deprived of their national sovereignty, and delivered into the hands of their oppressors.

Yet the Cherokees were still determined to remain in the land of their fathers. But at length, in 1835, a few of their chiefs were induced to sign a treaty for a sale of their lands, and a removal west of the Mississippi although this treaty was opposed by a majority of the Cherokees, and the terms afterwards—decided upon at Washington—rejected by them, yet as they found arrayed against them the certain hostility of Georgia, and could expect no protection from the general government, they finally decided upon a removal; but it was not until towards the close of the year 1838 that the business of emigration was completed.[16]

1889

With the frontier closing toward the late nineteenth century and the "Indian problem" coming to an end, some students began to read passages from textbooks that went to great pains to highlight the "civilized" qualities of the Cherokee.

The Cherokees were now the most powerful tribe of Indians in Georgia and Alabama, since the Creeks had been overthrown by Jackson. They were intelligent and educated; they had churches, schools, and newspapers of their own; and they refused to remove across the Mississippi. Finally, the State of Georgia became impatient, and decided to force the Indians to go.

President Adams, in 1827, interfered to protect the Indians, but Georgia declared its intention to resist the Federal Government, if necessary, by force. The State was at last successful in compelling the Cherokees to remove.[17]

1916

By the early part of the twentieth century, students began to have their attention focused on the fight between Jackson and Marshall, while the story of the Cherokee basically became a footnote to the event.

When Jackson came into office, the state of Georgia was still engaged in its struggle to remove the Creek and Cherokee Indians from its borders to the regions west of the Mississippi. In contrast to President Adams, who vainly attempted to defend the Indians against what he considered unfair treatment, Jackson, who knew from experience how the presence of the Indians hindered the settlement of the country, upheld the state at every step. To assert its jurisdiction over the lands of the Cherokees, the courts of Georgia tried a Cherokee, Corn Tassels by name, for murder, and found him guilty. Against the order of the Supreme Court of the United States the officials of the state put the culprit to death, and the President did not interfere. On another occasion a certain missionary was arrested and convicted by the state for entering, without state license, upon the lands held by the Indians, and was kept in prison in defiance of the Supreme Court of the United States. Again the President refused to uphold the court. "John Marshall has made his decision," he is reported to have said; "now let him enforce it." Disheartened, the Cherokees at last gave up their lands to the United States for a stipulated sum and consented to removal to Indian Territory, which Jackson recommended to be set aside for the Indian tribes.[18]

1947

Staying with the theme that these tribes had done nothing wrong to deserve what happened to them, many textbooks often tried to insinuate that the tragedy was due to the settlers' greed and Jackson's arrogance.

Jackson Removes the Indians to the West. The fate of the Indians was still unsettled when Jackson took office. Thomas Jefferson had believed we should civilize the red men and let them keep part of their land. This policy was not tried in the old Northwest, for there the white settlers advanced along a single wide front, pushing the Indians steadily westward. But in the old Southwest, where the white men settled chiefly along the great rivers, five powerful tribes were left on the lands in between. These tribes were accepting the Christian religion and taking up most of the white men's ways. They were known as the "Five Civilized Tribes." The Cherokees, for example, were excellent farmers and stock raisers, living in neat wooden houses surrounded by orchards. They built roads, kept inns, and made cotton and woolen cloth. They had an alphabet and kept written records. They had a constitution and a government much like ours. The United States had recognized them in treaties as an independent nation.

The people of Georgia wanted the Cherokee lands, so the state authorities announced that the Indians must move. The Cherokees appealed to the courts. The Supreme Court, under John Marshall, ruled that the Cherokees were a nation and that the laws of Georgia did not apply to them. Georgia refused to obey the Supreme Court and began to remove the Indians by force. This action was just as serious as South Carolina's refusal to obey the tariff law. Yet President Jackson did nothing about it. Like other frontiersman, he had no respect for Indians, and believed they should be driven to places set aside for them in the West, that is, to reservations. He is reported to have said, "John Marshall has made his decision; now let him enforce it." [19]

1974

While the historiography of the Trail of Tears has consistently put the Cherokee in a positive light, Jackson's reputation seemed to take the hardest hit in the 1970s.

When it came to Indian policy, Jackson sometimes took a states' rights stand. Like many other westerners, Jackson disliked and distrusted Indians. The Indians disliked and distrusted him, too, with reason. Jackson's two terms as President were marked by constant fighting with the tribes.

The government's, and especially Jackson's, aim in this period was to remove all Indians living in the area east of the Mississippi. Explorers had described the area west of the Mississippi as the "Great American Desert," unsuitable for farming. Thinking that white settlers would never want this arid land, government leaders decided it would be the perfect spot to put the Indians. Thus the government would end the seemingly endless cycle by which white settlers moved in to Indian Territory, fought over it, defeated the tribes, negotiated a treaty, pushed the tribes out, settled, filled up the territory, and moved toward more Indian land. By locating the Indians on land that no whites wanted, the leaders thought they would be giving the Indians a permanent territory. At the same time they would be getting rid of the tribes in areas that whites wanted for themselves.

The Bureau of Indian Affairs, which had been set up as part of the War Department in 1824, was expanded in 1832. Under Jackson, the BIA directed the signing of ninety-four treaties by which tribal peoples gave up some of their lands.

In the North, most of the tribes had already been moved west of the Mississippi. The last stand of the northeastern tribes was the Black Hawk War, in 1832. Led by the Sauk chief, Black Hawk, the Sauk and Fox resisted removal. They fought in northern Illinois and southern Wisconsin until they were finally beaten by the army.

Of the southeastern tribes, the Choctaw, Chickasaw, and Creek were fairly easy to move to the new Indian Territory. The Cherokee and Seminole, however, refused to sign treaties with the government. When the state of Georgia tried to make the Cherokee subject to the state, the Cherokee took their case to the Supreme Court. Although the Court upheld the Cherokee position, Andrew Jackson did not. The President refused to execute the court's orders. He is reported to have said: "John Marshall has made his decision; now let him enforce it."

The state of Georgia, at Jackson's urging, harassed the Cherokee until some of them signed a removal treaty. The tribe was moved west in 1838 and 1839, after Jackson had left office. A fourth of the tribe died during the journey, which came to be called the Cherokee "Trail of Tears." Some of the Cherokee fled to the hills of North Carolina, where their descendents still live.[20]

1995

In this passage, an economic motivation—the expansion of cotton—has been woven into the story of the Native Americans' removal. Also of note, this was one of the very few texts that, although extremely brief, mentioned the actual journey these people were forced to take in the 1830s.

President Jackson also used federal power negatively to support the relocation of the Cherokee, Choctaw, Creek, Chickasaw, and Seminole peoples to what is now Oklahoma. He had a deep prejudice against Native Americans and believed that they would prevent white people from moving west and opening up land for cotton production.

Many Americans shared Jackson's prejudice against Native Americans. In 1829 Georgia seized Cherokee land for cotton growers. After appealing to the United States Senate with little result, the Cherokee appealed directly to the American people in 1830. In that appeal, the Cherokee said:

> The people of the United States will have the fairness to reflect, that all the treaties between them and the Cherokee were made . . . for the benefit of the whites. . . . We wish to remain on the land of our fathers. We have a perfect and original right to remain without interruption. . . . The treaties with us and laws of the United States made in pursuance of treaties, guaranty [*sic*] our residence. . . . It cannot be that the community we are addressing, remarkable for its intelligence and religious sensibilities, and preeminent [admired] for its devotion to the rights of man, will lay aside this appeal.

Two years later, Chief Justice Marshall, in the case *Worcester v. Georgia,* ruled that Georgia's action was unconstitutional and should not be allowed. But Jackson and Georgia ignored the Supreme Court, which had no power to enforce its decision. In 1837 and 1838, the United States Army gathered about fifteen thousand Cherokee and forced them to migrate west.

On this nightmare journey, which has come to be called the Trail of Tears, about one out of every four Cherokees died of exposure or disease. In an added outrage, the $6 million spent by the federal government to relocate the Cherokee was charged against the $9 million that the Cherokee had been forced to accept for their lands.[21]

19

The Mormons

Early American history textbooks assumed that the United States was founded on a Christian basis, and that God had preordained the country to be an exemplary Christian nation in the world. Still, the Christian orientation did not mean that textbooks, particularly those written and used in the 1800s, would be tolerant of the numerous Christian sects developing in the United States. Of these, the Church of Jesus Christ of Latter Day Saints (aka Mormons) has attracted the most attention, and has most often tested America's conception of itself as a nation built on tolerance and religious diversity.

1866

In the 1800s, it was not uncommon for textbooks to openly express criticism of the Church of Jesus Christ of Latter Day Saints and its followers.

Another subject which early demanded the attention of Mr. Buchanan was the condition of the Mormons in Utah. This strange sect, whom we have already mentioned as causing some disturbance in Illinois, moved to the west in 1848, and established themselves in the vicinity of the Great

Salt Lake, amid the mountains which lie between the Western states and the region of the Pacific.

Notwithstanding the absurdity of the religious pretences on which this sect is founded, and their gross and immoral practice of polygamy, they have rapidly increased in numbers, and active missionaries are found propagating the faith in nearly every country of Europe. The whole number of the community is said to exceed two hundred thousand. In Utah there is probably a population of one hundred thousand, almost exclusively Mormons.

Near the Great Salt Lake they have commenced a city on an extensive plan, with sumptuous public buildings, and they have also covered large tracts of their territory with well-cultivated farms. Being on the main route of travel from the Western states to California, they derive great profit from the emigrants. Their government is in the hands of a few persons, and a man by the name of Brigham Young is now (1864) and for several years has been their prophet, priest, and king.[22]

1897

While this selection was still not a sweeping endorsement of the Mormons and their beliefs, it did take a much more positive viewpoint of their history than most other textbooks found in the 1800s.

Rise of the Mormons; Nauvoo

Toward the close of Van Buren's presidency, a new religious community, called Mormons, settled in Illinois. Its founder was Joseph Smith, a native of Vermont. While living in New York he declared that an angel from heaven gave him a number of golden plates—like sheets of tin—on which a new scripture was written called the "Book of Mormon."

Smith went to Ohio, to Missouri, and, finally, to Illinois, where he and his followers—the "Latter Day Saints" or Mormons—built the "Holy City" of Nauvoo on the banks of the Mississippi. There he stated that he received a revelation from God declaring that every true Mormon marriage would last forever, and encouraging all good Mormons to marry as many wives as they found convenient. Those, said he, who keep this law will, in the next world, "pass by the angels" in glory.

Shortly after this, several persons who had belonged to the Mormons began publishing a paper in Nauvoo, in which they accused Smith of leading an evil life. Smith broke up the paper. For this he was arrested, and while in jail at Carthage (1844) was shot by a mob who had no faith in him or his religion.

EMIGRATION OF THE MORMONS TO UTAH; WHAT THEY HAVE ACCOMPLISHED THERE

Brigham Young of Vermont—a man as keen-sighted in the things of this world as it was said Smith had been in those of the other—now became leader of the Mormons; but the people round Nauvoo forced the "Saints" to leave, and they crossed the Mississippi. In 1847 Young started for the far west, and, with about a hundred and fifty followers, reached Salt Lake, in what is now Utah. Later, he led a much larger number of Mormon emigrants to the same place. It was a journey of fifteen hundred miles through the wilderness. The country bordering on the lake was a desert. The hunters of that desolate region predicted that the Mormons would starve. But Young saw what could be done to prevent that. He set his company to work digging ditches to bring water from the mountains; every street in the village had two of these ditches running through the length of it, one on each side. The abundant supply of water soon made the dead, dry soil green with waving crops of wheat and corn. Industry transformed the desert into a garden. Since then the Mormons have prospered and grown strong. The village has become a city, and Utah now has a Mormon population of over a hundred thousand, largely made up of emigrants from Great Britain, Norway, and Sweden.[23]

1944

Throughout much of the first half of the twentieth century, the story of the Mormons changed: the Mormons were no longer bringing troubles to themselves; rather, outside agitators were causing them problems. Though the Mormon religion was still questioned (especially the act of polygamy), what the Mormons did in the Utah desert impressed history textbook authors enough to finally gain them some positive recognition.

The territorial settlement at the close of the Mexican War and the rapid progress of California in population and wealth affected the career of one of the strangest communities in the whole story of American pioneering. This was the Mormon colony in Utah. The Mormon sect had started on its course under the leadership of Joseph Smith, of New York, in 1830, and had been pushed from place to place by hostile neighbors before it settled finally in Utah. Its members had tried living in Missouri. From Missouri they moved to Illinois. Having now adopted the practice of polygamy, or "plural marriage," and given it an elaborate religious sanction, the Mormons seemed to multiply their enemies on every hand. When Brigham Young became their second leader, they decided to go to some remote region where they might live and work in their own fashion with no interference from outsiders. After inquiring about the distant West, Young selected a spot so far away and so arid, he supposed, as to invite few if any intruders; and in 1847 he led his flock to the Salt Lake Valley.

By hard labor and efficient management, the Mormons in Utah made that desert blossom like a rose, as Young had said they would, and built up a prosperous society. Their freedom in the wilds of the West was, nevertheless, soon curtailed. In organizing the territory of Utah the government of the United States brought them under its control; and the gold rush to California over the trail running through Salt Lake City introduced "foreigners" and the lure of gold into their midst. Moreover, many Gentiles insisted on settling down in Utah. Thus the Mormons' longed-for escape from the difficulties of relations with other people proved to be no escape at all. They were destined to be merged in the great Union as the tide of immigration rolled westward toward the Pacific.[24]

1966

This passage uniquely associated the Mormons' trek west with that of an earlier American religious dissident, Roger Williams.

The Mormons and Utah

One of the largest groups was the Mormons. The Mormon Church, or the Church of Jesus Christ of Latter-Day Saints, had been founded in western New York in the 1820's by young Joseph Smith. Smith announced that he had found golden plates on which sacred scriptures were engraved. When translated, these became the "Book of Mormon." Thousands of converts joined the new religious faith.

In three different places—Kirtland in Ohio, Independence in Missouri, and Nauvoo in Illinois—Mormons attempted to build an ideal society where they could live and worship in their own way. Each time, they were driven away by hostile neighbors who did not understand them and who disliked their idea that they were a chosen people with a special revelation of truth. Also, in Missouri, the fact that most Mormons were of "Yankee" background and did not favor slavery, called forth the opposition of the proslavery Missourians. The open acceptance of polygamy by the Mormons at Nauvoo was a further cause of disapproval.

The Nauvoo community prospered above the other two. By 1844 it had become a thriving town of 15,000 persons. In that year, however, nearby communities organized against the Mormons. Joseph Smith and his brother were thrown into jail and then murdered by a mob. Once again the Mormons were forced to move.

Under the able leadership of Brigham Young, the Mormons moved out of Nauvoo. Their long caravan of loaded wagons moved westward across the plains, through the towering Rockies, and finally came to a halt in 1847 on the southeastern shore of Great Salt Lake. There the Mormons plowed and irrigated the fields, learning many lessons about desert farming which they passed on to later western settlers. They laid out Salt Lake City on the Jordan River, and erected a famous temple. The Mormons also sent missionaries to the ends of the earth and organized ways of transporting converts to their new community in Utah.

For a number of reasons, Utah was not admitted to the Union until 1896. By that time it was a settled and prosperous region, born out of a desire similar to that which had driven the Pilgrims, Roger Williams, and others to worship God in their own way.[25]

1995

It was not until the late twentieth century that textbooks reflected a fully tolerant and historically nuanced view of the Mormons' presence in the American West.

Starting in 1847, hundreds of Mormons left their temporary camps in Iowa for new homes near the Great Salt Lake. Within three years, more than 11,000 Mormons had settled in the region. By 1860, about 30,000 Mormons lived in Salt Lake City and more than ninety other towns in present-day Utah.

Despite many difficulties, these settlements were orderly and prosperous. The Mormons skillfully irrigated their desert region and devoted themselves primarily to farming.

At first the leaders of the Mormon church established their own system of government. With the end of the Mexican War, however, Utah became an official territory of the United States and Brigham Young its first governor. Utah eventually entered the Union in 1896 as the forty-fifth state.

At the time of the Mexican War, the Mormons, one of the largest groups of migrants to head west in the 1840s, were finding a new home in present-day Utah. Mormons, or members of the Church of Jesus Christ of Latter-Day Saints, had been looking for a permanent home ever since Joseph Smith founded the religion in western New York in 1830. Harassed by neighbors who were suspicious of their beliefs, the Mormons moved to Ohio, then to Missouri, and finally to Nauvoo, Illinois.

Although the Mormons initially prospered in Illinois, relations with neighbors deteriorated after Smith revealed in 1843 that the Mormons accepted polygamy, a practice in which a family includes one husband and several wives. After a hostile mob killed Smith and his brother in 1844, the Mormons were forced to move on once again. The religion's new leader, Brigham Young, decided that the Mormons' only hope was to live beyond the borders of the United States of that time. He and other leaders chose the Great Salt Lake Basin as the Mormons' new home, largely because it was located nearly a thousand miles from other Americans.[26]

20

The Alamo

Few historical events in American history evoke as much legend, patriotism, and myth as the siege of the Alamo. Nevertheless, much of the mythology seems to have been created in the latter half of the twentieth century. The Alamo rarely received more than a mention in most nineteenth-century textbooks, but today there are often longer passages with the compulsory picture of the Alamo. One has to wonder what impact television and film has had on our collective memory of this historical event.

1867

In a textbook written just two years after the end of the Civil War, students learned that the Alamo was significant due to the "gallant" bravery of the Americans who fought there and that David (not Davy) Crockett was probably one of those killed.

The prosperity of these settlers awakened the jealousy of the Mexicans, and an unjust and oppressive policy was pursued towards them. Their remonstrances being disregarded, they declared their independence of Mexico, and made ready to support it by force of arms. Volunteers from

America hastened to their aid. In 1835, the revolution began with the battle of Gonzales, in which 1,000 Mexicans were defeated by 500 Texans. Goliad, and the strong citadel of Bexar, known as the Alamo, were soon after taken, and the whole Mexican army was dispersed. On the 6th of March, 1836, however, Santa Anna, having raised a new force of 8,000 men, attacked the Alamo, which had been left in charge of a small but gallant garrison. All night they fought, but superior numbers triumphed. Every man fell at his post but seven, and these were killed while asking quarter. Here died David Crockett, the famous hunter. Crockett had enjoyed but two months instruction at a country school; but his strong common sense and indomitable courage made him very popular among the people of Tennessee, who three times elected him to Congress. In 1834 he went to Texas, to strike a blow for freedom. The Alamo proved his last battlefield. He expired, covered with wounds, surrounded by a circle of Mexicans who had fallen by his sword.[27]

1878

In the nineteenth century, Mexican brutality and American courage were two consistent themes in the historiography of this event.

Santa Anna now invaded the country with nearly eight thousand men and laid siege to the Alamo, then held by only one hundred and forty Texans under Colonel Travis. The place was taken by storm, the Mexicans losing sixteen hundred soldiers. All the garrison fell fighting at their posts except seven who were put to the sword after having surrendered. Among them was David Crockett, the famous backwoodsman and hunter. Santa Anna then attacked Colonel Fanning, who was stationed at Goliad with five hundred men. Overwhelmed by superior forces, the soldiers surrendered on condition that they should give up their arms and return to the United States. In spite of this agreement, they were all massacred in cold blood.[28]

1899

Like most of the textbooks printed in the 1800s, the Alamo, as in this passage, was not even mentioned in the story of the Texas Revolution.

The southern people, therefore, in self-defense felt driven to acquire more territory. The republic of Texas was close at hand, a fine country as big as the Austro-Hungarian Empire, with Italy and Switzerland thrown in. Texas had once belonged to Mexico, but, in 1820, Moses Austin, a native of Connecticut, had obtained a grant of land there, and within a few years more than 20,000 people from the United States had settled in Texas. The government of Mexico was regarded as oppressive, and these Texans declared their state independent. In 1836, their commander, Samuel Houston, totally defeated the Mexicans under Santa Anna, in the battle of San Jacinto, and the independence of Texas was achieved. Next year, she asked for admission to the American Union, but nothing was done about it, and for some years she was known as the "Lone Star State."[29]

1905

This passage made a unique claim when it stated that "the Texans were too well organized and too good fighters ever to be conquered by Mexico." If this is historically accurate, then how exactly did they lose the battle for the Alamo?

By 1835 the spirit of independence was so strong that the Texans resisted a Mexican force under General Santa Anna, the Mexican dictator. In March, 1836, under Sam Houston, a friend of Jackson, they declared their independence, drew up a national constitution, and made slavery a fundamental part of the government. Four days later a fortified convent, the Alamo in San Antonio, was taken by a Mexican army after a brave defense, and every man within it was killed. This massacre sowed undying hatred, and the Texans were too well organized and too good fighters ever to be conquered by Mexico. They desired to be annexed by the United States; and it might have been brought about had not the North protested against an annexation which would strengthen the slave power. In October, 1836, the Texan congress claimed a boundary "to the mouth of the Rio Grande, thence up the principal stream of the said river to its source."[30]

1916

In the early twentieth century, students reading this passage probably did not miss the racial overtones.

Conflict with the Mexicans was an unavoidable consequence. It could not be expected that citizens of the United States, with Anglo-Saxon blood in their veins and with the independent spirit of frontiersmen, would feel loyalty to the weak and shifting government of Mexico. Once settled in the province of Texas, the immigrants quarreled with the native inhabitants, broke into open rebellion, and on March 2, 1836, declared Texas a free and independent state. The Texas War of Independence opened with a terrible massacre by the Mexicans of one hundred and fifty Texans at the Alamo, an old Spanish mission building in San Antonio, Texas, and closed with the battle of San Jacinto, in which the insurgents under General Sam Houston won a notable victory over President Santa Anna and his Mexican followers. Six hundred Mexicans were killed in the battle, two hundred injured, and Santa Anna made prisoner. Houston was made President of the new Republic of Texas, and in spite of the fact that Mexico still claimed Texas as her own, the President and Congress of the United States recognized the independence of the revolted state. After such an unfriendly act by the United States, the neighboring sister republic and the nations farther south began to question the sincerity of the Monroe Doctrine.[31]

1950

By midcentury, U.S. history textbooks began to give students the more "modern" agreed-on story.

Mexico tried to crush the revolt. General Santa Anna led troops into Texas to punish the Americans. The Texans suffered two horrible defeats, but they also won one final and glorious victory. The first defeat was at the Alamo in the city of San Antonio. The Alamo was an old Spanish mission surrounded by high walls. A force of 187 Texans, under the command of Colonel William Barrett Travis, barricaded themselves in the mission and were besieged by 3,000 Mexicans under Santa Anna. In spite of the unequal odds, the Texans held out for eleven days. When the battle was over, all of them were dead. "Remember the Alamo" became the battle cry of all Texans.[32]

1961

In this passage, the stereotypical images began to seep into the story, with the names of Colonel William Barret Travis, Davy Crockett, and James Bowie as well as the phrase "Remember the Alamo" all playing integral parts.

The Texans are defeated at the Alamo. Before the end of February, 1836, Santa Anna's invading army had encircled San Antonio. Texas was not prepared to meet his force. Her troops were scattered and out of touch with each other, and there was no plan of campaign. One band of Texans, led by William B. Travis, instead of retreating before Santa Anna's superior force, moved into the chapel in San Antonio, called the Alamo, and awaited the Mexican assault.

Surrounded by a force of 2,400 Mexicans, Travis' little group of men succeeded in holding out for more than a week. Every one of the 188 defenders, including such famous pioneers as David Crockett and James Bowie, as well as Travis, was killed. Among Texans, "Remember the Alamo!" became the popular battle cry.[33]

1995

By the mid-1990s, a different perspective was added to the historiography of the Alamo story. This passage questioned the "mythical bravery" of the Texas/ American forces inside the Alamo, and did not give Crockett his glorious last-stand death.

Within days after Texas declared itself a republic, rebels and Mexican troops in San Antonio fought the famous battle of the Alamo. Myths about that battle have magnified the rebels' valor at the Mexicans' expense. The story is based on fact—only 187 rebels fought a far larger number of Mexican soldiers for more than a week before eventual capitulation—but it is not true that all rebels, including folk hero Davy Crockett, fought to the death. Crockett and seven other survivors were captured then executed. Moreover, the rebels fought from inside a strong fortress with superior cannons against march-weary Mexican conscripts. Nevertheless, a tale that combined actual mythical bravery inside the

Alamo gave the insurrection new inspiration, moral sanction, outside support, and the rallying cry "Remember the Alamo."

The revolt ended with an exchange of slaughters. A few days after the Alamo battle, another Texas detachment was surrounded and captured in an open plain near the San Antonio River and was marched to the town of Goliad, where most of its 350 members were executed.[34]

2 1

The Start of the Mexican-American War

Current historiography blames the United States for starting a war with Mexico, primarily for expansionist reasons. Most students today learn that this was a war of aggression and greed; a young lieutenant by the name of Ulysses S. Grant is often quoted in this context, calling this war "one of the most unjust ever waged by a stronger against a weaker nation." But this part of the story is relatively new to students. In the nineteenth and early twentieth centuries, students frequently learned that America was just defending itself from Mexican hostilities, even if a preemptive strike into Mexico was needed in order to do that.

1849

In this passage, written immediately after the war concluded, there was little doubt as to who started the war. The Mexicans not only ignored the negotiating envoy; they were also, it was believed, assembling troops to retake Texas.

Scarcely had Mr. Polk taken his seat as president of the United States, when decided indications of a rupture with Mexico became apparent.

Mexico had long viewed the conduct of the American government, in relation to the acquisition of Texas, with exceeding jealousy and distrust: still claiming that country as a part of her own territory, she had declared that she would regard annexation as a hostile act, and that she was resolved to declare war as soon as she received intimation of the completion of the project. In accordance with this policy, immediately after the resolution of annexation had passed the American Congress, and received the sanction of the President, Mr. Almonte, the Mexican Minister at Washington, protesting against the measure as an act of warlike aggression, which he declared Mexico would resist with all the means in her power, demanded his passports and returned home.

On the fourth of July following, Texas assented to the terms of the resolution of annexation, and two days later, fearing that Mexico would carry her threats of war into execution, requested the President of the United States to occupy the ports of Texas, and send an army to the defence of her territory. Accordingly, an American squadron was sent into the Gulf of Mexico, and General Taylor, then in command at Camp Jessup, was ordered by the American government to move with much of the regular forces as could be gathered from the western posts, to the southern frontier of Texas, to act as circumstances might require. By the advice of the Texan authorities he was induced to select for the concentration of his troops the post of Corpus Christi, a Texan settlement on the bay of the same name, where, by the beginning of August, 1845, he had taken his position, and at which place he had assembled, in the November following, an army of little more than four thousand men.

On the 13th of January, 1846, when it was believed that the Mexicans were assembling troops on their northern frontiers with the avowed object of reconquering [sic] Texas, and when such information had been received from Mexico as rendered it probable, if not certain, that she would refuse to receive the envoy whom the United States had sent to negotiate a settlement of the difficulties between the two countries, the American president ordered General Taylor to advance his forces to the Rio Grande, the most southern and western limits of Texas, as claimed by herself: on the 8th of March following the advance column of the army, under General Twiggs, was put in motion for that purpose, and on the 28th of the same month General Taylor, after having established a depot at Point Isabel twenty-one miles in his rear, took his position on the northern bank of the Rio Grande, where he hastily erected a fortress, called Fort Brown, within cannon shot of Matamoras.

On the 26th of April, the Mexican general, Ampudia, gave notice to General Taylor that he considered hostilities commenced, and should prosecute them; and on the same day an American dragoon party of sixty-three men, under command of Captain Thornton, was attacked on the east side of the Rio Grande, thirty miles above Matamoras, and after the loss of sixteen men in killed and wounded, was compelled to surrender. This was the commencement of actual hostilities—the first blood shed in the war.[35]

1880

This selection cast the U.S.-Mexican conflict in the broadest possible terms, suggesting a racial conflict centuries in the making.

Mexico, the capital of the ancient Aztecs, the seat of the Spanish American empire in America—had passed from Aztec and from Spaniard to the Anglo American—the Northman of the Goths, the Saxon of Germany, the Englishman of America—the same bold, hardy, energetic, ingenious, invincible, ambitious, and adventurous being, whose genius the forms of civilization cannot confine and to whose dominion continents are inadequate. In what hour of time, or limit of space, shall this man of the moderns—this conqueror over land and seas, nations and governments—find rest, in the completion of his mighty progress? Commencing his march in the cold regions of Scandinavia, no ice chilled his blood—no wilderness delayed his steps—no labor wearied his industry—no armies arrested his march—no empire subdued his power. Over armies and over empires—over lands and over seas—in heat, and cold, and wilderness, and flood—amidst the desolations of death and the decays of disease—this Northman has moved on in might and majesty, steady as the footsteps of Time, and fixed as the decrees of Fate!

How singular—how romantically strange is this—his wild adventure and marvelous conquest in the valley of valleys! How came the Northman and the Moorish Celt here to meet, and here to battle, in this North American valley? Look at it! Inquire! Ask yourself how they came here! Are they the citizens, by nature, of this continent? Are they the aborigines of these wild and wonderful forests? Never! How came they, then, to be contending for the lands and groves of those whose children they are not? In the beginning of the sixteenth century, Cortez landed on the coast of Mexico, and, at the head of Spanish troops, marched on to the conquest of Mexico, over whose effeminate inhabitants the Spaniard has, for three hundred years, held undivided dominion. Not many years after, the Anglo-Saxon landed on the coasts of the northern Atlantic. He, too, marched on to conquest. The native citizens of the forest disappeared before him. Forests, mountains, and Indians, were ineffectual to oppose him. From the banks of the St. Lawrence to the Sabine of Texas, he is a conqueror over nature. And now, this Spaniard and this Northman meet, in battle panoply, in this valley of volcanoes, by the ancient graves of unknown nations, on the lava-covered soil where nature once poured forth her awe-inspiring flames. Three centuries since, these warrior-nations had left their homes beyond the wide Atlantic. Two thousand miles from each other, they had planted the seats of their empire; and now, as if time, in the moral world, had completed another of its grand revolutions, they have met in mortal conflict.[36]

1 9 1 1

The idea that U.S. military actions at the beginning of the war constituted a preemptive strike (anticipating a Mexican invasion) stood unchallenged in textbook narratives for over a century.

Texas had now come into the Union, but there was still trouble with Mexico. That country seemed bent on a quarrel. President Polk did not desire it, he made an effort to settle the question by treaty; and this might have been done had Mexico been willing to yield certain points. "Texas has no right as an independent state to seek and receive admission into the United States," she said. And then she insisted that the dividing line should be the Nueces River, while Texas laid claim to the Rio Grande.

President Polk, fearing an attack, sent General Zachary Taylor to the disputed territory. And not many days passed before General Taylor received a letter from the Mexican general, Ampudia. "Your Government has not only insulted but has provoked the Mexican nation," he wrote, "and in this case, by orders of my Government, I require you to break up your camp and retire to the other bank of the Nueces River. If you insist upon remaining upon the soil, it will clearly result that arms, and arms alone, must decide the question."

What was General Taylor's answer? "The instruction under which I am acting will not permit me to go back from the position I now occupy. I regret the alternative which you offer, but, at the same time, wish it understood that I shall by no means avoid such an alternative, leaving the responsibility with those who rashly commence hostilities." It was not long after this that war was declared. General Taylor did not wait for more soldiers to arrive, but marched on and defeated the Mexicans near the mouth of the Rio Grande, although they outnumbered him. The enemy fled across the river, but Taylor pursued them and captured Matamoros. He then moved up the Rio Grande to besiege Monterey, one of the most strongly fortified cities of Mexico.[37]

·   1966

In the 1960s, for the first time, American students were introduced to the idea of a historical discrepancy between the U.S. and Mexican versions of the war's origin.

War Breaks Out

President Polk was now sure that Mexico would never willingly give up its control of Upper California and New Mexico, or its claim to Texas. However, he intended that the United States should occupy the vast area and was ready to declare war to get it. Several members of his cabinet urged him to delay, saying that if he waited long enough, Mexico would probably commit some act that would justify a declaration of war by the United States.

In January 1846, however, Polk dispatched troops under General Zachary Taylor from the Nueces River to the north bank of the Rio Grande. Ever since Texas had declared its independence from Mexico, Texans had claimed that their southern border lay on the Rio Grande, but Mexicans had insisted that it must stop at the Nueces River. By sending troops into this disputed area, Polk could claim that he was acting defensively; but the Mexicans could claim that the United States was acting aggressively.

Weeks passed, with President Polk's impatience mounting daily. Finally, on May 9, the President notified his cabinet that he intended to recommend war with Mexico within a few days. But that very night the news came for which he had long been waiting. Mexican troops had crossed the Rio Grande and had fought with American forces. Convinced that the American people would approve his action, Polk sent his war message to Congress on May 11. "But now after reiterated menaces," he declared, "Mexico has passed the boundary of the United States, has invaded our territory and shed American blood upon American soil . . . War exists, and notwithstanding all our efforts to avoid it, exists by the act of Mexico herself. . . ."

Two days later, on May 13, Congress declared war. On the day that Congress made its formal declaration, Polk told his cabinet that "in making peace with our adversary, we shall acquire California, New Mexico, and other further territory, as an indemnity for this war, if we can."

Who started the war? Many people at the time and many people since have regarded the Mexican War as one of aggression on the part of the United States. One person who questioned the actions of the United States was Abraham Lincoln, a young Illinois lawyer then serving his only term in Congress. In 1847 he introduced in Congress his famous Spot Resolutions, questioning whether the "spot" on the north bank of the Rio Grande where American blood had been shed was really United States soil.

On the other hand, some historians have maintained that Mexico deliberately sent troops across the Rio Grande, hoping to start a war that it thought it could win. Despite the great difference in size between the United States and Mexico, it is true that many Mexican military leaders did not fear a war with the United States. The Mexican leaders were full of confidence. They had expelled the Spaniards in 1821 and had overthrown revolutionists in their own country since that time. Thus they were boastful of their military abilities. They also hoped that Great Britain, which had looked forward to developing its own trade with the Republic of Texas and had therefore opposed its annexation to the United States, would come to the aid of Mexico. The Mexicans believed, too, that the people of the United States would never support a war. As events turned out, Mexican hopes were misplaced. The Mexicans did not have the necessary military power. Great Britain did not support them. Although some north-

erners feared the expansion of slavery into the vast area that might be acquired as a result of the conflict, American people in general supported
the war.[38]

1995

*By the 1990s, while diminishing in size and importance in most textbooks, the story of
what caused the Mexican-American War had changed substantially. Besides main-
taining that U.S. forces sparked the war, this account also suggested a "plot to add
slave states to the Union."*

Sparking the War

In January 1846, Polk ordered General Zachary Taylor to cross the
Nueces River and set up posts along the Rio Grande. Polk knew that Mexico claimed this land and that the move might spark a war. In April 1846,
Mexican troops crossed the Rio Grande and fought briefly with the Americans. Soldiers on both sides were killed.

President Polk claimed that Mexico had "shed American blood upon
the American soil." At his urging, Congress declared war on Mexico.
Americans were divided over the war. Many people in the South and West
wanted more land and so were eager to fight. Northerners, however, opposed the war. They saw it as a southern plot to add slave states to the
Union.[39]

PART IV

The Civil War Era

22

Slavery in America

Slavery is arguably one of the most contentious issues in American history and one that many textbooks have had to treat rather gingerly since the 1800s. Textbooks authors in the early 1800s often did not want to face the subject head-on. Therefore, the reader will find a hodgepodge of stories here dealing with the issues of states' rights, the slave trade, and in the late 1900s, what life was like as an African slave. Most of the textbook selections reflect the sharp racial stereotypes of their time. For the most part authors, even those who were against slavery, must have reinforced the stereotypes that many white students already had—especially the image of the kindly master and the "happy-go-lucky" slave.

I 8 5 I

The ideological viewpoint of this selection should be clear: this book was printed for and used in the North, and it did not mince words when it came to dealing with slavery. While this passage did not explain the life of a slave, it gave the reader a good sense of the political and social atmosphere in the years before the Civil War.

Since the middle of the last century, expanded minds have been, with slow gradations, promoting the decrease of slavery in North America. The progress of truth is slow; but it will, in the end, prevail. The first voice raised against this uncharitable practice was by a Quaker, the amiable and enlightened John Woolman, of Mount Holly, in New Jersey. He wrote his sentiments on that subject in the year 1746; strenuously recommended its abolition, at the several stated meetings of his society; and, in 1754, published his "Considerations on the Keeping of Negroes"; a work admirable for its dispassionate and lucid style of argument; highly beneficial in his own time, and deserving most serious attention at the present. Anthony Benezet, of Philadelphia, though his writings were subsequent to Woolman's, has acquired a yet higher rank among philanthropists. His labours, in the same field, were singularly active, and conspicuously successful. St. George Tucker, of Virginia, also wrote an able dissertation against slavery. A duty on the importation of slaves was laid by New York, in 1753; by Pennsylvania, in 1762; and by New Jersey, in 1769. Virginia the first state concerned in their introduction, was also the first that set an example of their exclusion; having, in the year 1778, amidst the perplexing scenes of civil warfare, passed an act to discontinue their entry into her ports. In 1780, Pennsylvania made a law for the gradual abolition of slavery; a law which, although it did not allow all the natural rights declared in her constitution, has the merit of being the earliest legislative proceeding of the kind, in any nation; and, soon afterwards, there was instituted in the same state, a society "for promoting the abolition of slavery, for the relief of free negroes unlawfully held in bondage, and for improving the condition of the African race." All the other states, north and east of Maryland, have since made laws for their gradual emancipation. On the adoption of the federal government, congress was authorized to prohibit, at the end of twenty years, the importation of negroes, into any part of the United States; and, accordingly, no arrivals have legally occurred since 1807. In 1820, a society for colonizing free people of colour, began a settlement at Sierra Leone, on the coast of Africa. A heavy grievance, however, is yet to be removed. Virginia, as well as every other American republic that still sanctions domestic bondage, will, we confidently anticipate, at no distant period, make arrangements, to unloosen, by degrees, the fetters, which are not less alarming to the master, than galling to the slave. Let us not only declare by words, but demonstrate by our actions, "That all men are created equal; that they are endowed, by their Creator, with certain unalienable

rights; that, amongst these, are life, liberty, and the pursuit of happiness."
Let us venerate the instruction of that great and amiable man, to whom,
chiefly, under Providence, the United States are indebted for their liberties; the world, for a common home: "That there exists an, indissoluble
union between virtue and happiness, between duty and advantage."[1]

1856

*This textbook, written for an unquestionably Southern audience, was published dur-
ing the height of the pre–Civil War sectional controversy. Of particular interest is the
fact that students in the South learned that the sectional tension, from their perspective, had nothing to do with slavery, but rather the rights of each individual state.*

Does Either Government Exercise Any Dominion Over the Other?

Young persons sometimes imagine that the general government is, in
some sense, a government *above* the state governments, and that it exer-
cises a sort of superintendence [*sic*] over them; but this is not so in any
sense whatever. The general government extends its jurisdiction over a
wider field than the state governments, it is true, but it does not rise to any
higher elevation in respect to sovereignty and power. It is supreme in respect to the business intrusted [*sic*] to it, and so are the state governments
supreme in respect to the business intrusted to them.

WHAT EXAMPLE IS THERE OF THE EXERCISE
GOVERNMENT IN VIRGINIA?

The government of Virginia, for example, has founded a university in
the heart of the state for the education of young men. That is a business
that belongs to the state. Now neither the President of the United States,
nor the Congress, nor both combined, can touch that institution at all, no
matter how well or how badly the government of Virginia may manage it.
The education of the people of Virginia is a subject that belongs to the
state. In respect to that business the state is supreme, and the general government of the United States has no more power to touch it than has the
government of France, or England, or that of any other country.

WHAT EXAMPLE IS THERE OF THE EXERCISE OF THE POWER OF THE GENERAL GOVERNMENT IN VIRGINIA?

On the other hand, at Gosport, near Norfolk, in Virginia, is a navy yard, established and maintained by the government of the United States. Every thing that pertains to the navy belongs to the departments of national defense and foreign commerce, and those things are the business of the general government. The general government accordingly bought the land for that navy yard, and built the docks and piers, and hired the workmen, and, although the ground is within the limits of the State of Virginia, neither the governor of Virginia, nor the Legislature, nor both together, can touch the navy yard at all, no matter how well or how badly the general government may manage it.

HOW MANY SYSTEMS OF GOVERNMENT, THEN, HAVE THE PEOPLE OF THE UNITED STATES ESTABLISHED?

In other words, the people of the United States, having a variety of public business to perform, have divided the business into two great branches, and have adopted one system of government for one, and another system for the other. In respect to certain great subjects of general interest, they have formed themselves into one nation, and they have constituted one general government to attend to that business. In respect to another great branch of business, they deem it more convenient to have it transacted in a different way. In respect to this, they are not one nation, in any sense, but are divided into a great many independent states, each of which has supreme and sovereign control within its jurisdiction. . . .

WHAT HAS BEEN THE PROGRESS OF THE COUNTRY SINCE THAT TIME?

Since that time the country has advanced in population, wealth, and power with a rapidity which is entirely unparalleled in the history of the human race. The extent of its territory has been greatly enlarged, and many new states have been successively formed and added to the confederation, so that the new republic is rapidly rising to a very exalted rank among the nations of the earth, and is destined, perhaps, at no distant day, to surpass all the political organizations that have preceded her in population, and power, and to exert a vast influence upon the future destinies of the great human family.[2]

1889

Written in the post–Civil War era, when the United States had to try to come to terms with the war and the institution of slavery, this textbook attempted to help students figure out how such a thing might have happened. Obviously written for Northerners, this selection was unique in how it criticized both the former slaves and the South for many of their problems.

Negro Slavery in the colonies was one of the worst of these cases of bad judgment. The first mention of it is in Virginia, in 1619 when a Dutch man-of-war exchanged some negro slaves for provisions. Negroes were soon held as slaves in all the colonies, though they increased most rapidly in the warmer southern colonies. Labor is the most important thing in a state. Out where laborers are generally known as slaves, no free man likes to labor, because there labor is thought to degrade the laborer to the level of a slave. A wise government would therefore have forbidden slavery in the colonies: the king of England not only did not forbid it, but became an active partner in the slave trade, and refused to allow the colonies to forbid it. Thus the southern colonies came to believe that slavery and slave labor were absolutely necessary to them. . . .

Negro Slavery existed in the colony, though there were not so many slaves as in the southern colonies. In 1740, it was believed that the negroes in New York City had made a plot to kill all the whites. Before the excitement ceased, 4 whites and 18 negroes were hanged, 14 negroes were burned at the stake, and 71 negroes were banished. It is almost certain now, however, that there was in reality no such plot. . . .

The Effects of Slavery

The cause is now seen by every one to have been negro slavery, though the South could not see that in 1860. Slaves worked only because they were made to do so; they worked slowly, carelessly, and stupidly, and were fit for nothing better than to hoe cotton. In factories or on railroads they were of little use. The rich whites did not need to work; and the poor whites did not wish to work, because they had grown up in the belief that work was a sign of slavery. Here was the real reason for the backwardness of the South, compared with the North. In the North there was a general race for work, and everything was in active motion. In the South there was no great number of persons who really wanted to work, and everything stood still.[3]

1900

This passage adopted a fairly contemporary view of slavery, even if it took great pains to blame the British for "forcing" the American colonists to accept this institution and would not be considered "politically correct" in today's world.

The enslavement of man by his fellow man was almost universal among ancient peoples. The system in most countries gradually merged into the serfdom of the Middle Ages, and eventually disappeared, after being greatly ameliorated by the influence of Christianity. In ancient times slavery was usually the result of conquest in war. The enslavement of the African race on commercial grounds had its beginning in comparatively modern times.

Slavery in the English colonies of North America dates back to within twelve years of the founding of the first colony, Virginia; but it had existed in Central America and in South America for more than a century before that, and in southern Europe for about fifty years before the discovery of the New World by Columbus. Not long after the introduction of slavery into the colonies, the traffic in slaves became quite profitable, and was chiefly carried on by English traders. England was responsible, above all other countries, for slavery in the United States. At different times the colonies attempted to suppress the slave-trade, but the British government thwarted them at every turn simply because it was a profitable means of commerce.

As early as 1712 Pennsylvania passed an act to restrict the increase of slaves, but it was annulled by the Crown. Fourteen years later Virginia attempted to check the trade by laying a tax on imported negroes, but the colony was soon forced to repeal the law. South Carolina attempted to restrict the trade in 1761, and Massachusetts made a similar attempt ten years later. In each case the effort was summarily crushed by the British Crown. The traffic was a source of much profit to England, and she would listen to no promptings of humanity in the matter. There had been founded in England, more than a century before the Revolution, the Royal African Company, a great monopoly, which furnished slaves for all the British colonies throughout the world. Queen Anne owned one-fourth of the stock in this company during her reign, and she especially enjoined Parliament to suffer no interference with the slave trade.

Thus England, while not permitting slavery on her home soil, not only encouraged, but enforced it, in her colonies. But the mother country was not alone to blame for the increase of the traffic in North America. The colonists purchased the slaves; if they had not, the traffic would have died out. Virginians made the first settlement in North Carolina, and took their slaves with them. Sir John Yeamans introduced them into South Carolina from the Barbadoes [sic], and from South Carolina they were carried into Georgia.

The Society of Friends, or Quakers, took the lead in opposing slavery, beginning about 1688. The Pennsylvania Germans also entered their protest against the evil at an early date. John Wesley called slavery the sum of all villanies [sic]. At the time of the Revolution all the colonies but one, Massachusetts, had slaves. The Continental Congress of 1774 pronounced against the slave trade. This was repeated two years later, only three months before the Declaration of Independence. The people were so jubilant over their own prospects of freedom that they were disposed to extend the blessings of liberty to their slaves; but this feeling was temporary with many, and subsided after the war was over. Jefferson in writing the Declaration of Independence put in a clause condemning the slave trade, but South Carolina and Georgia demanded that it be struck out, and it was done. But they could not prevent that grand sentiment in the Declaration: "All men are created equal"—not equal in mental gifts nor in worldly station, but equal in their right to life, liberty, and the pursuit of happiness. If the colonists had followed out that noble principle, it would have freed every slave in America; and indeed it did furnish a powerful weapon in the hands of the opponents of slavery down to its overthrow in the sixties.

Soon after the Revolution the northern States took hold of the matter and began to emancipate, Pennsylvania leading in 1780. Virginia came very near it two years before. New Hampshire became a free state in 1784, New York in 1799, and so on until all the northern States had abolished slavery. New Jersey had a few left as late as 1840. In 1787 an ordinance was framed for governing the territory northwest of the Ohio River, afterward Ohio, Indiana, Illinois, and Michigan. In this document, known as "The Ordinance of 1787," slavery was forever prohibited in that territory. Had it not been for this prohibition Ohio, Indiana, and Illinois would no doubt have become slave States, as they were largely settled by emigrants from Virginia and Kentucky. Even then efforts were made by Governor William Henry Harrison and others to break down that ordinance and to make Indiana and Illinois slave States; but they were not successful. In 1784 Jefferson introduced in the old Congress a similar ordinance to prohibit slavery in the new States south of the Ohio, afterward Kentucky, Tennessee, Mississippi, etc. Had this motion carried and been effective, how great would have been the results; slavery would have been confined to the few Atlantic States in the South, and would no doubt have died a natural death. This would have prevented the seventy years of slavery agitation and the great Civil War. But the measure was lost by one vote. A member from New Jersey who would have voted for it was absent, and for want of his vote the measure was lost. Thus the entire course of our history was changed by the absence of one man from Congress on a certain day in 1784!

Here let me say a word about the slave trade, especially the smuggling trade. This was certainly one of the most nefarious pieces of business ever carried on. A vessel would go to the African coast and secure a cargo of negroes. These were packed in the ship almost like sardines in a box, and so inhuman was the treatment that sometimes thirty percent of them died before reaching America. A smuggling vessel, pursued, would sometimes throw its entire cargo of negroes overboard! This occurred on various occasions. But when a smuggling ship was caught, it seldom brought relief to the poor blacks, as the laws were persistently against them, and often a whole cargo of negroes was sold to pay the cost of investigation. There was always a way found to enslave the black man; sending him back to his home in Africa, or giving him his freedom in this country was almost unheard of. A committee of Congress recommended that a free colored man on trial and proving himself free, must pay the cost of the trial, and if unable to do so must be sold into slavery to defray the expenses! But fortunately this did not become a law.[4]

1933

The image of the kindly old master and his happy-go-lucky slaves is a part of the slave narrative that existed well into the twentieth century in a great many U.S. history textbooks.

The Slaves

Although he was in a state of slavery, the negro of plantation days was usually happy. He was fond of the company of others and liked to sing, dance, crack jokes, and laugh; he admired bright colors and was proud to wear a red or yellow bandana. He wanted to be praised, and he was loyal to a kind master or overseer. He was never in a hurry, and was always ready to let things go until the morrow. Most of the planters learned that not the whip, but loyalty, based upon pride, kindness, and rewards, brought the best returns. If a slave was overworked or was ill-treated, he was apt to run away.[5]

1950

Beginning in the mid-twentieth century, many history textbooks explained to students what plantation life was like for the slave. In many instances, such as the one below, these passages probably reinforced more stereotypes and prejudices then they helped destroy.

How did the slaves live? All the hard work on the plantation was done by the slaves. The field hands worked from early morning until nightfall. The more fortunate slaves were personal and house servants. On a large plantation, each member of the family had his own slave as a personal servant. On each plantation there were also a few slaves who worked as carpenters and blacksmiths or who took care of the horses. The great majority of the Negro men, women, and children, however, were field hands. . . .

Slaves were owned by their master, of course, and were absolutely subject to his will. Yet life in the slave quarters on many a plantation was not too unhappy. During the day the small children played merrily, often with the younger white children from the "great house." In the twilight young and old gathered to sing and dance. The Negroes have given us some of our most beautiful folk songs and spirituals, such as *Deep River; Roll, Jordan, Roll;* and *All God's Chillun Got Wings.* On special occasions the slaves were allowed to attend picnics or to hunt 'coon' and 'possum.' Of course there were some harsh masters who treated their slaves cruelly. In general, however, slaves were too valuable to be mistreated. The greatest fear of the slave was that he and his family would be sold. When this happened, families often became separated, and great suffering resulted.[6]

1961

Even in this 1960s' textbook, slavery was not considered an "absolute" evil.

Treatment of slaves varies. The treatment that a slave received depended upon the owner and the kind of work performed by the slave. Farmers with only two or three slaves lived and worked alongside them and often regarded them much as northern farmers regarded their hired help. On the larger plantations, the slaves were usually well treated. After all, they were valuable property and it was foolish to overwork or injure them. House servants were better off than field hands. Slave families lived in log cabins, "the quarters" on the master's plantation. They received clothing and rations of cornmeal, pork, and molasses, and were encouraged to raise vegetables and poultry for themselves. During the busy season, working hours were from sunrise to sunset, with two hours off at noon. They were given most of Saturday, as well as Sunday, off. Plantation owners insisted that the life of the average factory worker in the North was far worse than that of their slaves.

Nevertheless, the slave was the property of the planter, who was free to do as he wished with him. It was difficult, and in some states illegal, for slaves to acquire freedom or to secure an education. Free Negroes, who were most numerous in Virginia and Maryland, were subjected to increasingly severe restrictions as time went by.[7]

1974

In this passage, the author moved away from the questions about how well the slaves were treated and focused on the repression that masters forced on their slaves in order to protect Southern white society.

Free the slaves or repress them? These were two of the choices that white southerners faced. Out of fear, habit, self-interest, and belief, they chose repression.

One reason for this choice was a slave revolt in Virginia. Nat Turner, a black preacher, led other slaves in an insurrection in 1831. They killed fifty-seven whites before they were captured. In the long chase by soldiers and sailors, perhaps as many as one hundred blacks were killed. Turner and twenty other blacks were tried and executed.

A shudder ran through the entire South, and afterward, white planters always wondered which slaves could be trusted. More than any other event, the Turner revolt led to the passage of a nightmarish series of laws, codes, and restrictions.

Every state with slaves had a slave code. This set up the legal position of the slave in relation to his or her master as well as to society. Most codes also prescribed minimum living conditions.

According to most codes, a slave was not to be away from the owner's land without a written pass. This pass had to be shown to any white who asked to see it. A slave could not preach, except to other slaves, and then only in the presence of a white. A slave could not own a gun, blow a horn, or beat drums. A gathering of five slaves or more was an unlawful assembly.

No one might teach a slave to read or write, and it was against the law to give books, pamphlets, newspapers, or other reading matter to slaves. A slave could not give drugs or medicine to whites.

In individual communities, the slave codes often included other rules. A curfew might be imposed. Some codes prohibited dancing or even any outward signs of joy.

The laws set up different standards for blacks than for whites. For example, in every southern state there was harsher punishment for blacks than for whites for the same offense. A crime that carried imprisonment for a white often carried a death penalty for a black.

The laws were, however, very harsh on any white who aided a slave. The stiffest penalties were given to those whites who hid a runaway or helped plan a rebellion. Death was the usual punishment.

The slave codes reflected a "closed society" in which any criticism of slavery could not be tolerated. Southerners who opposed slavery found it necessary to move north. Even in entertainment, such as plays, slaves had to be shown as servile. Although there had been slave codes in colonial times, they had been relaxed during the first years of the new republic. The Turner revolt and the rising tide of abolitionist activity led to tighter controls.[8]

1995

Many current textbooks now incorporate a fairly sophisticated analysis of American slavery, in all of its variations and complexity.

Life on Small and Large Farms

The life of enslaved Americans varied depending on circumstances. The typical slaveholder owned only a few African Americans. On small farms, enslaved people often worked side by side with their owners and their families. They sometimes ate together and slept in the same house. Close personal relationships sometimes developed; but, just as often, enslaved workers endured all manner of cruelties without a larger community to turn to for support and protection.

Most enslaved Americans, however, did not live on small farms. Because a few white men owned most of the enslaved people of the South, most enslaved African Americans lived on plantations. There they had the benefits of a sizeable community of people, usually including twenty or more African Americans. But plantation life had serious drawbacks in contrast to life on a small farm. Labor could be harsher, for example. Plantation workers frequently toiled in gangs under the supervision of foremen and slave drivers.

For enslaved women in particular life could be extremely difficult. In addition to bearing and caring for their own children and taking care of their households, they cooked and served food, cleaned houses and clothes, and labored in the fields. Especially hard work was required of them at harvest time in the late summer and fall. In addition to the drudgery of plantation life, they also had to endure rape or the threat of rape by slave owners.[9]

23

Abraham Lincoln's Character

Most historical characters found in history textbooks only appear when they are historically significant. We hear of Meriwether Lewis during his exploration west and Admiral George Dewey during the Spanish-American War, otherwise, according to textbooks, there is nothing else we need to know about them. On the other hand men such as George Washington and Abraham Lincoln are two of the lucky few who are usually given at least a paragraph to several pages dedicated to both their characters and lives before they came onto the national scene. Yet there is a significant difference between the two narratives. While Washington is viewed as a near "saint," Lincoln is your average man of the people. Washington, it seems, was predestined to lead the nation, while Lincoln had to work from the bottom-up to get where he was going. Finally, Washington was blessed with a wealthy family and natural abilities, whereas Lincoln's parents were people of the soil and he struggled to earn everything he received.

1866

News of Lincoln's assassination could not have reached this author long before his textbook went to press. Not only is Lincoln compared to Washington, but it seems his character was also forever solidified.

Abraham Lincoln was loved by the people as no man had been loved since Washington; all felt as if some member of their own family, some kind and trusted friend, had been taken away. His loss was lamented not only in America, but throughout the civilized world. For a time, all local differences, all national jealousies, were hushed in the presence of the great calamity; and Abraham Lincoln passed into history acknowledged by friend and foe a statesman, patriot, and martyr.[10]

1899

The message to students in this selection was fairly clear: it does not matter who your parents are, where they were born, or how much money you come from, if you work hard enough and remain honest as well as loyal, you too can be president of the United States.

In 1858, Senator Douglas was a candidate for reelection to the Senate, and the Republicans of Illinois put forward Abraham Lincoln as rival candidate. Abraham Lincoln was then forty-nine years old. Descended from Virginian ancestors, he was born in Kentucky, February 12, 1809. His parents were so poor and ignorant that they are often spoken of as belonging to the "poor white" class. Of schooling Lincoln had but little. He served as a flatboat hand, as a clerk and storekeeper in a country village in Illinois, as a postmaster, and as a surveyor, and, at length, having taught himself law, he was admitted to the bar, and soon won distinction as a lawyer. He was several times elected to the Illinois Legislature, and served for a short time in Congress. Long before 1858, his local reputation was that of one of the ablest men in Illinois. He was extremely clearheaded and sagacious, with wonderful insight into men's characters. As an orator, although his tall figure (six feet and four inches) was somewhat ungainly, he excelled in commanding dignity and in persuasiveness; and he was a consummate master of pure English speech. As a debater he could not be surpassed. He was very kindhearted, unfailing in tact, and abounding in droll humor; and he was also, when occasion required, as masterful a man as ever lived. Unselfish, and always to be depended upon, he was everywhere known in homely parlance as "Honest Abe." For winning people's confidence and keeping it, he was much like George Washington.[11]

1916

Written during the Progressive era, this textbook praised Lincoln's ascent from lowly beginnings yet also held him accountable for mistakes he may have made.

The leader of the North during the war period was President Abraham Lincoln. He was born of poor parents February 12, 1809, in a log hut in the slave state of Kentucky, and was reared on the frontier in the free state of Illinois, where he was successively rail-splitter, flatboatman, clerk in the country grocery store, and captain in the state militia, until by his own efforts he succeeded in obtaining sufficient education to practice law. Beyond membership in his own state legislature and one term in the national House of Representatives at Washington during the Mexican war, he had no official training for the chief magistracy. Sometimes as President he proved unfortunate in his choice of advisers, occasionally his favorite measures failed of enactment in Congress, such, for example, as compensated emancipation in the Border States and the colonization of the negroes outside the United States, and from time to time he made mistakes. His use of the patronage was certainly not in accordance with the standards of the civil service of the present day. Yet in spite of his limitations and mistakes he was the greatest President since the time of Washington, and by his broad sympathies, his firmness, judgment, patience, freedom from resentment, and tact, he brought the ship of state safely through the troubled waters. Nature endowed him with a keen intellect, a large heart, a strong will, and a gentleness of character that enabled him to command at the same time the love and the respect of his fellowmen.[17]

1950

By studying Lincoln and his life, students were taught that hard work, perseverance, and fortitude would help them achieve any goal.

Who was Abraham Lincoln? The man who had won the election of 1860 was one of the most remarkable men in all our history. Reared among the hardships of the frontier, he lacked the advantages that many of our Presidents have enjoyed. Because he was poor, he had to turn his hand to various ways of making a living. Before he became a lawyer, he cleared and tilled the soil, split rails, worked on a flatboat on the Mississippi, and tended store. Lacking schooling, he had to educate himself in spare moments during the day and by the flickering firelight during the evenings. Even his physical appearance—unusual height, awkward movements, and high-pitched voice—was against him.

In spite of these handicaps he won recognition amongst his neighbors. People liked and respected "Abe" Lincoln. His honesty, clear thinking, ability to tell stories, friendliness, and trust in the common people were qualities which made him popular. When he decided to go into politics, he proved a popular candidate. Lincoln served several terms in the Illinois legislature. In 1846, he was elected to the House of Representatives, where he served two years.[13]

1995

Contrary to most historical narratives, few things have changed in Lincoln's story in over two hundred years. The image of the self-made man who starts out at the lower end of society and makes it all the way to the White House seems to be a story that textbook authors have wanted students to learn for a long time.

The man elected to the White House in 1860 was striking in appearance—he was 6 feet 4 inches in height and seemed even taller because of his disproportionately long legs and his habit of wearing a high silk "stovepipe" hat. But Abraham Lincoln's previous career provided no guarantee he would tower over most of our other presidents in more than physical height. When Lincoln sketched the main events of his life for a campaign biographer in June 1860, he was modest almost to the point of self-deprecation. Especially regretting his "want of education," he assured the biographer that "he does what he can to supply the want."

Born to poor and illiterate parents on the Kentucky frontier in 1809, Lincoln received a few months of formal schooling in Indiana after the family moved there in 1816. But mostly he educated himself, reading and rereading a few treasured books by firelight. In 1831, when the family migrated to Illinois, he left home to make a living for himself in the struggling settlement of New Salem, where he worked as a surveyor, shopkeeper, and local postmaster. His brief career as a merchant was disastrous: he went bankrupt and was saddled with debt for years to come. But he eventually found a path to success in law and politics. While studying law on his own in New Salem, he managed to get elected to the state legislature. In 1837, he moved to Springfield, a growing town that offered bright prospects for a young lawyer-politician. Lincoln combined exceptional political and legal skills with a down-to-earth, humorous way of addressing jurors and voters. Consequently, he became a leader of the Whig party in Illinois and one of the most sought after of the lawyers who rode the central Illinois judicial circuit.

The high point of his political career as a Whig was one term in Congress (1847–1849). Lincoln did not seek reelection, but he would have faced certain defeat had he done so. His strong stand against the Mexican War alienated much of his constituency, and the voters expressed their disaffection in 1848 by electing a Democrat over the Whig who tried to succeed Lincoln. In 1849, President Zachary Taylor, for whom Lincoln had campaigned vigorously and effectively, failed to appoint him to a patronage job he coveted. Having been repudiated by the electorate and ignored by the national leadership of a party he had served loyally and well, Lincoln concentrated on building his law practice.[14]

24

John Brown at Harpers Ferry

One of the main historical questions that U.S. history textbooks have had to deal with since the 1860s is, What caused the American Civil War, 1861–65? Slavery, states' rights, Lincoln's election, and westward expansion are all usually found in any U.S. history textbook trying to answer this question. Another cause that every textbook also covers is the issue of John Brown's raid on Harpers Ferry and its impact as a catalyst for the war. It should be added that the issues of Brown's sanity and the justness of his cause are as alive today as they were in 1859.

1874

Less than a decade after the Civil War had ended, this U.S. history textbook argued for mental instability as one of the chief reasons why Brown acted the way he did.

In October, 1859, an event occurred which created great excitement throughout the country, and added to the sectional animosity which already prevailed to an alarming extent at the south. This was a mad attempt of John Brown to free slaves in Virginia and Maryland.

John Brown had been prominent among the free-state men of Kansas as a bold and resolute leader, and had suffered deeply from pro-slavery invaders of that territory. On the night of October 16, with twenty-one associates, he seized the United States arsenal at Harpers Ferry, intending to arm from its stores such slaves as might be induced to join him. He, however, failed to excite a revolt, and was overpowered by the militia of the neighborhood and a party of United States marine, under the command of Colonel Robert E. Lee. Of the insurgents, thirteen were killed, two escaped, and the rest, with their leader, were tried, condemned, and executed, at Charlestown, Virginia. Many persons in the south believed that Brown was merely the agent of a large number at the north, who had conspired to create an insurrection among the slaves. At the next session of Congress, the Senate appointed a committee to investigate the subject; but no evidence was elicited to implicate any one in the scheme except Brown and his immediate associates.[15]

1899

With words such as "fanatic," "grim work," and "insane," this author left little to question for young readers as to his belief about Brown's mental stability.

Differences Past Healing

The next year something happened that so enraged people of the South as to make them more ready to secede from the Union if a Republican president should be elected. John Brown was a Connecticut man by birth, and a religious fanatic by nature, a curious compound of self-devotion and ruthlessness. In 1855, he had moved from Ohio to Kansas, and in the bloody struggle there had done his full share of grim work. In the summer of 1859, he left Kansas and settled in the neighborhood of Harpers Ferry, in Virginia. One night in October, with not more than twenty followers, he attacked the arsenal at that place, in the hope of getting weapons and setting up in the wild mountains about there an asylum where fugitive and rebellious slaves might congregate. He was captured of course and hanged. His attempt found but little sympathy or approval in the North, where it was generally regarded as an insane piece of folly. But to the southern mind it brought up all the possible horrors of negro insurrection, and many persons may have feared that the election of a Republican as president would countenance the repetition of such lawless and dangerous proceedings.[16]

1912

By the early 1900s, Brown's reputation had not improved a great deal.

The report that John Brown, with his twenty-two followers, had seized the United States arsenal at Harpers Ferry (October 16, 1859) aroused the entire country. As a leader in Kansas, Brown had freed a number of slaves by force and now he proposed to bring about the total destruction of slavery. His plan was to advance from a spot in the Virginia mountains with a small company of men, liberate slaves and arm them or send them to Canada. In this way, with an enlarged force he thought to make slaveholding insecure, and thus the owners would ready to give up all their slaves.

Prominent antislavery leaders assisted him with money. The scheme to attack Harpers Ferry was unknown to them, and was disapproved by his two sons and all of the other men. In defending themselves against the militia which had been hastily summoned, a number of men on both sides were killed. Four of Brown's followers escaped, and the survivors were made prisoners by United States troops. In a fair trial, Brown was found guilty and was ordered to be executed on the charge of treason and conspiracy "with slaves and others to rebel and murder." The act was that of a man who had brooded so long over freeing the slaves that his mind had become unbalanced on that one question. At the South, it was believed that the deed was the outcome of the teachings of the "Black" Republican party. That party in its National Convention condemned the deed as "among the gravest of crimes." Emerson expressed the thought of the men of more extreme views when he declared: "I wish we might have health enough to know virtue when we see it and not cry with the fools, 'madman' when a hero passes." [17]

1966

In this 1960s' selection, the issue of Brown's sanity was not deemed extremely important.

John Brown's Raid

In the fall of 1859, John Brown undertook to start a rebellion of slaves in Virginia. With money obtained from a number of New England and New York abolitionists, Brown armed a party of eighteen men. On October 16 he seized the federal arsenal at the town of Harpers Ferry, in what is now West Virginia. He planned to seize the guns stored in the arsenal, hand them out to slaves nearby, and lead the slaves in what he hoped would be a widespread rebellion.

It was a wild idea, certain to fail. Brown and his followers were captured by Colonel Robert E. Lee of the United States Army in command of a unit of marines. After a trial that Brown admitted was more fair than he had reason to expect, he was hanged for "murder, criminal conspiracy, and treason against the Commonwealth of Virginia." Many southerners believed that Brown's action represented northern opinion and concluded that slavery was no longer safe from direct attack. As a matter of fact, northern politicians and the majority of northerners were shocked at the news of John Brown's raid and quickly condemned it. But extreme abolitionists regarded Brown as a heroic martyr. Emerson declared that Brown was a "new saint" who would "make the gallows glorious like the cross."

Southern newspapers quoted this small minority of abolitionist opinion as typical of what the whole North was thinking. To southerners John Brown's raid was convincing evidence that the North was determined to abolish slavery. By 1860 the ties binding the two sections had almost disappeared.[18]

1986

In this version, Brown's mental state once again came to the forefront, and students learned that he was "almost certainly insane."

At this point John Brown again appeared on the national scene. Brown was never punished for his part in the Pottawatomie massacre. He believed that God had commanded him to free the slaves by force. Kansas had seemed the best place to wage this battle. But violence was no longer necessary to keep slavery out of Kansas, and its settlers had little interest in fighting to get rid of it anywhere else.

Brown had to develop a new scheme. He decided to organize a small band of armed followers, march into the South, and seize land in some remote area. What would happen next he never made clear. Apparently he expected slaves from all over the region to run away and join him. With their help he would launch raids throughout the South aimed at rescuing more blacks from slavery.

Brown managed to persuade six important Massachusetts abolitionists to give him enough money to organize and supply his attack force. The goal of his miniature 18-man army was a United States government armory in the town of Harpers Ferry, Virginia, on the Potomac River northwest of Washington.

On the evening of October 16, 1859, Brown and his commandos crossed the Potomac. They overpowered a watchman and occupied the armory and a government rifle factory. Brown then sent some of his men off to capture two local slaveholders as hostages. One of these was Lewis Washington, a great-grandnephew of George Washington. When workers began to arrive in the morning, Brown also took some of them prisoner. Then he sat back to wait for local slaves to rise up and join his rebellion. Not one slave did so. But the local authorities reacted promptly. In a matter of hours Brown's force was under siege, pinned down in the armory. A detachment of marines commanded by Lieutenant Colonel Robert E. Lee arrived from Washington. Brown refused to surrender. On October 18 Lee sent the marines forward with fixed bayonets. They quickly overwhelmed the rebels.

Ten of Brown's men were killed, but he was taken alive. He was charged with murder, conspiracy, and treason. After a fair but swift trial he was convicted and sentenced to be hanged.

John Brown was almost certainly insane. He was so disorganized that he did not even attempt to let the slaves know that he had come to free them. The affair might have been dismissed as the act of a lunatic if Brown had acted like a disturbed person after his capture, but he did not do so. Indeed, he behaved with remarkable dignity and self-discipline.

Even Brown's judge and jailers admired his calm courage. When he was condemned to death, he said that he had acted in the name of God. "To have interfered as I have done . . . in behalf of His despised poor, is not wrong, but right. Now, if it is . . . necessary that I should forfeit my life for the furtherance of the ends of justice . . . I say, let it be done." And he added calmly, "I feel no consciousness of guilt."

Brown became a hero to the abolitionists and to many other northerners. They considered him a noble freedom fighter. His bloody murders in Kansas and his wreckless assault at Harpers Ferry were conveniently forgotten. When northerners made Brown a near saint, white people in the slave states became even more concerned. They began to think that northerners intended to destroy slavery, not merely limit its expansion. Once again, northerners and southerners looked at each other with suspicion, fear, and even hatred.[19]

1995

By the 1990s, Brown's historical reputation had been substantially restored. While this passage did not specifically discuss the issue of mental competency, presumably the authors would argue that he was perfectly sane since they referred to him as a "prophet."

Other factors increased tensions in the late 1850s. One was an economic downturn called the Panic of 1857. Another was the continuing growth of the American population. Many people were uneasy; there was a sense that Americans were at sea, that their country was growing and changing so rapidly that it could be controlled no longer. John Brown, however, was not one to resign himself to the twists of fate. He would control his own destiny and that of his nation if he could. On October 16, 1859, three years after his nighttime raid along Pottawatomie Creek in Kansas, Brown attacked the federal arsenal at Harpers Ferry, Virginia (now West Virginia). With him were twenty-two men, including two African Americans—Shields Green and John Anthony Copeland, a college student. Supported by abolitionists in the North, Brown and his followers hoped to seize the weapons in the arsenal and give them to enslaved people. They had a dream of a massive uprising of enslaved Americans that would end slavery, punish slaveholders, and lead the United States to moral renewal.

Alerted to the attack, United States troops under the command of Colonel Robert E. Lee bore down on Harpers Ferry and surrounded

Brown and his men in the arsenal. The troops killed half of Brown's men—including two of his sons—before the rest surrendered. Convicted of treason against the state of Virginia, John Brown was sentenced to be hanged by the neck until dead.

Just before his execution, Brown wrote a brief note. Although he had failed as a soldier, his final message proved him a prophet. Northerners hailed Brown as a martyr to the cause of justice and freedom. Southerners denounced him as a terrorist and a tool of Republican abolitionists. In short, his raid and his trial only deepened the division between North and South.[20]

25

The Dakota Conflict of 1862

While the U.S. government was primarily focused on the Civil War, another war developed between whites and Native Americans in Minnesota that distracted Lincoln from his main aim of defeating the South. The Dakota Conflict, which started over the issue of land and treaty rights, forced Lincoln and his generals to send in military forces. Once the uprising was put down, Lincoln approved the death sentence for thirty-nine Dakota leaders (one was given a last-minute reprieve). The final thirty-eight were hanged in Mankato, Minnesota, on December 26, 1862.

Simultaneously a major challenge for the Union and a major turning point in Native American history, the Dakota Conflict of 1862 has long since faded from U.S. history textbooks. By the early 1900s this once significant event is either ignored entirely or treated as a historical footnote in most history textbooks.

1874

This selection appeared while the United States was still struggling with the Sioux [aka Dakota] for control of the Great Plains. Although this author found fault with both sides, his warning at the end made it clear that Native Americans were still not to be trusted.

The Sioux War. The summer of 1862 was sadly distinguished in Minnesota by frightful massacres perpetrated by some bands of Sioux Indians, under Little Crow and other chiefs. They began their outrages about the middle of August, and kept them up for more than a month, when they were driven into Dakota, except several hundred who were captured, thirty-eight of whom were hung in punishment for their murders. It has been estimated that more then seven hundred whites were slain, and twenty-five thousand were driven from their homes; and, for some time, a third of this number was dependent upon charity for support. The next summer the savages renewed their outrages, which were not suppressed till after a tedious campaign, lasting into September.

For a long time the Indians had been dissatisfied. They especially complained of the course pursued by the traders, and of the delay of the national government in making the annual payment due them by treaty. On the 17th of August a party of Indians murdered some whites near the town of Acton, and this taste of blood was followed the next day by a general massacre of the settlers on the Upper Minnesota River. Successful in an encounter with a few troops who first went against them, the savages urged on the work of death throughout the whole western part of the state, and in Iowa and Dakota. Every species of fiendish atrocity was perpetrated on their victims. A fierce attack made upon New Ulm, an isolated town containing some fifteen hundred persons, was repulsed with difficulty. The place was then abandoned by its inhabitants. Fort Ridgely, after enduring a siege for several days, was relieved by Colonel (since General) Henry H. Sibley, who led an expedition up the Minnesota Valley to suppress the ravages of the Indians. After some fighting, Little Crow and his followers fled far into the Dakotas. Meanwhile General Pope was sent to take command in this department. Renewing their outrages the next year, the savages were hunted down; their chief, Little Crow, was killed; and an expedition, under General Sibley, pursued the hostile tribes, and, after considerable fighting, drove them across the Missouri River. Yet the Indians remained restive and troublesome, and ready for another outbreak.[21]

1889

The fact that some of the violence was directed at women and children seemed to be a major point in most textbooks of this period.

The Sioux War

During the summer of 1862, the Sioux Indians, in western Minnesota, revolted. They had made many complaints of their treatment by the government, and in August they burst suddenly upon the outlying settlements, killing men, women, and children without mercy. Troops were hurried back from the western armies, and the Indians were driven out of the State. Thirty-eight of them were tried, convicted of murder, and hanged.[22]

1899

This selection indicated that the "red men" invaded Minnesota. In fact, the Dakota were living in this region when the first white settlers started exploring in the seventeenth century.

The Sioux Indians had for some time complained, probably with reason, of ill treatment at the hands of white settlers and government officials. In the summer of 1862, while the Union armies were busy at the South, these red men invaded Minnesota and Iowa, and massacred nearly a thousand men, women, and children, with circumstances of the most horrible barbarity. A small Federal force soon suppressed these Indians, and several of their leaders were convicted of murder and hanged.[23]

1994

For most of the twentieth century, U.S. history textbooks fell silent on this event—a one-time major historical event all but erased from our historical consciousness. Here is an example of its rare reappearance.

During the Civil War the Sioux of Minnesota, facing starvation and taking advantage of the sectional quarrel, went on the warpath and murdered several hundred settlers. The uprising was finally crushed by federal troops, and nearly forty of the Sioux Indians, after a summary trial, were hanged at a well-attended mass execution.[24]

26

Sherman's March to the Sea

One of the most contentious issues emerging from the Civil War, besides the role of slavery, was General William Tecumseh Sherman's March to the Sea. When Sherman brought his concept of total war to the South, it forever left an indelible mark on Southerner memory and Southern history.

1876

Sherman's famous paraphrased quote, "War is Hell," resonated throughout this selection (taken from a Northern textbook), which clearly supported Sherman and his tactics.

Sherman's first point of attack was Atlanta in Georgia, an important center of railway communication. It was about a hundred miles from Chattanooga, Sherman's point of departure. He set out early in May. His line of march lay along a railway which kept up his communication with Chattanooga. His army numbered nearly a hundred thousand. The Confederate force opposed to him, under Johnston, was barely half that number. Johnston gradually fell back, impeding Sherman's advance and harassing him on every occasion, but avoiding a pitched battle. The march was, in Sherman's own language, "one gigantic skirmish." Johnston had never stood well with the Southern Government, and his present policy met with no favor. On the 17th of July the command of the Confederate army was transferred to Hood. Whatever may be thought of Johnston's policy, it was hardly a well-chosen time for such a change. All the mischief that might result from Johnston's caution had now been done. His previous career showed that his retreat was not the result of weakness or indecision, but part of a deliberately arranged plan. To make a change now was to suffer all the mischief of such a plan and to forego the compensating gain. Hood at once adopted a bolder policy, but with no good result. He was defeated with heavy loss in a series of engagements round Atlanta. Sherman then marched to the west of Atlanta, and by threatening Hood's communication with the rear, forced him to evacuate the place. On the 2nd of September Sherman telegraphed to Washington "Atlanta is ours." His total loss in the campaign which ended thus was about thirty thousand, that of the enemy some ten thousand more. Merciless severity in his dealings with the inhabitants of the South, when the operations of war seemed to need it, was Sherman's fixed and deliberate policy. He was not wantonly, or even revengefully, cruel; but he went on the principle that the South could be crushed only by bringing home to the inhabitants a full sense of the miseries of war, and that no feeling of pity for them ought to stand in the way of any arrangement which could bring the war to a speedy end. In his own words, "war is cruelty, and you cannot refine it." In this spirit he ordered that all the inhabitants, without regard for sex, age, or sickness, should quit Atlanta, and he destroyed the buildings of the town, sparing only churches and dwelling-houses. The capture of Atlanta was but a step towards further ends. To penetrate into the heart of the Southern Confederacy was Sherman's ultimate aim. With this view he quited [sic] Atlanta, abandoning his communications with the rear, and determining to maintain his army, nearly seventy thousand men, on the resources of the country and such supplies as he could carry with him. Hood, instead of opposing him, resolved to invade Tennessee; thus two invasions were going on simultaneously. The object of Sherman's march was the city of Savannah. On the 14th of November he started, and from that time till he arrived at the sea no clear tidings of his army reached the North. On the 20th of December a division of the army appeared before

Fort McAlister, some fourteen miles from Savannah. The Federals had made more than one unsuccessful attack on this place from the sea, but it now fell at the first assault. General Hardee, who was in command of the Confederate forces at Savannah, found that it would be impossible to hold the place, and evacuated it. Sherman sent a message to the President announcing that he presented him, as a Christmas gift, with the city of Savannah. He had marched more than three hundred miles in thirty-six days, with a loss of little more than five hundred men. His own report stated that he had done damage to the amount of a hundred millions of dollars, of which eighty millions was sheer waste and destruction.[25]

1911

This passage took an overtly pro-Northern stance, which reflected the sharp turn in race relations after 1900, deciding on a more stereotypically negative portrayal of African Americans.

Another great general of the war was William T. Sherman. He was with Grant at Vicksburg. It was later decided that General Grant should go east and take command of the Army of the Potomac. General Sherman then became the chief commander in the West. Grant was to advance upon Richmond while Sherman with an army of sixty thousand men was to capture Atlanta and thence to march across Georgia to the sea.

General Sherman thought by this march that he would cut the Confederacy again, and thus hasten the end of the war. He destroyed railroads and telegraph lines, and thus cut off supplies. "Better to lose property," he said, "than to lose life."

There were several severe battles fought before General Sherman's army entered Atlanta. He took this city and sent the despatch [sic] to Washington: "Atlanta is ours and fairly won." The city had large factories and iron foundries. "We must burn these," said Sherman, "for it will stop the manufacture of articles that the Confederacy needs to carry on the war." And what was done? Atlanta was burned, bridges and railroads were destroyed, and telegraph wires were cut.

It was November 15th when the army began its long march from Atlanta to the sea—a distance of three hundred miles. "Your army will starve," Sherman was told. "Georgia has a million of inhabitants. If they can live, we should not starve," was the reply.

The soldiers, too, hoped that this march would bring the war to a close. On both sides they had not only suffered hardships by the cruelties of war, but they had seen many a life destroyed before its time. And as General Sherman rode past the long lines, they called out: "Uncle Billy, we guess that Grant is waiting for us at Richmond."

They were to march fifteen miles a day, beginning at seven o'clock in the morning. They accordingly set out in four columns, cutting a swath from forty to sixty miles wide. And thus they marched on day after day.

Foraging parties accompanied the army. They were called "bummers," and they provided the food for the soldiers. They started in advance and went out for miles on each side of the army to gather poultry, vegetables, or forage of any kind. But they had certain instructions. They must not enter dwellings or commit any trespasses, and in all foraging they must endeavor to leave with each family a reasonable portion for their maintenance. Some of them broke these rules and treated the people of Georgia cruelly, without General Sherman's knowledge. Narrow lines of men on horseback were on each side of the army. They were called flankers, and it was their duty to prevent any surprise by the Confederates. Last of all in the march came those whose work was to destroy railroads and burn bridges.

The army was followed by crowds of negroes; but many of them did not know what the march meant. "We'se gwine along, we'se free," they exclaimed. At one time a colored woman with a child in her arms walked along among the cattle and horses. "Where are you going, aunty?" asked an officer. "I'se gwine whar you's gwine, massa," was her reply. The people in the North were anxious to know how General Sherman and his army were faring; and no one was more anxious than President Lincoln. But there was no way of knowing, for the telegraph lines had been cut. It is said that at a morning reception at the White House the President was very absentminded. His silence was noticed. "Pardon me if I am a little preoccupied," he said; "to tell the truth, I was thinking about a man in Georgia." At last a message came on Christmas eve, and it was from General Sherman. The despatch said: "I beg to present you as a Christmas gift the city of Savannah, with one hundred and fifty guns and plenty of ammunition, also about twenty-five thousand bales of cotton."[26]

1914

In this textbook, written by a Southerner and more than likely marketed in the South as well, students learned that Sherman's march may have caused an undue amount of destruction throughout the South.

General Grant planned two great campaigns, one under himself against Lee in Virginia, with the purpose of capturing Richmond; the other under Sherman against Johnston, with the purpose of capturing Atlanta. In this way Grant proposed to enfold the Confederacy within the coils of two mighty armies, and to end the war by a campaign of destruction.

The two campaigns began at the same time in May, 1864. On the day after Grant crossed the Rapidan to attack General Lee, Sherman left Chattanooga, on his long march through the Confederate States. He had an army of a hundred thousand men and two hundred and fifty cannon. Johnston's army was half the size.

As Sherman advanced, Johnston interposed his army at every point. There was sharp fighting almost every day. For over two months Johnston slowly retired as Sherman's lines threatened to flank his army. By July Johnston had reached Atlanta and fortified himself in the city. Sherman had lost about thirty-two thousand men. Johnston had lost about twenty-two thousand.

At this juncture General John B. Hood was put in command of the Confederate army, with directions to attack the Federals and drive them back. This Hood tried to do in the bloody battles around Atlanta. He failed, however, and then took his army into Tennessee, to threaten Sherman's line of supplies. Here his army was severely defeated in the battles around Nashville. This left Sherman unopposed to enter Atlanta and to continue his march through the South.

It was the policy of General Sherman to bring the war to a close by making the South "feel the hard hand of war." When he set out on his "March to the Sea," he set fire to the city of Atlanta, and out of four thousand houses, only four hundred were left standing.

With sixty thousand men Sherman set out for Savannah. His army covered a front of forty miles, and the soldiers lived on the country as they moved. Farmhouses, gin houses, cotton crops were burned; horses, cows, hogs, sheep, were killed for the soldiers' use, or left dead in the fields;

barns were rifled of their content; slaves were carried away; railroads were destroyed by tearing up the tracks, heating the rails, and twisting them around trees. Sherman estimated the damage done to the State of Georgia at about one hundred million dollars.

From Savannah Sherman turned through South Carolina, and thence on to Goldsboro, N.C. Following his army was a crowd of stragglers that did more damage than the soldiers themselves. They were called the "bummers of the army." At Columbia, S.C., a few of the soldiers and bummers broke into the saloons, became drunk and lost all restraint. Nothing could stay them. The city was set on fire and was soon reduced to a heap of ruins.*

Sherman's army marched eight hundred miles in six months, and cut a path of destruction and desolation through the heart of the South. Often in the wake of his army the people were glad to eat the corn left by his horses.

1933

By the 1930s, when a great many publishers were trying to market their textbooks to larger audiences, outright blame for specific events during the Civil War began to disappear and were replaced by passages that gave credence to both historical perspectives.

On November 15, 1864, Sherman began his march from Atlanta to the sea. With no strong army before him, he spread his men out over a zone sixty miles wide. As they advanced the soldiers destroyed the railroads, burned many buildings, tore down fences, and destroyed the crops. Late in December the army entered Savannah. Sherman stayed there for more than a month. He then began an advance through South Carolina, destroying property over a wide area. His object was to cripple the South so that the war could be brought to a speedy close, but his ruthless warfare

---

* [Original footnote] In regard to the burning of Columbia, ever since the occurrence there has been a difference of opinion as to whether General Sherman ordered, or consented to, the unfortunate affair. General Sherman insists that it was done by "the bummers of the army." The people of Columbia are strong in their belief that he was aware of the intention of his soldiers, that it was a prearranged affair, and that nothing was done to prevent it. In any event, it appears to have been an unnecessary and an unfortunate destruction of a large part of a beautiful city.[27]

left painful memories that long lingered in the minds of Southern people. The Union army moved on into North Carolina. Johnston was then put in command of the Confederate troops in the Carolinas. Gathering all the soldiers that he could, he made an effort to stop Sherman's advance. But it was all in vain. Confederate hopes were being shattered before Richmond, and Johnston's army was not powerful enough to cope with Sherman's forces.[28]

1973

In the 1970s, the focus on Sherman's March to the Sea shifted from what he did on his campaign to what the lasting effects were on the South as well as the Southerners' "hearts and minds."

After the election Lincoln's generals moved quickly. Sherman cut loose from his supply base, letting his army feed off the countryside. Leaving Atlanta behind, he headed southeast for Savannah. Lonely chimneys of burned homes and a charred, desolate landscape sixty miles wide marked the route of his famous journey to the sea. Behind his army followed a throng of black refugees seeking freedom. But in the hearts and minds of the people of the South, this modern soldier left the strongest impression of all. The social system of the South could not withstand the economic might that Sherman's vast well-equipped and well-armed army represented, and after his passing the will to fight died. Hood's futile effort to distract Sherman from his march across Georgia ended in the destruction of that hapless officer's army at the hands of General Thomas in the battle of Nashville. At Christmas Sherman telegraphed Lincoln the news of Savannah's fall.[29]

1995

By the end of the twentieth century, the narrative of this story had been severely stripped down, leaving a number of details out. Furthermore, this contemporary textbook questioned the ultimate purpose of Sherman's action and emphasized the historical impact of this event on future animosity between the North and the South.

Sherman's March to the Sea

As it turned out, Sherman could not catch the army he was sent after. Instead he besieged Atlanta, Georgia, in September 1864 and captured it. Then he proposed a new plan of his own. He would march his troops from Atlanta to the sea, gathering the food he needed from the land and destroying everything he could not take with him. He told Grant:

> If we can march a well-appointed army right through [Jefferson Davis's] territory, it is a demonstration to the world, foreign and domestic, that we have a power which Davis cannot resist.

With Atlanta in flames behind him, Sherman set out for the seacoast city of Savannah, Georgia. Cutting a sixty-mile-wide swath across the red earth of the state, he burned the harvest, plundered plantations, uprooted railroad tracks, and smashed bridges, factories, and mills. By December 22, he had reached the coast and captured Savannah. He had succeeded in his purpose to make the people of Georgia "so sick of war that generations would pass away before they would again appeal to it." But his march would also make the hatred between North and South still more difficult to heal.[30]

27

African Americans and Reconstruction

In the years following the Civil War, the United States had to go through a painful process of healing. One way of doing this was to teach succeeding generations of Americans what the war was about, how and why it was fought, and maybe most important, what its effects were on American society at large. The key issue going into the war, as well as at its conclusion, was the status of the slaves. While the Thirteenth Amendment formally freed African Americans from bondage, it did nothing to solve the issue of the role of these newly freed people in society. The following U.S. history textbook selections examine what happened to African Americans in the immediate aftermath of the war.

1878

Published on the heels of Reconstruction, this excerpt is striking for the complete absence of former slaves or the accomplishments of the Reconstruction governments.

The close of the war found at least one million five hundred thousand men under arms. The opening of the new era was marked by the disbanding of this vast armament. A grand review of the armies of Grant and Sherman, two hundred thousand strong, took place in the presence of the President and his cabinet. For twelve hours this triumphal procession, thirty miles long, massed in solid column twenty men deep, rolled through the broad avenues of the capital. With no disturbance, no excitement, the men laid down their arms and returned to their homes. Soon there was nothing to distinguish the soldier from the citizen, except the recollection of his bravery. Never had the world seen such a triumph of democratic institutions.

Now came the task of reconstruction. It presented more difficult problems than the war itself. Johnson took the position that a State could not secede, and therefore none of the Southern States had ever been really out of the Union. Having laid down their arms, it was only necessary for them to submit to the national authority to be in all respects as they were before the war. He recognized the State governments that had been formed in Virginia, Tennessee, Arkansas and Louisiana under the protection of the Federal army. In the others, he appointed provisional governors, and authorized the calling of conventions to establish loyal governments.

The conventions, which were accordingly held, repealed the ordinances of secession, repudiated the Confederate war debt, and ratified the thirteenth amendment. April 29th, the President removed restrictions on trade with the South, and a month later he issued a proclamation of amnesty to all who would take the oath of allegiance to the United States. A few classes of individuals were excluded, but many persons thus debarred were pardoned on special application to the President.

The thirteenth amendment abolishing slavery having been ratified by the legislatures of twenty-seven States, on the 18th of December it was declared to be a part of the Constitution of the United States. . . .

Though the nation was still agitated by political strife—the groundswell, as it were, of the recent terrible storm—the country was rapidly taking on the appearance—and ways—of peace. The South was slowly adjusting herself to the novel conditions of free labor. The soldiers retained somewhat their martial air; but "blue-coats" and "gray-coats" were everywhere to be seen engaged in quiet avocations. The ravages of war were fast disappearing. Nature had already sown grass and quick-growing plants upon the battlefields where contending armies had struggled.[31]

1 8 9 7

Almost twenty years later, Reconstruction historiography had changed a great deal. Students were told of the corruption and scandals brought to the South by Northern "carpet-baggers" and the newly freed slaves.

Six States Re-admitted; Negro Legislators and "Carpet-Baggers"

In some of the restored states, especially in South Carolina, there were more negroes than white men. The negroes now got control of these states. They had been slaves all their lives, and were so ignorant that they did not even know the letters of the alphabet. Yet they now sat in the state legislatures and made the laws. After the war many industrious Northern men settled in the South, but, besides these, certain greedy adventurers went there eager to get political office and political spoils.

These "Carpet-Baggers," as they were called, used the ignorant freedmen as tools to carry out their own selfish purposes. The result was that the negro legislators, under the direction of the "Carpet-Baggers," plundered and, for the time, well-nigh ruined the states that had the misfortune to be subject to their rule.*

After a time the white population throughout the South resolved that they would no longer endure this state of things. Partly by peaceable and partly by violent means they succeeded in getting the political power into their own hands, and the reign of the "Carpet-Bagger" and the negro came to an end.[32]

1 9 1 2

In the early twentieth century, U.S. history textbooks helped develop the racist mythology of the Reconstruction era. One went so far as to claim that slavery might have been a positive thing in the long run. It is essential to realize that this account reflected respectable, informed opinion at the time.

* [Original footnote] In 1868 the total debt of South Carolina was about $5,000,000. Under four years of "Carpet-Bag" government, or rather misgovernment, the debt was increased to no less than $30,000,000. Much of the debt represented simply what was stolen from the people of the state.

One-third of the white breadwinners had been either killed or disabled. But the most difficult problem in the situation involved the negroes, who comprised one-half of the population. Could they prove their fitness for freedom? Under slavery they had been elevated from barbarism to at least a semblance of civilization; but they had had no experience in working under any other incentive than the fear or the love of a master who was at the same time owner. It is not strange that they should have developed little power of self-control and that, emerging from slavery, they should have been, on the whole, both indolent and shiftless.

During the war the mass of the slaves had remained on the plantations, quietly guarding the women and the children and raising crops. For their admirable conduct they had won the gratitude of their masters. If this benevolent attitude could have continued, all might have been well; but that was not to be. As the victorious Union armies advanced, particularly after the issuance of the Emancipation Proclamation, multitudes of negroes flocked to them for protection. Many of them followed the troops, while others left their plantations and went to the neighboring towns and cities. All were without means of subsistence, and consequently the Federal Government was forced, for humane reasons, to begin the practice of issuing rations and clothing to them. In March, 1865, a special bureau was created in the War Department, known as the Freedman's Bureau, with officers and agents in all parts of the South. Its purposes were: (1) The distribution of food, clothing, and fuel to destitute freedmen; (2) the distribution among them of abandoned or confiscated lands; (3) the establishment of schools for their instruction. During the summer of 1865 and the winter that followed, multitudes of freedmen were without occupation; against the advice of the Freedman's Bureau officials, they continued flocking to the towns and wandering from place to place. Petty larceny became very common. Many, indeed, took advantage of their new freedom to assume insolent airs toward their former masters.[33]

1933

In the early 1930s—on the eve of the Great Depression and amid the early stirrings of civil rights activity in the South and the North—textbooks such as this one hewed closely to a deeply racist version of U.S. history.

The Negroes Are Demoralized

After Lee's surrender many a white-haired planter called his slaves around him to tell them of their freedom. They came always respectfully, hat in hand, crowding around the front portico—old men, burly field hands, buxom women, half-naked boys and girls. "You are now free," said the master, "and you may go if you please, or if you wish you may stay with me and work for a share of the crop." "Yes, master," was the usual reply, "we want to stay right here with you." Yet many left. Freedom for these simple souls meant release from work, and during the summer of 1865 the roads were full of negroes on their way to the Freedman's Bureau or the nearest federal garrison. They had heard that rations were handed out there, and many believed that each negro was to have forty acres and a mule. Thousands of idle men and women were concentrated in camps, or wandered over the country living by raiding barns or chicken-coops. Lawlessness, idleness, immorality, sickness resulted, while many plantations were uncultivated for lack of workers. The Freedman's Bureau did much to alleviate this situation, by caring for the negroes and sending them back to work at fair wages. But the problem was too great to be handled by this bureau, and called loudly for action by the state governments.

THE BLACK CODES ARE MISUNDERSTOOD IN THE NORTH

When the new legislatures in the Southern states assembled, they met the situation in a practical way, but a way which proved unwise because it was misunderstood in the North. They passed laws fixing the status of the negro, and providing penalties for vagrancy and lawlessness. In some states he had to have a license to preach or to engage in trade, in others he could own no land. For seditious speech, rioting, or vagrancy he was subject to fine. If he could not pay the fine he might be handed over to a white man and forced to work. If he failed to support his children, they might be apprenticed to an employer, who must clothe and feed them, teach them to read and write, and keep them employed. When these Black codes were published in the North they aroused great indignation. "Are we going to permit the South to re-establish slavery under a different name?" it was asked. "After fighting a long war to abolish this evil, is it to come back under the guise of laws for vagrants and apprentices?" [34]

1950

By midcentury, the narrative of Reconstruction was remarkably intact. Many U.S. history textbook authors were as harsh in condemning the carpetbaggers and scalawags for the failure of Reconstruction as they were the freed slaves.

Selfish Adventurers Gain Control of State Governments

By the Reconstruction Act, men who only a few brief years before had labored as slaves were enabled to vote and hold office. Many of them could neither read nor write, and did not understand the workings of government. Therefore, they became easy victims of selfish white men who sought to gain control of the southern governments. These white men were known as *carpetbaggers* and *scalawags*. The carpetbaggers were Northerners who saw a chance to get rich quickly. They earned their name from the fact that they rushed to the South with their belongings hastily packed in old-fashioned traveling bags called "carpetbags." The scalawags, on the other hand, were southern white men who had opposed secession or who now thought they could gain something by favoring the North. Both carpetbaggers and scalawags were more interested in wealth and power for themselves than in rebuilding the South.

RECONSTRUCTION IS CARRIED OUT UNDER CARPETBAG GOVERNMENTS

How did the carpetbaggers gain control of the state governments? They joined with the scalawags and the Negroes to form a Republican Party in the South. By promising the Negroes money and power, they got themselves elected to offices in the state governments. Negroes and scalawags were elected to the state legislatures. It was those carpetbag governments which carried out the provisions of the Reconstruction Act. By 1870, all the southern states had been admitted once more to the Union.

Under the carpetbaggers and scalawags, the southern legislatures wasted huge sums of money. The capitol building in South Carolina was furnished with $650 French mirrors, $60 chairs, $600 clocks, and $60 imported china spittoons! Huge amounts of money were voted for buildings, roads, schools, and railroads, and much of this money was spent foolishly. In order to raise these sums, heavy taxes were voted. The heavy taxes fell chiefly on the southern whites who owned property. Many had to sell their lands because they could not pay the taxes.[35]

1974

For the first time, textbooks in the early 1970s began to suggest some of the positive benefits of the Reconstruction governments. Many such texts attempted a historical balancing act, weighing evidence of corruption and "Northern interference" against the social and political improvements that Reconstruction tried to implement.

Through the Reconstruction acts, the Republicans in Congress intended to put members of their party in control of the South. Since there had been no Republican party in the South before the war, the party had to be organized as a new combination of political elements. It came to consist of black men and of two groups of white men, the so called scalawags and carpetbaggers.

Black men made up the largest bloc of Republican voters in most of the states under Radical Reconstruction. Negroes served as state and local officials, legislators, and as United States representatives and senators, but they never held a majority of offices except in the South Carolina legislature. Although some attained state offices as high as lieutenant governor, none was ever elected governor. Many of the black officeholders had received no schooling and did not know how to read and write. Others, most of whom were free before the war, and some of whom had been born and reared in the North, were well educated. Several were eloquent speakers and effective leaders.

The scalawags were native white southerners who, temporarily at least, joined the Republican party. Some were farmers who had never owned slaves, who had long disliked the planter aristocracy, and who had given the Confederacy little or no support during the war. Others were wealthy or once wealthy planters and businessmen who had opposed secession but had "gone with their states" and had served in the Confederate army. Having once been Whigs, they did not feel quite at home as Democrats. They were willing to join once more with former Whigs (now Republicans) of the North. Moreover, they believed they could advance their own interests by cooperating with blacks and working to control black votes.

The southern white Republicans did not, of course, call themselves scalawags. They were called that by the Democrats, who viewed them as scoundrels. The Democrats held the same view of the carpetbaggers northern Republicans who took part in southern politics after the war. The Democrats termed them carpetbaggers in order to give the impression that they were fortune seekers who had gone south with all their possessions in a carpetbag (at that time a common kind of traveling bag).

Actually, the carpetbaggers included a variety of men from the North, well-off and poor, honest and dishonest. Nearly all were veterans of the Union army. Most of them came south during the war or within a year or two after its close. Some had arrived as Freedmen's Bureau agents or as federal officials. Others had come as planters, businessmen, or professional men who thought they saw a new frontier of economic opportunity in the postwar South. Though not numerous enough to be important as voters, the carpetbaggers were clever and courageous enough to be extremely influential as leaders. More willing than the scalawags to mingle socially with Negroes, the carpetbaggers were more successful in winning black confidence and support.

Under Radical Reconstruction, the old political order in the South seemed to be turned upside down, with recent slaves imposing laws upon their former masters. White Democrats complained of "Negro rule." Yet, in fact, Negroes alone never ran the southern states. For a time, they helped govern, but they did so in cooperation with white men, some from the North, a much larger number from the South.

The Republican state governments did not change relations between blacks and whites as much as some people expected. For example, they refrained, except in a few cases, from legalizing interracial marriages or requiring integrated schools (in New Orleans, some of the schools were racially integrated for a brief period). Nevertheless, these governments were quite different from those that preceded them. The new ones undertook to do things that their predecessors had not done at all or had done only on a small scale.

One of these things was to provide education for masses of children, black as well as white. Before the war, every southern state had adopted some kind of public educational system, at least on paper. But none except North Carolina had actually established public schools throughout the state. In trying to educate hundreds of thousands of persons who had never been educated before, the Republican government faced an expensive task. They had to build many schoolhouses. Most of the teachers had to be attracted from the North at high salaries.

The new state governments also tried to improve and expand the means of transportation. The Republicans—and many Democrats—believed that the South could prosper only if trade were encouraged by the construction of additional railroad lines. They believed that the states must give financial aid to railroad companies in order to encourage rapid expansion. Some of the governments under Johnsonian reconstruction had helped finance railroad construction, but the Republican governments did much more.

The states also borrowed money (by issuing bonds) for other purposes, such as the building of schools and the rebuilding of streets, roads, bridges, levees, and courthouses. Consequently, the state debts increased, some of them to a level several times as high as the prewar debts. Taxes also went up, both to pay interest on the debts and to meet increased running expenses.

Unfortunately, not all the money raised by taxing and borrowing was used for public improvement or the general welfare. Some of the money (no one can say how much) was wasted or diverted for private gain. Negroes, scalawags, and carpetbaggers were not the only ones involved. Black men were no more corrupt than white men, Republicans no more corrupt than Democrats, northerners no more corrupt than southerners. During the postwar years, political corruption was widespread throughout the nation. In the years after Reconstruction, however, the memory of corruption under the Reconstruction governments grew until it became the chief thing for which Reconstruction was remembered.[36]

1995

By the 1990s, a new generation of influential scholars had turned the traditional view of Reconstruction on its head. This text argued that while there may have been some corruption, it was not above the norm. Students also learned that while some parts of Reconstruction may have failed, there were some African American leaders who were successful.

Significant problems faced the Republican for Reconstruction in the South. After all, the party had had virtually no support in the region before the mid-1860s. And it was unlikely to win large numbers of converts among whites in the post–Civil War years.

WHITE REPUBLICANS IN THE SOUTH

For these reasons, the Republicans depended for their support in the South on African Americans and on people who are now known as carpet-baggers and scalawags. Both of these terms were originally insulting names given to these groups by southerners. *Carpetbaggers* were northern Republicans who moved to the South after the Civil War. Their name referred to a kind of suitcase, and it implied that these northerners had hastily migrated into the region to take advantage of the political situation. Carpetbaggers were mainly former Union army officers and Freedmen's Bureau officials. *Scalawags,* a term that means "rascals," were southern whites who became Republicans. They tended to be men who had been Whigs, who were interested in economic development, or who lived in the more isolated areas. Many scalawags were poor.

AFRICAN AMERICANS IN OFFICE

African Americans were key, though underrepresented, members of the Republican party in the South. Determined to win their share of political power, they organized to promote the interests of their community. In 1865 the African American state convention addressed these words to the people of South Carolina:

> Now that we are free men, now that we have been lifted up by the providence of God to manhood, we have resolved to come forward, and, like MEN, speak and act for ourselves.

Many southern whites criticized the presence of African Americans in Reconstruction governments. They accused African American officials of being corrupt or incompetent. In reality, the South's African American officials appeared to have been no worse and no better than their white counterparts. Many served with distinction. Between 1867 and 1869, approximately 1,000 men attended state constitutional conventions throughout the South. Some 265 of them were African Americans; at least 107 were former slaves. Many were veterans of the Union army, ministers, artisans, farmers, and teachers.

African Americans held high office in the South during Reconstruction, though the number of such officials was small relative to the African American population. African Americans were, after all, a majority in Louisiana, Mississippi, and South Carolina. One African American, P.B.S. Pinchback, briefly served as governor of Louisiana. Six African Americans were lieutenant governors, and several others held high state office. Meanwhile, sixteen African Americans went to Congress, and Hiram Revels, an educator and minister, became a United States senator from Mississippi in 1870. Mississippi also sent former sheriff Blanche K. Bruce to the Senate in 1874. In addition, 600 African Americans were members of various state legislatures and hundreds of others held local offices. While some were illiterate—70 percent of African Americans could not read or write in 1880, compared to under 10 percent of whites—many were educated and virtually all were capable of making informed judgments about major issues.[37]

28

Birth of the Ku Klux Klan

Originally founded in 1865, the KKK was intended as a social organization, but it quickly turned to violence when its members began to resist congressional Reconstruction. This meant that the KKK focused its attention on carpetbaggers, scalawags, and the newly freed slaves, and by using violence and intimidation tried to keep these people out of the post–Civil War governments. How U.S. history textbooks dealt with the birth of the KKK (and other similar organizations) since the 1860s seems to be a litmus test of what America's young people have been taught about race relations.

1889

After the passage of the federal Ku Klux Klan Act of 1871, the Klan began to diminish in size and power. The Klan, as a national organization with political clout, would not truly reemerge until 1915. This textbook, published in a time when the KKK was not so influential, argued against the KKK and seemed to give credence to the newly freed slave.

The Ku Klux Klan was a secret society of whites, extending all through the Southern States. It was originally formed as a sort of police, to keep the freedmen in subjection. It then attacked the white Republican, the "carpetbaggers" or "scalawags." Finally it seems to have gone into the work of committing murders for pay or spite, so that the better class of whites were compelled to aid in putting it down. Before this took place, Congress passed a number of severe laws, intended to put an end to the society and its practices of riding by night in masks and disguises to terrify, whip, or murder freedmen and white Republicans.

Reconstruction, so far as it aimed to make freedmen voters, was thus a failure in all but three States before 1876; and even in these three States, South Carolina, Florida, and Louisiana, it became a failure in 1877. And yet, in spite of this failure, it has been a success in other respects. As a slave, the negro had been only a thing, a piece of property, without any rights. Reconstruction has given him every right but that of voting; and even this right is being obtained slowly but surely, as the negro shows himself worthy of it.[38]

1914

Although published in Chicago, this textbook was written by Lawton B. Evans, a Georgian who also wrote a series of textbooks on Georgia history. While it is possible that this textbook was sold north of the Mason-Dixon Line, it would have arguably been more popular in the southern states in the first half of the twentieth century.

The Negroes After the War

In the North business went on as before; in the South the people had to face new conditions. The negroes were no longer slaves who had to work; they were free to work or not as they chose.

Most of them stayed on the farms and worked for wages. There were some, however, who wandered idly from place to place, and became a menace to the peace of the country. Soon they had no money, no food, and nobody to care for them. Some of them became vicious and even thought they could take by force what they needed.

To protect themselves against these idle and lawless negroes, who were often led away by evil white men, a secret order known as the "Ku Klux Klan" was formed by the white people of the South. Its members met in the woods or on the outskirts of the town. They wore masks and hideous disguises, and had a password and secret signs. Whenever a bad negro or white man began to give trouble a sign was nailed on his door, or a note was sent to him, ordering him to leave the community or suffer the consequences.

The "Ku Klux" riders were a great terror to the negroes. Whenever they appeared, the frightened blacks scurried to their cabins. The threats of this organization held the negroes in check, kept them in their houses, forced the evil ones to behave, and made the idle ones work.[39]

1916

Again, in the 1910s, students were introduced to the stereotype of the superstitious, ignorant former slaves.

The self-respecting Southerners, before Congress would allow them to vote, found two ways of fighting against their oppression. First, they formed secret societies to intimidate the black voters and frighten them away from the polls. The members of the most notable of these societies, the Ku Klux Klan, would ride about among the negro huts at night, attired in fantastic costumes, to frighten the occupants and bind them by solemn oath to do the bidding of the whites. They resorted not only to actual violence but also to grotesque devices. Drawing up before one hut and requesting a drink of water, a horseman, who carried a tank concealed beneath his robes, would drink three bucketfuls [*sic*] of water, with the words, "That's good; the first I've had since Shiloh." Another would ask a frightened negro to hold his horse, and then taking off what was apparently his own head would bid the black hold that too. It was easy to frighten the superstitious ex-slaves. In 1870 and in 1871 by "Force Acts" Congress adopted extreme measures against such methods and the Ku Klux Klan was broken up.

Furthermore, the disfranchised whites, through their Northern friends, carried on a persistent agitation in Congress in favor of giving them back the suffrage. Congress, as we have seen, yielded but slowly, and lent its favor rather to the negroes than to their old masters. It was not till 1872 that a law was passed by Congress wholly removing from the Southern whites the political disabilities resulting from the war. From that time the "carpetbagger," the "scalawag," and the negro gradually lost their political domination.[40]

1936

The historiography of the KKK took a turn in the 1930s when, instead of cheering on the organization's exploits, most U.S. history textbooks began to back the "law-abiding citizens."

The Beginning of the Ku Klux Klan

As the carpetbaggers encouraged the negroes to assert more and more authority in the South, the Ku Klux Klan was organized to combat this influence. The K.K.K., as it is often called, was a secret society first formed in Tennessee. Its purpose was to frighten negro voters so they would keep away from the polls. "Dens" were established in many places in the South where men met to plan raids against negroes of the neighborhood. It served its purpose against the negro, but it did not stop there. Men were murdered, many were whipped, and others driven from their homes. Finally, law-abiding citizens were obliged to put down the organization and stop its disorderly conduct.[41]

1948

In the late 1940s and 1950s, students would have read this passage in the context of a new wave of Klan violence against the Civil Rights Movement in the South.

The Ku Klux Klan

Deprived of any legal means of defense against such iniquitous government, the South naturally resorted to intimidation. Secret organizations, chief of which was the Ku Klux Klan, took advantage of the Negroes' superstition and fear to force them back into a position of social and political obscurity. Bands of young men on horseback, robed in ghostly white sheets, spread terror through the Negro quarters at night and posted on trees and fences horrible warnings to carpetbaggers and scalawags to leave the country if they wished to live. Negroes were beaten and scalawags were shot. Exaggerated reports of these deeds of violence were spread through the North and used by the radical politicians to justify the tightening of military rule in the South.[42]

1961

Written while the Civil Rights Movement was in full swing, this textbook told students that the KKK was nothing more then a terrorist group.

The Ku Klux Klan Supports White Supremacy

Southern whites became increasingly resentful of Radical reconstruction. In the beginning, some Southerners had been willing to grant suffrage to the Negro. They believed that the Negroes, with education and property qualifications, could be made to take an interest in the affairs of the South and its welfare. However, the methods used by the Union League to assure Republican rule in the South turned many of these people against Negro suffrage. Southern whites of all classes became united in their opposition to the whole reconstruction program. Their aim was to restore the Democratic Party to power. Since it was impossible to achieve their objectives by legal means, many Southerners resorted to methods outside the law. One of the most effective of these was the organization of such secret societies as the Ku Klux Klan, the Knights of the White Camelia, and the Society of the White Rose.

The most important of the secret societies was the Ku Klux Klan. The name was taken from a Greek word, *kuklos,* meaning a band or circle. The Klan was organized in 1866 by a group of young men in Pulaski, Tennessee, who put on white masks and robes and frightened Negroes by pretending to be ghosts. Although it started as a prank, the Klan soon developed into a powerful instrument for restoring white supremacy in the South. The organization spread rapidly throughout the southern states. In the spring of 1867, at a secret meeting in Nashville, Tennessee, the local Klans were united into the "Invisible Empire of the South." Members were pledged to oppose equality of the races and to work for the restoration of the southern whites to political power.

THE KLAN TURNS TO TERROR AND MEETS OPPOSITION

Thus began a reign of terror against the freedmen and the Radical political leaders. There were strange disguises, midnight rides and drills by white-sheeted horsemen, and dire warnings written in blood and decorated with coffins, skulls, and crossbones. These were calculated to scare the freedmen away from the polls and to drive reconstruction officials out of town. If fear and threats did not work, the Klan turned to violence. Local Klans came increasingly under the control of reckless and lawless elements. In 1869, General Nathan Bedford Forrest, Grand Wizard of the Klan, ordered that it be dissolved. After this, most respectable and law-abiding Southerners left the organization.

To suppress the Klan, Congress passed the Ku Klux Klan Acts in 1870 and 1871, which were designed to enforce the Fourteenth and Fifteenth Amendments. These acts gave the President military power to uphold the carpetbag governments and authorized him to declare a state of war when he considered it necessary. President Grant made use of this power only once. In October, 1871, he declared nine counties in South Carolina centers of "armed combinations," suspended *habeas corpus* there, and sent in regular army troops and federal marshals.[43]

1996

Contrary to what students might have found in textbooks in the late 1800s and early 1900s, by the end of the twentieth century there was no doubt that the KKK had done nothing to boast about. Rather, in the late twentieth century, the Klan's history was portrayed as having a negative impact on the South while the KKK members themselves were depicted as "masked thugs on parade."

The Radical Republican governments were able to remain in power in the south only so long as blacks voted for them. Some Southern whites decided to make sure that blacks did not vote. The South was now at war with itself. Southerners said that they were really fighting against their fellow Southern blacks who wanted to be free and equal.

Before long, certain Old Confederates in the South had organized a secret army. Its purpose was to carry on the Civil War under another name.

Although slavery was abolished by law, many Southerners still hoped to preserve as much as possible of their former way of life.

This secret army called itself the Ku Klux Klan—perhaps from the Greek word *kyklos,* meaning circle. Soon many branches, or circles, appeared all over the South. Klan members traveled the countryside flogging, maiming, and sometimes killing blacks who tried to vote or who in other ways presumed to be the white man's equal. The Klan uniform was a pointed hat with a white hood to conceal the face, and a long white or black robe.

Scores of other organizations joined in the bloody work—the Tennessee Pale Faces, the Louisiana Knights of the White Camelia, the North Carolina White Brotherhood, the Mississippi Society of the White Rose, the Texas Knights of the Rising Sun, the Red Jackets, and the Knights of the Black Cross. In 1871 alone, in a single county in Florida, 163 blacks were murdered, and around New Orleans the murders came to over 300. These organizations kept the lists of their members secret to save them from punishment for their crimes. Thousands of blacks were driven from their homes, maimed, or tortured. Whole communities were terrorized by masked thugs on parade, by burning crosses, by kidnapping and tar-and-feathering.

Under pressure from Northern Radical Republicans, some Southern states passed laws against these outrages. On December 5, 1870, President U.S. Grant delivered a special message to Congress. "The free exercise of franchise," he warned, "has by violence and intimidation been denied to citizens of several of the States lately in rebellion." Congress then passed the Ku Klux Klan Acts to outlaw these organizations and to protect all citizens.[44]

PART V

---

*Industrialization,
Imperialism, and War*

29

Eugene V. Debs and the Pullman Strike

The concepts of modernization, progress, and industrialization figure prominently in most U.S. history textbooks written over the past hundred years. American students have been taught that it is a combination of these three things that
made the United States great. While most textbooks focus on the positive aspects of Industry, others take a social perspective, discussing how immigrants
were often treated in factories, the living conditions for America's poor, and the
development of the labor unions as a counterbalance to industrialism. A key
player in the early labor movement was Eugene V. Debs, a unionist from Indiana;
he would later become a Socialist and made five attempts at running for president of the United States. This section looks at Debs and the Pullman strike, and
how history textbooks have treated the issue of laborers who were not pleased
with the "Captains of Industry" and their companies.

1912

*On the heels of a period of sharp labor unrest, strikes featured prominently in text-
books of this era.*

One of the most notable strikes in our history had its center in Chicago in 1894. Employees of the Pullman Palace Car Company struck for the restoration of wages that had been reduced. These workmen were members of the American Railway Union. Although advising against the strike, the Union supported its members when the Pullman Company refused to arbitrate the questions at issue, or to "recognize" the Union. A sympathetic strike was ordered, in which train men refused to move trains containing Pullman cars. Within a few days there was a general paralysis of commerce centering in Chicago. In spite of the efforts of city officers, state militia, and special United States marshals to maintain order, and to facilitate the movement of trains by nonunion men, there was great danger to life and much destruction of property in Chicago. Finally, President Cleveland ordered Federal troops to the scene for the purpose of preventing the obstruction of mail trains and interstate commerce. This was done against the protest of Governor Altgeld of Illinois. An injunction was issued by a Federal Court against the officers of the American Railway Union, forbidding them to issue further orders in pursuance of the strike. The President of the Union, E. V. Debs, and other officers, were convicted for disobedience of this injunction. The strike was a failure, but a United States Commission of investigation condemned the refusal of the Pullman and railroad to arbitrate.[1]

1920

This history textbook was published just as the "Roaring Twenties" were about to take off—a time when most business leaders were seen as heroic historical actors in many history textbooks.

The Pullman Strike

There was nothing farcical, however, in the conflict between capital and labor which broke out in Chicago that same month of May. The Pullman Palace Car Company, whose business had been seriously injured by the hard times of 1893, discharged a number of employees for whom it had no immediate use and cut the wages of the rest. But in view of the fact that the company was paying 7 percent dividends, that it had accumulated a surplus of $25,000,000 on a capital of $36,000,000, the workers could not see that the company was suffering, and a committee of the docked men waited on Mr. Pullman to remonstrate. For this "impertinence" three men on the committee were discharged. Then nearly all the employees struck. About 4,000 of the Pullman employees were members of the powerful American Railway Union, an organization founded in 1893 under the presidency of Eugene V. Debs. The union took up the matter at its June meeting in 1894 and demanded that the company submit the question of wages to arbitration. This Mr. Pullman refused to do. The union then forbade its men to "handle" the Pullman cars. The boycott extended to 27 states and territories, affecting the railroads from Ohio to California. But the dire conflict came in Chicago. Early in July only 6 of the 23 railroads entering the city were unobstructed. United States mail trains carrying Pullman cars were not allowed to move. President Cleveland ordered troops to the seat of disturbance, and an injunction was issued by the federal court ordering the strikers to cease obstructing the United States mails. The reading of the injunction was received with 'hoots and jeers.' Debs had appealed to the strikers to refrain from violence and the destruction of property, but they could not be restrained. Trains were ditched, freight cars destroyed, buildings burned and looted. At one or two points it became necessary for the federal troops to fire on the mob to protect their own lives. Debs and his chief associates were arrested and imprisoned for contempt of court in not obeying the injunction.[2]

1966

By the 1960s, many history textbooks began to side with the unions. Students were also given more detail about the role the U.S. government played in suppressing the labor movement.

The Courts Support Industry

The courts, no less than governors and Presidents, generally used their powers on behalf of ownership and management in the late 1800's. For example, during the famous Pullman strike of 1894, the owners asked a federal court in Chicago to issue an injunction, or court order, forbidding Eugene Debs and other labor leaders from continuing the strike. The court issued the injunction. It justified this action on the ground that the strikers had entered into "a conspiracy in restraint of trade," and that they were therefore violating the Sherman Antitrust Act, passed in 1890, which declared such conspiracies illegal.

Debs defied the court order. Instead of calling off the strike, he called upon the leaders of other unions to call a general strike as a token of sympathy for the Pullman strikers. Although organized labor was firmly in sympathy with Debs and the American Railway Union, the union leaders refused to respond to Debs' call for a general strike. Debs was promptly arrested for "contempt of court." He was sentenced to six months in jail for his refusal to obey the injunction. Labor denounced this conviction as "government by injunction." But the Supreme Court in 1895 upheld the Federal Circuit Court, Debs was placed behind bars, and the strike was broken.

President Cleveland consistently aroused the opposition of organized labor. Labor had been angered in 1893 when Cleveland appointed as Attorney General a man who had been a corporation lawyer and who was an avowed opponent of the Sherman Antitrust Act. Cleveland's role in the Pullman strike and other strikes further aroused the antagonism of organized labor. Thus organized labor vigorously supported the farmers in the Populist Party during the early 1890's. And they rallied enthusiastically to the support of William Jennings Bryan in the election of 1896.

After 1895 the injunction became a powerful weapon against organized labor since employers were often successful in securing injunctions to prevent or break up strikes. Labor complained bitterly, but the only relief it could hope for was (1) that the Supreme Court would reverse its decision of 1895 or (2) that Congress would modify the Sherman Antitrust Act so that it could not be used against labor unions.

But despite setbacks in its struggle, organized labor continued to fight for its aims and for public recognition and support. By the early 1900's, as you will see there were signs that the lot of American workers was beginning to improve.[3]

1982

In the post–Vietnam War, Reagan 1980s (a time when the headlines were dominated by the mass firings of air traffic controllers following the strike by the Professional Air Traffic Controllers Organization), a classroom discussion on the following topic would have been interesting. Would students support the workers protesting against big business and government (much like students did in the 1960s and 1970s), or would they be more sympathetic to the capitalists?

In 1894, workers at the Pullman Palace Car Company walked out in protest over exploitative policies at the company town near Chicago. The paternalistic company head George Pullman tried to do everything for the twelve thousand residents of his so-called model town. His company owned and controlled the land and all buildings, the school, the bank, and the water and gas systems. It paid workers' wages, fixed their rents, determined what prices they would pay for the necessities of life, and employed spies to report on disgruntled workers. One laborer grumbled, "We are born in a Pullman house, fed from the Pullman shop, taught in the Pullman school, catechized in the Pullman church, and when we die we shall be buried in the Pullman cemetery and go to the Pullman hell."

One thing Pullman would not do was negotiate with workers. When the depression that began in 1893 threatened his business, Pullman managed to maintain profits and pay dividends to stockholders by cutting wages 25–40 percent but holding firm on rents and prices in the model town. Workers, squeezed into debt and deprivation, sent a committee to Pullman in May 1894 to protest his policies. Pullman reacted by firing three of the committee. The enraged workers, most of whom had joined the American Railway Union, called a strike. Pullman retaliated by shutting down the plant. When the American Railway Union, led by the charismatic young organizer Eugene V. Debs, voted to aid the strikers by boycotting all Pullman cars, Pullman stood firm and rejected arbitration. The railroad owners' association then enlisted the aid of U.S. Attorney General Richard Olney, who obtained a court injunction to prevent the union from "obstructing the railways and holding up the mails." In response to further worker obstinacy, President Grover Cleveland sent federal troops to Chicago, supposedly to protect the mails but in reality to crush the strike. Within a month the strike was over, and Debs was jailed for six months for contempt of court in defying the injunction. The Supreme Court upheld Debs's sentence on the grounds that the federal government had the power to remove obstacles to interstate commerce.[4]

1995

Although Debs continuously shows up as a "workingman's hero" in textbooks discussing his role in the Pullman strike, in general he is usually a footnote in most U.S. history textbooks. One main reason for this was briefly explained in this section. After World War II, with the onset of the Cold War, few, if any, textbooks were going to give much space to an American leader, no matter how significant, if they had fallen in line with the Socialist ideology.

The great Pullman strike. One of the largest strikes in the country's history began just a few days after Coxey's arrest when the employees of the Pullman Palace Car Company, living in a company town just outside of Chicago (a town in which everything was owned and meted out by the company), struck to protest wage cuts, continuing high rents, and layoffs. On June 26, 1894, the American Railway Union (ARU) under Eugene V. Debs joined the strike by refusing to handle trains that carried Pullman sleeping cars. Within hours, the strike paralyzed the western half of the nation. Grain and livestock could not reach markets. Factories shut down for lack of coal. The strike extended into twenty-seven states and territories, tying up the economy and renewing talk of class warfare. In Washington, President Grover Cleveland, who had been reelected to the presidency in 1892, decided to break the strike on the grounds that it obstructed delivery of the mail.

On July 2, he secured a court injunction against the ARU, and he ordered troops to Chicago. When they arrived on the morning of Independence Day, the city was peaceful. Before long, however, violence broke out, and mobs, composed mostly of nonstrikers, overturned freight cars, looted, and burned. Restoring order, the army occupied railroad yards in Illinois, California, and other points. By late July, the strike was over; Debs was jailed for violating the injunction. Many people applauded Cleveland's action, "nominally for the expedition of the mails," a newspaper said, but "really for the preservation of society."

The Pullman strike had far-reaching consequences for the development of the labor movement. Working people resented Cleveland's actions in the strike, particularly as it became apparent that he sided with the railroads.

Upholding Debs's sentence in *In re Debs* (1895), the Supreme Court endorsed the use of the injunction in labor disputes, thus giving business and government an effective antilabor weapon that hindered union growth in the 1890s. The strike's failure catapulted Debs into prominence. During his time in jail, he turned to socialism, and after his release he worked to build the Socialist party of America, which experienced some success after 1900.[5]

30

Immigration

The historical story of the poor immigrant who comes to the United States without a dime to his or her name and climbs the social ladder is as much a part of American folklore as any other tale in U.S. history. Between 1870 and 1920, nearly twenty million immigrants arrived, looking for this golden opportunity that textbooks so love to talk about. Ironically, that image of the hardworking, industrious immigrant ran into the belief of a number of "old-stock" Americans that these new immigrants from Europe and Asia were actually destroying U.S. culture.

1905

This textbook was published amid the great wave of European immigration, between 1870–1920. In the historiography of immigration, there has always been two competing stories: the positive narrative and the darker view, which usually overshadowed the former in most early twentieth-century history textbooks.

The supply of labor was affected by a wave of immigration of races which, up to 1870, were not much known in America—Italians, French

Canadians, Poles, Bohemians, Hungarians, Russian Jews, Slovaks, Armenians, Greeks, and Syrians. The workingmen secured from Congress a series of acts somewhat restricting immigration. (1) Convicts, idiots, and like unfit persons were shut out, and a head tax of fifty cents was laid on all immigrants admitted (1882). (2) Congress excluded "contract laborers" who might come over under an agreement to take a specified job when they arrived (1885). (3) Polygamists, diseased persons, and persons unable to support themselves were shut out (1891). (4) The immigrant head tax was raised to two dollars (1903).

That some foreigners were dangerous to society was shown by an anarchist outbreak in Chicago (May 4, 1886). After weeks of violent speeches, principally by foreigners, urging people to resist the government, a dynamite bomb was thrown in the Haymarket and killed seven policemen.[6]

1916

While most textbooks focused on European immigration, the "threat" of immigration from Asia, to some textbook authors, seemed even more troubling. According to this author, if action was not taken against the continuing growth of Asian immigrants, soon they "might some day rival in difficulty the Negro or the Indian problem."

Organized labor, bent on keeping down the supply of labor in order to maintain as high a standard of wages as possible, had long stood consistently opposed to foreign immigration, but only after the labor unions had become a powerful factor in national life did Congress pay attention to their demands. The first law of the United States for the restriction of immigration, marking the end of the country's traditional policy of welcome to all foreigners, was passed in 1882. Previous to this time there had been some few restrictions on immigration by such states as were directly affected; for example by New York, which had excluded certain classes. By the national law, which was in many respects a copy of existing state laws, lunatics and convicts were excluded, all who were liable to become a public charge, and, by an act of 1885, all contract laborers, that is, all laborers coming into the country under a contract. At this time most of the immigrants were from the countries of Northern Europe.

The presence of thousands of Chinese laborers on the Pacific coast, attracted by the prospects of work in the gold mines and in the construction of railroads, was highly objectionable to the labor unions. The Asiatics worked for low wages, lived in squalid quarters on a few cents a day, and in general competed with the whites on terms which to the latter were intolerable. Their presence, too, threatened to create another race problem, which might some day rival in difficulty the Negro or the Indian problem. President Hayes vetoed a bill passed in his administration to exclude the Chinese altogether, as contrary to the existing treaty with China; but before he went out of office he succeeded in making a new treaty with China, which gave to the United States discretionary power to "regulate, limit, or suspend" but not to "absolutely prohibit" the coming of Chinese laborers into the country. Under this treaty, in the administration of Arthur, Congress passed a law to exclude the Chinese for twenty years, which seemed to the President too long a term, and he refused his approval. A compromise bill, fixing the term of exclusion at ten years, was then passed and received the signature of the President. This was renewed later under another president, and the exclusion is still in force. Though the law seems harsh, every nation undoubtedly possesses the right to expel from its shores any aliens whose presence may be considered dangerous to its interests, and likewise to refuse admission to all whom it may consider undesirable.[7]

1933

Oddly enough, this textbook condemned Chinese immigrants by claiming that although they are hardworking and law-abiding, they cannot be trusted since they do not "intermarry with other races."

An influx of Chinese causes alarm in California. The westernmost region, the new world facing the old Oriental world across the Pacific, had also its race problem. Chinese laborers came to San Francisco as early as 1849, where the scarcity of labor won them a hearty welcome. Industrious and law-abiding, they occupied themselves with mining, farming, making cigars, and working on the railways. But when they continued to arrive in increasing numbers, sentiment toward them changed. "Are we to convert California into an Oriental region?" men asked. "Are we to permit these Chinese to run American laborers out of the West by working long hours for small wages? You cannot make Americans out of these people; they will not become Christians, do not intermarry with other races." Scenes of violence and bloodshed ensued. Everywhere Chinese were persecuted and abused. Legislatures and city councils vied in passing laws denying them citizenship, excluding them from schools, restricting their rights to work. In 1882 this movement culminated in a federal act, excluding all Chinese except visiting merchants, travelers, and students. Although this law was frequently defied, the desire of many Chinese to return to their native land brought about a gradual decline in their numbers.

California discriminates against Japanese settlers. With the subsiding of the Chinese problem, the Japanese problem became acute. In 1900 there were 24,000 Japanese in the United States; ten years later there were three times that number. They were mostly unmarried young men, who showed a great willingness to learn the language of the country and adopt its customs. But the readiness with which they acquired land, together with the fact that their marked racial traits made assimilation unlikely, brought them into disfavor. Matters reached a crisis when San Francisco excluded Japanese from the public schools. This brought a protest from the Japanese government. Japan was just emerging as a world power and was jealous of her dignity and the rights of her citizens. While political candidates in California pledged themselves to an anti-Japanese policy and hoodlums attacked Japanese residents without interference, President Roosevelt took up the matter with the government at Tokyo. The exclusion act of 1907 resulted. In 1911 this was superseded by a "gentleman's agreement" whereby Japan herself limited emigration to this country, in return for the removal of the formal restrictions.[8]

1936

The author of this textbook made a distinction—common for its time—between good and bad immigrants. It should also be noted that this textbook would have been used in U.S. schools in the mid- to late 1930s, and many of the young men who read textbooks such as this one might have served during World War II in the Pacific.

Good Types of Immigrants

The immigrants before 1880 were largely from Great Britain, Ireland, Germany, and the Scandinavian countries. They were desirable people.

Many of the Germans went to the farms in Michigan, Illinois, and Wisconsin. Most of the Scandinavians-Danes, Swedes, and Norwegians settled in Wisconsin, Minnesota, and the Dakotas. The prosperous country in those regions is a monument today to their thrift, industry, and intelligence.

THE CHINESE EXCLUSION ACTS

The Chinese were not welcomed when it began to appear that they might fill places in industries which were sought by the American laborer. The Chinaman's habits of living were such that he could afford to work for much less than our laborers and still prosper. There was a good deal of agitation against the Chinese in the western states during the '70's. The feeling became so intense that a Chinese Exclusion Act was passed in 1902 making the exclusion of Chinese effective for all time.

IMMIGRANTS FROM SOUTHERN EUROPE

After 1880 the majority of European immigrants to the United States came from Russia, Austria, Hungary, and Italy. In 1882 nearly 789,000 were admitted. Many of this number were Russians, who left their native country on account of persecution; others were Italians and Austrians, who found it convenient to emigrate to America after direct steamship lines had been opened between the United States and the Mediterranean ports. The southern European countries soon surpassed the northern in number of immigrants because the Irish, Germans, and Scandinavians were unwilling to live as cheaply and to work for as small a wage as the immigrants from southern Europe.

THE NEW TYPE OF IMMIGRANT CREATES ALARM

The character of the new immigration marked a change not only in habits of living but also in education and readiness to adopt the democratic institutions in the United States. Many had lived so wretchedly in Europe that any conditions of living and working were an improvement over what they had had. There were some among the new immigrants who were quickly Americanized, but a large percentage of them were illiterate and did not soon change their habits of life. They gathered into communities of Italians and Hungarians and "Little Italies," and "Little Hungaries" and the like sprang up in large cities where the customs of Europe, rather than of America, prevailed.

The public schools and compulsory attendance laws made a great change in the second generation of the newcomers. There was, however, such a constantly swelling tide of immigrants to the United States that many feared that democratic America would be flooded with Europeans with all sorts of radical notions about government. The next step was the adoption of some restrictive measures to keep out undesirables, and also to cut down the total number of immigrants.

JAPANESE IMMIGRATION

In 1900 there were about twenty-four thousand Japanese laborers in the United States. Most of these people were in the Pacific states, though some were in other Western states, particularly Colorado, about one-half of them were in California. At first the Japanese were welcomed in the salmon canning factories, on the farms, in the mines, and in domestic service. In 1909 the Immigration Commission discovered that the Japanese owned over sixteen thousand acres of land in California and leased over one hundred thirty-seven thousand acres. After this information was made public, the Californians became very hostile to the Japanese. They feared domination by a race that showed so much ability. The anti-Japanese policy found its way into politics and candidates were pledged to oppose further immigration. Bills were passed which resulted in an agreement by Japan to keep her people out of the United States. In 1924 the law expressly forbade Japanese and Chinese immigration. President Coolidge recommended to Congress while the law was being considered that such harsh measures against Japan should not be adopted. There seemed no necessity for it. The Japanese government did not wish her people to go where they were not wanted and she particularly did not want them regarded as inferior to other people. There were street riots against Americans in Japan and many threats were made to boycott American goods. The feeling between the two countries seems to be adjusted now, however.[9]

1950

In the aftermath of World War II, the historiography of immigration took a sharp turn. The bad guys in the story were now close-minded Americans or cruel factory owners. Part of the reason for this change may be due to the fact that the earlier waves of immigrants had lived in the United States for a generation or two, and were sending their children to public schools. A wise textbook publisher would want to market well-received books in traditionally "immigrant" areas.

Immigrants Must Work Hard

Many immigrants did not have an easy time earning a living. Those who had been farmers at home and became farmers here got along with the least difficulty. Even though they might not own their own farms, at least they were doing familiar work. As we have seen, many immigrants, particularly those who arrived before about 1890, did become farmers. They and their descendants are among the most successful American farmers. Immigrants seeking other jobs, however, often found that they had to accept the hardest work, with the longest hours, at the lowest pay. This was particularly true in the late 1800's and early 1900's. Unless the newcomer had a special skill which was needed by employers, he had to accept hard labor. Because these immigrants at first were not familiar with American ways, greedy and selfish men were able to cheat them in business and to take advantage of them in general.

IMMIGRANTS ARE DISLIKED BY SOME AMERICANS

It is unfortunate but true that immigrants were often received in an unfriendly way by older Americans. Some people dislike anybody or anything which seems strange to them. Most of the new immigrants, of course, did seem strange. They did not have the speech, the manners, or the customs of Americans. Also, although the people of the United States had much work to do in building the country, immigrants sometimes seemed to cause unemployment. Some of them were willing to take jobs at lower wages than those which people who had been here for some time would accept. Americans feared that this would lead to lower wages for them, too. These things caused some Americans to dislike immigrants.

SHOULD IMMIGRATION BE RESTRICTED?

Many Americans believe that this policy of limiting immigration is unwise. They point out that progress in the United States has been helped greatly by newcomers to our shores. They also believe it is undemocratic to deny completely the right of some people (from Asia and Africa) to settle in the United States. They believe that immigration should be limited on some other basis than that of birthplace—possibly on education or the ability to earn a living.[10]

1961

The key to a successful immigrant story, according to this textbook, was for the immigrants to assimilate to American values and ideas as rapidly as possible.

The immigrants become part of America. During the twentieth century, the immigrant was being successfully assimilated into American society. Because of the immigration restrictions put into effect after World War I, the proportion of foreign-born Americans has decreased. In 1900, approximately 13 per cent of the American population was foreign-born. In 1960, the foreign-born made up approximately 6 percent of the population. One heard foreign languages spoken in American cities and industrial towns far less often in 1960 than in 1900. The foreign-language press and theater declined steadily and among some groups disappeared entirely. Foreign-language hours on the radio also became less frequent.

Sons and daughters of immigrants attended public schools, tried to live by American standards, and acquired American customs and manners. They discarded the traditions which their parents had brought from the Old World and adopted the traditions of the *Mayflower* and the Declaration of Independence, which they learned in school. Grandchildren of immigrants, with English-speaking parents, considered themselves as American as descendants of seventeenth-century Pilgrims. The public school provided the means by which many different national and racial groups were unified.[11]

1986

As with other topics covered in this book, note the distinctly different tone of this text-book in comparison with earlier excerpts. Rather then just explaining to students all the negative images and stereotypes of the immigrants who came during this time, by the 1980s textbooks showed that all the groups that immigrated to the United States ran into some problems, but most were hardworking and in search of the American dream.

Before the 1880s most immigrants had come from western and northern Europe, especially from England, Ireland, Germany, and the Scandinavian countries. We have already noted that established Americans frequently resented these newcomers. However, people from western Europe had certain advantages that helped them to adjust in their new homeland. British and Irish immigrants spoke English. Many German immigrants were well educated and skilled in one or another useful trade. Scandinavians were experienced farmers and often came with enough money to buy land in the West. Except for the Irish, most of these immigrants were Protestants, as were most Americans. In the 1880s the trend of immigration changed. Thousands of Italians, Poles, Hungarians, Greeks, and Russians flocked in. After 1886 the immigrants' first sight of America was often the Statue of Liberty. The words at its base, written by the poet Emma Lazarus, began "Give me your tired, your poor . . ." Most were indeed poor. They had little or no education and no special skills. They knew no English. Their habits and cultures were very different from those of native-born Americans. The majority were Roman or Greek Orthodox Catholics or Jews.

Many of these immigrants came from areas where money was seldom used. People there exchanged food for cloth, a cow for a wagon, and so on. It was difficult for such people to adjust to life in a large industrial city.

The immigrants from each country or district tended to cluster together in the same city neighborhood. In 1890 a New York reporter wrote that a map of the city showing where different nationalities lived would have "more stripes than the skin of a zebra, and more colors than any rainbow." These ethnic neighborhoods were like cities within cities. They offered people newly arrived in the strange new world of America a chance to hold on to a few fragments of the world they had left. There the immigrants could find familiar foods, people who spoke their language, churches and clubs based on old-country models.

Many native-born Americans resented this new immigration. They insisted that the newcomers were harder to "Americanize" than earlier generations. Workers were disturbed by the new immigrants' willingness to work long hours for low wages. A new nativist organization, the American Protective Association, blamed the hard times of the 1890s on immigration. Nativists charged that the new immigrants were physically and mentally inferior. They were dangerous radicals, the nativists said, who wanted to destroy American democratic institutions.

In the 1890s the Immigration Restriction League called for a law preventing anyone who could not read and write some language from entering the country. The League knew that such a literacy test would keep out many immigrants from southern and eastern Europe.

In that part of the world many regions did not have public school systems. Congress passed a literacy test bill in 1897, but President Grover Cleveland vetoed it. He insisted that America should continue to be a place of refuge for the world's poor and persecuted. Many employers opposed any check on immigration for less humane reasons. They knew that unlimited immigration would assure them a steady force of low-paid but hardworking laborers.

Congress *did* exclude one type of immigrant during this period: the Chinese. By 1880 there were about 75,000 Chinese immigrants in California. They were extremely hardworking people. Because of language and cultural differences, the Chinese tended even more than most immigrants to stick together. They seemed unwilling to try to adapt to American ways, to *assimilate*. Older residents feared and resented them. In 1882 Congress responded to the demands of Californians by passing the Chinese Exclusion Act. It prohibited Chinese workers from entering the United States for a period of ten years. Later the ban was extended. It was not lifted until 1965.

By 1900 there were about 80,000 Mexican-Americans in the southwestern part of the nation. Unlike most other immigrants, these newcomers seldom settled in large cities. Many found jobs as laborers building the Southern Pacific and Santa Fe Railroads. When the lines were completed, they became section hands-men whose job it was to maintain the railroad right of way and repair damaged tracks. This work kept them moving from place to place. Many families had to live in railroad boxcars. Other Mexican immigrants worked as cowhands on cattle ranches. Still others became farm laborers. Like so many immigrants, the Mexican-Americans were poorly paid and oftentimes badly treated.[12]

31

Women's Suffrage

Over the past two hundred years, few, if any, U.S. history textbooks seem to have made overtly sexist remarks about women, as compared to, for example, racist comments about African Americans or Native Americans. And as far back as the early 1800s, individual women were often accorded significant positive attention. Still, women as a group, obviously deserving of serious historical analysis, did not seem to exist in U.S. history until the 1970s, when students were introduced to such textbook topics as "Women in the Colonies," "The Seneca Falls Movement," and "Women's Suffrage."

1920

The ink on the Nineteenth Amendment was barely dry when this textbook reported the passage of the amendment that finally gave women the right to vote.

Woman Suffrage

The House passed an amendment granting women suffrage in January, 1918, but, in spite of the President's repeated recommendations, it was not until eighteen months later that the necessary two-thirds majority was secured in the Senate by the narrow margin of 56 to 25 votes. By the close of 1919 only 22 states had ratified the amendment; but the National Woman Suffrage Association was determined that the necessary 36 states should be secured before the opening of the presidential campaign. Their untiring zeal won state after state, until Tennessee, on August 28, 1920, completed the list. Thus the electorate of the country was enlarged by some eight million voters in the presidential contest of 1920 between Senator Warren G. Harding and Governor James M. Cox, both of Ohio.[13]

1933

This selection mentioned the often-overlooked role of Republican legislator Harry T. Burn in changing the course of women's history in the United States.

The Nineteenth Amendment Is Passed Enfranchising Women (1920)

Nationwide enfranchisement of women was at hand. In 1919 an amendment to the Constitution was proposed in Congress, forbidding any state to deny the right of citizens to vote on account of sex. The resolution passed the House of Representatives 304 to 89, and the Senate 56 to 25. By August, 1920, thirty-five states had assented, and one more only was needed to make the amendment effective. The final battle was fought in Tennessee. On August 18, 1920, the Hall of Representatives at Nashville was crowded with legislators and interested spectators. The suffragists wore yellow flowers, the anti-suffragists red roses. The Senate had voted for ratification, and the House was now debating a motion to concur. Suddenly Speaker Walker resigned the chair, and, taking the floor, said: "I move that this measure go where it belongs, to the table." In the midst of great excitement the vote was taken, and resulted in a tie, 48 to 48. When a second vote had the same result, the anti-suffragists demanded a vote on the resolution itself, realizing that if the tie continued, ratification would be lost. When the roll was called there was no change until the teller came to the name of Harry T. Burn, of McMinn County. This young man, at this critical moment, switched his vote, and the Amendment was ratified. There was an uproarious demonstration. Women threw their arms around each other's necks and danced, hundreds of banners waved, while from the gallery came a shower of yellow flowers. The century long battle, to all intents and purposes, was over, and 27,000,000 American women had the right to vote.[14]

1961

Forty years after the passage of the Nineteenth Amendment, students were introduced to the struggle for women's suffrage as just one part of a larger struggle for women's equality in the United States.

Women Seek New Rights

Although American women could not vote, had few legal rights, and few educational opportunities, many of them had always taken an interest in the affairs of their country. American women helped in many ways during the American Revolution, and they followed the work of the Constitutional Convention of 1787 with keen interest. In March, 1776, Mrs. John Adams wrote her husband, then in the Continental Congress, that she hoped that "independency" would come soon and that the new nation would make laws "generous and favorable" to women.

During the reform period of the early nineteenth century, women were active in the temperance and abolition movements. But when they tried to attend conventions or make speeches, they always ran into opposition. A woman's place, it was generally believed, was in the home, and the idea of a woman appearing on a public platform shocked most people. When two American abolitionists, Mrs. Lucretia Mott and Mrs. Elizabeth Cady Stanton, went to London to attend an anti-slavery convention, they were not permitted to take part in the meetings. With great indignation, Mrs. Mott and Mrs. Stanton returned to the United States and decided to launch a women's rights movement.

WOMEN SUCCEED IN GETTING MORE LEGAL RIGHTS

Mrs. Mott and Mrs. Stanton organized their forces; and, in 1848, they called a convention at Seneca Falls, New York, to issue a "Declaration of Feminine Independence." The convention demanded political, economic, and intellectual equality with men, and presented 18 grievances against "male tyranny." Most people were shocked. Others laughed at "The Reign of Petticoats," but many prominent men, like the writers John Greenleaf Whittier and Ralph Waldo Emerson, supported the movement. Even Abraham Lincoln, on the western frontier, declared he favored sharing government with women.

After the Seneca Falls convention, Mrs. Mott and Mrs. Stanton, joined by Susan B. Anthony, worked tirelessly to improve the position of women in the United States. It was many years before they achieved their main goal: the right to vote. But they did persuade a number of states to pass laws giving women more legal rights.[15]

1978

This discussion of the women's suffrage movement would have been read by students at the height of the modern feminist movement, and just before the ratification deadline for the Equal Rights Amendment.

Women Win the Right to Vote

As women became more active outside the home, there seemed less and less reason to deny them the right to vote. Susan B. Anthony and Elizabeth Cady Stanton were leaders of the National Woman's Suffrage Association. They carried on their efforts to win equal rights for women in the face of scorn and strong opposition. By 1900, four states west of the Mississippi River had approved woman suffrage; that is, they had granted women the right to vote. But leaders in the battle for women's rights had to fight long and hard to win suffrage for all American women. Women wrote newspaper articles and gave lectures. They even paraded before the White House to awaken the public to the need for this reform. In 1920, the Nineteenth Amendment was added to the Constitution, extending to women the right to vote. Women in all parts of the country voted in the election of 1920. Since that time they have taken more and more interest in government. Women today not only vote but hold many offices in our national, state, and local governments.[16]

1995

This dispassionate account of the women's suffrage movement was written years after the failure of the Equal Rights Amendment and a decidedly more conservative political swing in the United States starting in the 1980s.

The struggle for women's suffrage went back many years. . . . After the Civil War, Elizabeth Cady Stanton and Susan B. Anthony led a renewed drive to win the vote. In 1869, they formed the National Woman Suffrage Association. This group worked to amend the Constitution to give women the vote.

"WE WILL COME IN WITH OUR WOMEN"

Most politicians opposed women's suffrage. Still, in the late 1800s, women gained the right to vote in four western states: Wyoming, Utah, Colorado, and Idaho. Pioneer women had worked alongside men to build the farms and cities of the West. By giving women the vote, these states recognized women's contributions.

When Wyoming applied for statehood in 1890, many members of Congress wanted the state to change its voting law. During the debate, Wyoming lawmakers wired Congress: "We may stay out of the Union for 100 years, but we will come in with our women." Wyoming barely won admission.

SUFFRAGISTS

In the early 1900s, the women's suffrage movement gained strength. More than 5 million women were earning wages outside the home. Although women were paid less than men, wages gave women a sense of power. Many demanded a say in making the laws that governed them.

Carrie Chapman Catt spoke powerfully in favor of the cause. Catt had worked as a school principal and a reporter. Later, she became head of the National American Woman Suffrage Association. Catt was an inspired speaker and a brilliant organizer. She devised a detailed battle plan for fighting the war for suffrage. Around the country, other people who campaigned for women's right to vote followed her lead.

The efforts of Catt and other suffragists slowly succeeded. Year by year, more states in the West and Midwest gave women the vote. For the most part, they were allowed to vote only in state elections. In time, more and more women called for an amendment to the Constitution to give them a voice in national elections. Some suffragists took strong measures to achieve their goal.[17]

32

The Sinking of the USS Maine

The role of the United States as a world superpower has its roots in the Spanish-American War's conclusion. Although there were a number of causes for this war, the sinking of the USS *Maine* has come to represent the primary catalyst that pushed the United States over the edge, and therefore it has taken on enormous symbolic significance. Indeed, the debate over what exactly sank the USS *Maine* in Havana Harbor still rages on. How a textbook answers this question says a lot about how it represents America's role in the world to students.

1905

In this 1905 account, there seemed to be little question as to who was to blame for this tragedy.

Demonstrations against the Americans in Havana led our government to send the battleship the *Maine* to that city. On the night of February 15, 1898, the *Maine* was blown up by an explosion, which killed 260 of the men; and an American naval board of inquiry later reported that the ship was destroyed by a submarine mine. Our consul-general, Fitzhugh Lee, said: "I do not think it was an act of four or five subordinate officers." Yet there was a widespread feeling in the United States that the Spanish government was responsible.[18]

1920

By 1920, blame had been spread in a more evenhanded fashion. History textbooks began adding some of the other individuals or events that were considered the main protagonists for war in 1898: Señor Dupuy de Lome, the yellow journalists, and an anti-Spanish attitude in the country all aided in getting the United States involved in this war.

Our Intervention in Cuba

Prudence and humanity alike forbade the continuance of these horrible conditions at our very doors. The platforms of both the great parties in 1896 expressed sympathy for the Cuban insurgents, and both Houses of Congress passed resolutions for the recognition of Cuban independence. President McKinley labored hard to get Spain to grant the island some degree of self-government and spoke in a hopeful tone in his message to Congress of December, 1897. But in the early weeks of 1898 events occurred which roused public indignation to a pitch where it drowned the voices of diplomacy. On February 9, a New York paper published the facsimile of a private letter written by the Spanish minister at Washington, Senor de Lome. The letter characterized President McKinley as a "cheap politician who truckled to the masses." The country was still nursing its indignation over this insult to its chief executive when it was horrified by the news that on the evening of February 15 the battleship *Maine,* on a friendly visit in the harbor of Havana, had been sunk by a terrific explosion, carrying two officers and 266 men to the bottom. The Spanish government immediately accepted the resignation of Senor de Lome and expressed its sorrow over the "accident" to the American warship. But the conviction that the *Maine* had been blown up from the outside seized on our people with uncontrollable force. Flags, pins, and buttons with the motto "Remember the *Maine!*" appeared all over the land. The spirit of revenge was nurtured by the "yellow journals." Congress was waiting eagerly to declare war.[19]

1933

By the 1930s, some textbooks called into question the idea that the Spanish were to blame for the destruction of the USS Maine.

The Battleship "Maine" Is Blown Up in Havana Harbor (1898)

At this juncture the United States sent the battleship Maine to Havana to protect American interests. This formidable sea-fighter arrived in January, 1898, and steamed past the battlements of Morro Castle to her anchorage in the harbor. On the evening of February 15, when most of the crew of the Maine had turned in, there came a blinding flash, accompanied by a roar. Fragments were seen flying through the air. From the crew's quarters came groans, and cries for help. There followed a lurching motion, then a heavy list, and the ship began to sink. Captain Sigsbee directed the lowering of the boats, and gave the order: "Abandon ship." Two officers and 266 men found their graves in the mass of twisted steel. A cry of horror arose in the United States. "Can it be that the Spaniards anchored the Maine over a mine with the purpose of destroying her?" they asked. "Is this their method of diminishing our naval power?" When a board of experts reported that the condition of the armor-plates showed that the Maine had been blown up from the outside, war was inevitable. "Remember the Maine" became the slogan of the nation. It has never been proved that the destruction of the Maine was due in any way to the Spanish government.[20]

1961

This textbook was written in the midst of the Cold War, a time when most Americans would have considered communist Cuba a more significant concern than the nation of Spain—perhaps explaining why this textbook takes a slightly different view then earlier ones.

America Went to War with Spain in 1898

At midnight on February 15, 1898, while the battleship *Maine* was at anchor in Havana harbor, an explosion sent her to the bottom. More than 250 officers and sailors died. Next morning, American newspapers told in banner headlines how the battleship had been "blown up" and American sailors "murdered" in time of peace. From the commander of the *Maine* came a quiet word asking Americans to "withhold judgment"—that is, to accuse no one until the cause was known.

To this day, no one knows how the ship was destroyed. Spanish officials claimed the *Maine's* sides were blown out by an explosion of her powder magazine. Other investigators stated her sides were blown in by a torpedo or a bomb. There was a possibility that Cuban rebels might have set off the explosion, hoping the United States would blame Spain and so give the Cubans support in their fight for freedom. Many people jumped to the conclusion that Spanish officials had planted a mine beneath the *Maine*. This was almost certainly not true. Spanish leaders were trying desperately to avoid war with the United States. They had nothing to gain by destroying the *Maine*. Unfortunately, people did not stop to think and reason. In the streets, in the newspapers, even in the halls of Congress, there rose a clamor for war. "Remember the *Maine!*" was the cry that echoed throughout the country.[21]

1986

In the 1980s, students learned that there may have been a number of reasons why the USS Maine sank that evening as well as why the United States and Spain ended up in a war. What was missing, as in every textbook that discussed the event, was an analysis of whether the United States had the right to go to war over what might have been an accident. In the end, U.S. history textbooks all seem to agree that since the country ended up becoming a world power following this war, the ends justify the means.

Both President Cleveland and President McKinley had tried to persuade Spain to give the Cuban people more say about their government. They failed to make much impression. Tension increased. Then, in January 1898, President McKinley sent a battleship, the U.S.S. Maine, to Cuba. There had been riots in Havana, the capital city. McKinley sent the Maine to protect American citizens there against possible attack.

On February 15, while the Maine lay at anchor in Havana Harbor, a tremendous explosion rocked the ship. Of the 350 men aboard, 266 were killed. The Maine sank to the bottom.

To this day no one knows for sure what happened. Many Americans jumped to the conclusion that the Spanish had sunk the ship with a mine, a kind of underwater bomb. The navy conducted an investigation. It concluded that the Maine had been destroyed by a mine. Another American investigation in 1911 also judged that an explosion from outside had destroyed the ship.

The Spanish government claimed the disaster was caused by an explosion inside the Maine. This is certainly possible. A short circuit in the ship's wiring might have caused the Maine's ammunition to explode, for example. It is difficult to imagine that the Spanish would have blown up the ship. The last thing Spain wanted was a war with the United States.

Emotions were inflamed on all sides. The Spanish government, or some individual officer, may indeed have been responsible. Or it is possible that the Cuban rebels did the job, knowing that Spain would be blamed.

In any case, a demand for war against Spain swept the United States. In New York City a man in a Broadway bar raised his glass and proclaimed, "Remember the Maine!" This became a battle cry similar to "Remember the Alamo!" during the Texas Revolution of the 1830s.[22]

33

The Philippine-American War

While the Korean War (1950–53) has often been nicknamed the "Forgotten War," the war that took place in the Philippines, one of the longest in America's history (1899–1913, according to some historians), truly deserves that title. It made Americans seriously debate the issues of imperialism, colonialism, global economics, race relations, and the role of the United States in the world. The war also saw a great many atrocities committed by both sides. In the end, it cost the United States nearly seven thousand soldiers, either killed or wounded, while the Filipinos lost nearly sixteen thousand soldiers and anywhere from a quarter million to one million civilians, who died due to starvation, famine, war, or disease. On "completion" of this war, the United States gained its first real colony and found itself firmly planted on the global stage. Despite all this, the Philippine-American War has been given scant attention in history textbooks and barely figures in our historical memory.

1903

On July 4, 1902, President Theodore Roosevelt made the announcement that the war in the Philippines had ended and America was victorious. This selection, written in the midst of the war, offered a succinct account of events up to that point and left little doubt for students that the war was all but over soon after it started.

The Philippines

Unlike Porto Rico [*sic*] and Guam, which welcomed American authority, some of the Philippines objected to any sovereignty foreign to themselves. Many of the Filipinos had fought bravely against the tyranny of Spain, and now, under the lead of Aguinaldo, they looked for absolute independence for themselves and their neighbors.

The war in the Philippines arose when there was no active sovereignty over the islands, during the long interval between the signing and the confirmation of the Paris treaty. General Merritt was succeeded by General Elwell S. Otis, who occupied Manila, while the insurgent Filipinos controlled most of the remainder of Luzon. On February 4, 1899, the Filipinos began the war by attacking the defenses of Manila; they were repulsed, with a loss of 2,000 men, and General Otis then directed an aggressive campaign. Malo'los, the Filipino capital, was captured (March 31); the army of the Filipinos was broken up; and within two years most of the insurgents surrendered.

In 1899 a commission appointed by the President visited the Philippines and reported upon their condition. Early in 1900 the President appointed a new commission of five members to control and take charge of all matters connected with the construction of a government, and to appoint all necessary civil officers. This commission, of which Judge William H. Taft of Cincinnati was made president, entered upon its duties in the Philippines in June. Schools were encouraged, local governments were established, and the Filipinos were given a large share of self-government.[23]

1916

Nearly a decade and a half after the "official" ending to the war in the Philippines, this U.S. history textbook barely conveyed even the most basic information about the conflict.

The War in the Philippines

While the treaty with Spain was under consideration, native troops, under Aguinaldo, on the night of February 4, 1899, made an unsuccessful attack on the Americans at Manila. War now followed; but by the beginning of the year 1900 the main army of the Filipinos had been completely broken up, and the only forces still opposing American authority were small bodies of bandits and guerillas. These held out persistently, and continued the warfare for more than a year. In 1900 the President sent a commission to the Philippines to organize civil government in such localities and in such degree as it should deem advisable; and in 1902 Congress enacted a plan of government under which the Philippines are constituted a partly self-governing dependency.[24]

1927

In the 1920s, students were taught about the positive consequences of the war and subsequent occupation that followed—a historical theme that continues to be a major part of this story up to the present.

The Philippines Present a New Problem

Possession of the Philippines presented a new problem. Some people opposed the annexation to the United States of territory in tropical regions and thousands of miles from American shores. They held that our country should not assume the difficult task of governing a people of different race, who were only partly civilized and knew nothing of American ideals of government. Others declared that annexation would help us secure trade in China and in other parts of the Far East. They added that after we had driven Spain out of the islands, we should not leave the natives without protection and guidance, because they were not ready to govern themselves and would be helpless if left alone. "Moreover," as these people reasoned, "if we withdraw from the Philippines, other powers seeking new territory will be likely to seize the islands." There was prolonged discussion in the Senate before the necessary two-thirds vote could be secured. Finally on February 6, 1899, the treaty annexing the Philippines was ratified and became effective. . . .

THE PHILIPPINES COME UNDER AMERICAN CONTROL

While the treaty of peace at the end of the Spanish-American War was still under discussion, some of the Filipinos, led by a native chief, Aguinaldo, rebelled against the authority of the United States. Before the war began the natives had tried to drive Spain out of the islands, and at first on the arrival of the Americans they were friendly. When, however, they learned that they were not to receive their independence, but only to change old masters for new ones, they determined to strike again for freedom. They made a desperate struggle, but after prolonged guerilla fighting which lasted for nearly three years they were subdued.

HOW WE HAVE GOVERNED AND HELPED THE FILIPINOS

The islands remained under military rule until July 1, 1901, when civil government was established. As soon as practicable the United States gave the natives a share in their government by allowing them to elect the lower house of their legislature (1907), and by the same act Congress allowed Philippine products to come into this country free of duties. The governor and the upper house, however, were to be appointed by the President and the Senate. Great efforts were made to guide the Filipinos to improved methods of administrating their affairs. Harbors, highways, and railroads were constructed; better methods of tilling the soil than the islanders had known were introduced; more healthful ways of living were taught; and, perhaps best of all, a free public school system like our own was organized and put into operation. Hundreds of American teachers have been sent over to guide the Filipinos to a more civilized life.

Meanwhile it has remained a debated question with the American people whether it was better to grant the Filipinos independence or to keep them under the control of the United States as their protector, guide, and teacher until they were ready to take care of themselves.

As the Democratic party had all along opposed making the Filipinos a subject people, the Democratic Congress of 1917 passed a law which provided (1) that they should elect the upper as well as the lower house of their legislature, and (2) that they should have their independence as soon as they proved themselves capable of home rule.[25]

1950

In the 1950s, the United States found itself in an idealistic battle against perceived Communist expansion around the world. Students reading this textbook, and many like it, learned that nations such as the Philippines that had accepted American rule came in the long run to believe that U.S. culture and politics were probably the best thing for them.

The United States Improves Conditions in the Philippine Islands

Conditions in the Philippines were not encouraging. In its thousands of islands lived peoples of many tribes and many languages. The largest island, Luzon, with its capital at Manila, was inhabited by Spanish-speaking natives. But on other islands lived tribes of savage people. Most of the Filipinos were poor and lacked education. Moreover, they did not welcome American control, for they had believed that the United States would give them freedom as we had done for the people of Cuba. After the Spanish forces surrendered in the Philippines, it was necessary to put down a revolt of the natives against the American forces. Indeed, it took years of jungle fighting which cost many lives on both sides before the revolt was finally ended.

In spite of these difficulties, the United States was able greatly to improve conditions in the Philippines. A bureau of health did much to stamp out disease and to teach the Filipinos the simple rules of healthful living. To provide education, schools were built and teachers were sent from America. Many Filipino teachers were also trained. By the 1930's, more than 7,000 schools had been set up. Local government was organized in towns and villages. Good roads were built. To provide more farms for the people, the government bought great stretches of land which were divided into small plots. Modern ways of farming and better tools were introduced. All these improvements cost large sums of money, most of which was furnished by the United States. In addition, Americans bought great quantities of Philippine sugar, hemp for making rope, and tobacco. Beginning in 1909, no tariff duties were placed on these products when they entered the United States. The Filipinos were better off than they had ever been before. Most of them no longer feared American rule.[26]

| 9 6 |

While still not affording it as much attention as other major American conflicts, this 1960s' textbook did at least explain what the fighting in the Philippines was like and how the Filipinos felt about their new foreign conquerors.

The war left many problems. War always brings far-reaching changes. While it may settle a few questions, it almost always raises new and more difficult ones. The Spanish-American War of 1898 was no exception. It involved the United States in problems no one had foreseen.

For one thing, Americans found they had to fight a long, bloody war in the Philippines. Like most other people, the Filipinos wanted to govern themselves. They expected to become independent when Spain was defeated. But President McKinley and his advisers felt the Filipinos lacked education and experience, and therefore the United States decided to keep control for a while.

The Filipinos had a capable determined leader named Emilio Aguinaldo. He had been fighting Spaniards for years. Now he organized resistance against the United States. The Filipinos knew they had no chance of winning a regular battle so they split up into small groups of guerillas. They hid in the mountains and jungle and struck suddenly when least expected. The guerilla were savage fighters. The warfare dragged on for two years. It was an ugly struggle, much like the Indian wars of colonial days. Aguinaldo was finally captured and his followers surrendered. But it took years to win the friendship of the Filipinos.

Americans built schools and roads, fought disease and developed industries, but still the Filipinos were dissatisfied. They admitted a government of their own probably would not be so efficient as American rule, but they preferred an inefficient government of their own to foreign control. American leaders promised the Filipinos they would become independent as soon as they proved able to govern themselves. Step by step, the Filipinos were allowed to take more power in running the islands.[27]

| 9 9 6

In concise fashion, this textbook let students know that a war was fought in the Philippines, and that for some reason or another it was fairly "brutal." But nearly one hundred years after the Philippine-American War started, the historiography, rather than focus on the negative aspects, remained true to the argument that U.S. occupation of these islands was beneficial in the long run to their inhabitants.

The anti-imperialists were especially disturbed by the situation in the Philippines. The Filipinos did not want to be ruled by the United States any more than by Spain. Led by Emilio Aguinaldo they fought against the Americans. Guerilla warfare went on for three years. The United States used more troops and spent more money than in the entire war against Spain. Many Americans were shocked by the brutal methods we used to put down the Filipinos.

It was not until April 1902 that the last rebel surrendered and the Philippines were officially declared "pacified." Even before then, however, in 1900 under the direction of William Howard Taft, first as head of the Philippine Commission and then as civil governor, the large land holdings of the Catholic friars were distributed to the people. Under Taft's wise direction roads were built, harbors and sanitation improved, and the Philippines started on the path of self-government.[28]

34

The Espionage Act

A controversial issue even when it was passed in 1917, the Espionage Act was seen by some as a wartime measure needed to keep the United States safe from external and internal threats. Others viewed it as unconstitutional and an invasion of privacy. It ended up being such a sensitive topic that many of those who argued against the legality of this act were imprisoned. This section looks at the historiography of this controversial piece of legislation, with an eye to how U.S. history textbooks wanted students to learn about the role of the government, citizens' rights, and patriotism.

1920

This U.S. history textbook explained the controversy over the Espionage Act of 1917, informing students that the few people who were "disloyal" and/or "agitators" were either paid agents, Socialists, or members of a labor union.

Opposition to the War

Though there was considerable activity among the confirmed advocates of peace to keep us out of the war up to the very eve of our decision, when that decision was once made opposition ceased, except for some aliens and that small and disloyal part of our citizens made up of I.W.W. agitators, certain sections of the Socialists, and the partisans or paid agents of Germany and Austria. To counteract the work of enemy aliens in obstructing the draft, destroying property, and advocating treason to the United States, a severe Espionage Act was signed by President Wilson on June 15, 1917. Conscientious objectors to war were allowed to perform noncombatant service in the medical, the quartermaster's, and the engineering corps. Those drafted men whose conscience would not permit them to serve in military uniform were allowed to work on farms under surveillance of the War Department. Less than 500 men refused to comply with the military laws of the country. They were imprisoned, along with those who obstructed the draft or plotted disloyal acts.[29]

1948

Following on the heels of World War II, this selection told students that in order to protect the United States during times of war, people who spoke out against the war or the draft were imprisoned—most notably, Eugene V. Debs.

The Espionage Act

It would be impossible to describe all these measures in detail, but we may select three laws of the extra session of April–October, 1917, as examples. The Espionage Act, of June 15, gave the President the authority to control the exports of commodities necessary for the Allies and conferred upon him certain powers of censorship. Direct trade with Germany had been prevented from the beginning of the war by the British blockade; but the Central Powers had still been able to draw large supplies from neutral countries. The Exports Board under the Espionage Act was therefore given the right to regulate trade with neutrals. For example, in the midsummer of 1917 one could see several Dutch ships, loaded with grain, lying for weeks in the Hudson River because they were unable to get clearance papers allowing them to sail until they gave assurance that their cargoes were not eventually destined for Germany.

The act also imposed severe penalties upon persons disclosing information concerning places connected with the national defense, "enemy aliens" (that is, Germans or Austrians not naturalized in the United States) being forbidden to go up in airplanes or balloons, to come within a hundred yards of wharves or piers, or to be found in waters within three miles of the shore. It was made a penal offense to advocate resistance to the laws of the United States, to refuse to do military duty, or to obstruct the draft. Provision was made for the "conscientious objectors." Drafted men who could prove that they belonged to "any well organized religious sect whose creed or principles forbade its members to participate in war in any form" were allowed to enter the various types of noncombatant service, such as the Medical Corps and the construction and repair departments. All but about five hundred conscientious objectors who were drafted accepted one or another of these assignments. Altogether some fifteen hundred to two thousand offenders against the Espionage Act were sent to prison, among them Eugene Debs, who ran for President for the fifth time on the Socialist ticket in 1920 while still serving his sentence in the Atlanta jail for encouraging resistance to the draft.[30]

1982

In a complete break from the earlier texts, this excerpt about the Espionage Act was couched in terms such as abusive, feverish atmosphere, and intimidation.

The Wilson administration also sponsored the Espionage Act (1917) and the Sedition Act (1918). The first statute forbade "false statements" designed to impede the draft or promote military insubordination and banned from the mails materials considered treasonous. The Sedition Act made it unlawful to obstruct the sale of war bonds and to use "disloyal, profane, scurrilous, or abusive" language against the government, the Constitution, the flag, and the military uniform. These loosely worded laws gave the government wide latitude to crack down on those with whom it differed. Fair-minded people could disagree over what constituted false or abusive language, but in the feverish home-front atmosphere of the First World War and under the threat of federal prosecution, the Justice Department's definition prevailed. Over two thousand people were prosecuted under the acts and many others were intimidated into silence.

Stories of arrests and an intellectual reign of terror began to fill the newspapers. Three Columbia University students were picked up in mid-

1917 for circulating an antiwar petition. The liberal-left journal *The Masses* and Tom Watson's *The Jeffersonian* were denied use of the mails and forced to shut down. Jane Addams was put under Justice Department surveillance, causing her, by her own admission, to moderate her appeals for peace. The producer of *The Spirit of '76,* a film about the American Revolution complete with redcoats shooting minutemen, was given a ten year prison sentence for, according to the judge, questioning the "good faith of our ally, Great Britain." Congressman Victor Berger of Wisconsin was indicted during the war for violating the Espionage Act and in the spring of 1920 the leader of a newly formed organization decided to hire two public-relations experts to help in recruiting members.[31]

35

The League of Nations

The Great War (1914–18) was such a horrible affair that many truly believed at the time that it would be the "war to end all wars." In order to make this happen, the leaders of the Allied powers met in Versailles to sign a treaty aimed at preventing a second catastrophe. This resulted in the founding of the League of Nations, with the mission to stop aggressive nations from causing another international conflict. President Wilson, a Democrat, needing the approval of the U.S. Senate in order to ratify the Treaty of Versailles (and hence the League of Nations), ran into a Republican Congress that was not in favor of some of its provisions. What was supposed to be an answer to the problem of global conflict ironically led to a huge domestic political debate between people who wanted the United States to remain isolationist and those who held a more internationalist perspective.

1920

The issue of the Treaty of Versailles and the Great War (obviously not referred to as World War I as of yet) were two of the biggest topics that this textbook covered. In the debate over who killed the treaty politically in the U.S. Senate, this selection pointed the finger at both parties as having made mistakes.

The League of Nations

A covenant of a League of Nations prepared by a committee of ten was reported to the conference by President Wilson in February and in slightly amended form was incorporated into the peace treaty. The chief provisions of its 26 articles concern the reduction of armaments, the publicity of treaties, the arbitration of international disputes, and the punishment of nations that go to war in defiance of the covenant. The famous Article X declares that "the members of the league undertake to respect and preserve as against external aggression the territorial integrity and existing political independence of all members of the league." Article XVI gives the council the right to recommend to the various governments what military and naval forces they shall contribute to enforce obedience to the covenant. The executive power of the League was intrusted [sic] to a council of nine members, of whom five were to be always representatives of the United States, Great Britain, France, Italy, and Japan. As soon as the provisions of the covenant were known in America more than one-third of the Senate (that is, enough to defeat the treaty) signed a round-robin declaring their opposition to the document "in the form now proposed," and advocating making peace with Germany first and then discussing plans for a League of Nations. But Wilson insisted on the immediate establishment of the league. On the eve of his return to Paris in March, 1919 (after a brief visit to the United States), he said, "When the treaty comes back, gentlemen on this side will find the covenant not only in it, but so many threads of the treaty tied to the covenant that you cannot dissect it from the treaty without destroying the whole vital structure."

OPPOSITION TO WILSON IN THE SENATE

The peace treaty was signed at Versailles on June 28, 1919, and the President immediately brought it home to lay before the Senate for ratification. Opposition was strong from the beginning. In the first place the 66th Congress, which Wilson had called in extra session by cable from Paris (May 19, 1919), was Republican in both Houses. Wilson had made the mistake of appealing to the public just before the autumn elections of 1918 to return a Democratic Congress—after having said in a message six months earlier, "politics is adjourned." The result of the President's partisan appeal was a Republican majority of 45 in the House and 2 in the Senate. Futhermore, the Senate had not been taken into the President's confidence in the negotiation of the treaty. Not a senator was appointed on the peace commission and it was only as guests at informal luncheons at the White House, during the President's brief "vacation" in America (February–March, 1919), that some of the leading senators were acquainted with his plans. The President later sent word from Paris that he did not want the treaty discussed until he returned to America. The treaty was published in Europe, and copies reached private citizens here before the official copy was presented to the Senate.

CRITICISM OF THE LEAGUE OF NATIONS

But aside from any feeling of resentment that they had been "ignored" by the President, many senators were opposed to various articles in the treaty and especially in the covenant of the League of Nations. The points of complaint were that the sovereignty of the United States was sacrificed, that we were pledged to make war at the bidding of the council of the league, that we would be eternally embroiled in the quarrels of Europe, that purely domestic questions like immigration laws and the tariff were subjected to the interference of other nations, that Great Britain was represented by six times as many votes in the assembly of the league as we were. About a dozen senators, led by Borah of Idaho, were opposed to the treaty altogether; but the majority, led by Henry Cabot Lodge of Massachusetts, chairman of the Foreign Relations Committee, were in favor of ratifying with certain amendments or reservations. The administration senators, obeying the behest of the President, insisted that the treaty must be ratified without any modifications. The amendments and reservations proposed would, said Wilson, "take the teeth out of the treaty."

THE TREATY REJECTED

In September President Wilson started on a tour across the country to explain the treaty to the people at large and create a public sentiment which should force the Senate to ratify. In the midst of the trip the President suffered a severe physical breakdown, due to many months of mental overstrain, and was hurried back to Washington, where he was completely removed from public business. His spokesman in the Senate, Mr. Hitch-cock of Nebraska, carried on the fight for unconditional ratification. Nei-ther side would budge. When the vote was finally taken (November 19, 1919) on the treaty with fifteen Lodge reservations attached, it was de-feated by a vote of 39 to 55. The extra session came to an end the same day, with each party in the Senate throwing on the other the blame for the deadlock. When the first regular session of the 66th Congress convened on December, President Wilson announced from his sick room that he would not resubmit the treaty to the Senate, but would shift the responsi-bility for its adoption to the shoulders of his countrymen. In other words, unless the Senate should choose to reconsider its position, the treaty might become the issue of the presidential election of 1920. The Senate again took up the treaty, the debate centering chiefly on Article X. Both Mr. Lodge and the administration senators seemed more anxious to arrive at a compromise; but again (March 19, 1920) the treaty was rejected by a vote of 49 in favor to 35 against.[32]

1946

A fairly constant theme in the historiography is that Wilson was a bit overzealous in his passing of the entire treaty. Most textbook authors seem to agree that with a bit of compromise between Wilson and the Republicans, something might have been ac-complished.

A Plan for a League of Nations Was Made a Part of the Treaty of Versailles

The purpose of the League was to provide for settling disputes between nations and to promote friendly relations and co-operation among na-tions. The plan was written into the treaty at the insistence of President Wilson. Greatly disappointed in not being able to have peace terms based on his "fourteen points" program, he hoped that the imperfections of the treaty might be corrected by the League in future years. It had long been his dream to see such a League formed, and he felt that he had the support of many Americans of all parties.

The plan for the League of Nations led to the refusal of the United States Senate to ratify the Treaty of Versailles. Under our Constitution the

Senate must give approval to (or ratify) all treaties made by the President. But many Senators felt that the United States should now withdraw entirely from the affairs of Europe and try to live apart from Europe, as in the past. Others felt that we should join the League, but only if the plan could be so modified that our nation would be in no danger of being drawn into European or Asiatic quarrels. Many others objected to the plan of the League, especially the provisions for representation in its Council. They feared that a few powerful nations might, by voting together, control the policies of the League. The debate was long and bitter. Possibly if President Wilson had been willing to accept certain modifications of his League plan, the treaty would have been ratified. This he refused to do and chose instead to appeal to the American people for support of his wishes. While on a speaking tour of the West, he collapsed in an illness from which he never fully recovered. In a short time the Senate defeated the treaty. Some time later a separate peace was made with Germany.[33]

1966

Following World War II, the historiography concerning the League of Nations changed forever. Historians began to focus on the failures of the League (and the Treaty of Versailles) as a major cause for World War II. Textbooks followed this trend after 1945 by usually explaining how the League of Nations failed in preventing World War II and how the United Nations would improve on past mistakes.

Weaknesses of the League

The League of Nations was not, of course, a perfect organization. It had several serious weaknesses. For one thing, taking action against an aggressor was almost impossible for a number of reasons. First, the term "aggressor" was not defined. Second, the Council could only recommend that nations take action, and no member could be compelled to act upon these recommendations. Third, any member of the Council could block the wishes of the other members because all important decisions of the Council had to be reached by unanimous vote. In brief, the work of the League depended upon the willingness of its members to co-operate.

Another basic weakness of the League was its guarantee of existing political boundaries. When the map of the world was redrawn, some peoples found themselves living in the country of their choice, but others did not. Those who did not had no way to secure further changes in their national boundaries.

A third weakness was the League's failure to provide adequate machinery for recommending solutions to economic problems that might lead to war. Trade rivalries and tariff barriers still existed, as did imperialism, yet the League was not equipped to do much more than study such problems. Finally, the League was in no position to tackle the problem of reducing armaments.

Despite its shortcomings, however, the League of Nations was a promising beginning in the difficult task of creating a new co-operative world order, dedicated to international peace and justice. In the 1930's, about 60 nations belonged to the League, which was bringing an important new ingredient into international affairs: the organized moral judgment of a majority of the nations of the world.

THE SENATE REJECTS THE LEAGUE

Early in July 1919 President Wilson returned confidently from Paris to ask the Senate to approve the Treaty of Versailles, and thereby to bring the United States into the League. The Senate shattered his high hopes by rejecting the treaty.

Senator Henry Cabot Lodge of Massachusetts, chairman of the important Committee on Foreign Relations, and other Republican Senators were annoyed that Wilson had not invited any of them to participate in the peace negotiations. They felt that a problem as important as the creation of a world organization should have been considered by both Republicans and Democrats.

But opposition to the League was based on more than such partisan considerations. Many Americans thought that the Treaty of Versailles was unjust, and they were unwilling to have the United States join a League which pledged its members to carry out the provisions of the treaty. Others were afraid that Great Britain, supported by the votes of its five self-governing dominions, might control the League.

But the greatest opposition to the League of Nations arose out of a general postwar reaction against American involvement in the affairs of Europe. Many Americans who were influenced by this reaction pointed with alarm to Article Ten of the League Covenant, which pledged each member to guarantee the existing political boundaries of the other members. Those who opposed the League of Nations for this reason argued that such a pledge might involve the United States in war.

WILSON REFUSES TO COMPROMISE

Despite the opposition to the League of Nations in the Senate and throughout the country, the Senate might have voted for it if President Wilson had been willing to accept a number of amendments proposed by Senator Lodge and others who shared his views. These amendments were designed to safeguard American interests and to prevent the United States from being drawn into European conflicts. Wilson believed, however, that these amendments would weaken the League so much that it would become ineffective, and he refused to compromise.

In an effort to win public support, he traveled across the country making speeches in defense of the League. Finally, exhausted by the long strain, in the fall of 1919 he collapsed, and for seven months lived in seclusion. His one remaining hope was that the public would support his cause by electing a Democratic President in the 1920 election. But the Republican landslide of that year and the election of President Harding seemed to indicate that the American people preferred to forget all about the League of Nations and world problems in general. They paid no heed to Wilson when he warned, "Arrangements of the present peace cannot stand a generation unless they are guaranteed by the united forces of the civilized world."

The rise of Japanese, Italian, and German expansionism in the 1930's proved Wilson's words to have been prophetic. But by that time, as you will see, the League, without the United States as a member, had become too weak to take actions which might have prevented the outbreak of World War II.[34]

1995

The moral of the story in the Clinton years was: political compromise and internationalism is good, isolationist tendencies are bad.

Wilson's Successes

For Wilson, his greatest success was including the League of Nations in the peace treaty. "A living thing is born," he declared. "It [the League] is definitely a guarantee of peace." When the President returned home, he faced a new battle. He had to convince the Senate to approve the Versailles Treaty.

Many Americans opposed the peace treaty. Some said that it was too soft on the defeated powers. Many German Americans felt that it was too harsh. Isolationists—or people who wanted the United States to stay out of world affairs—opposed the League of Nations.

HENRY CABOT LODGE

Critics of the treaty found a leader in Senator Henry Cabot Lodge of Massachusetts. Lodge, a Republican, was chairman of the Senate Foreign Relations Committee. Although he accepted the idea of the League of Nations, he wanted changes in the treaty.

Lodge objected to Article 10. It called for the League to protect any member whose independence or territory was threatened. Lodge argued that Article 10 could involve the United States in future European wars. He wanted changes in the treaty that would ensure that the United States remained independent of the League. He also wanted Congress to have the power to decide whether the United States would follow League policy.

NO COMPROMISE

Wilson was sure that Lodge's changes would weaken the League. When advisers urged the President to compromise, he replied, "Let Lodge compromise." He refused to make any changes.

As the battle grew hotter, the President took his case to the people. In early September 1919, Wilson set out across the country to defend the League. He made 37 speeches in 29 cities. He urged people to tell their senators that they supported the treaty.

In September 25, the weary President complained of a headache. His doctors canceled the rest of the trip. Wilson returned to Washington. A week later, his wife found him unconscious. He had suffered a stroke that left him bedridden for weeks.

THE TREATY IS DEAD

In November 1919, the Senate rejected the Versailles Treaty. "It is dead," Wilson mourned, [and] "every morning I put flowers on its grave." Gone, too, was Wilson's cherished goal—American membership in the League of Nations. The United States did not sign a peace treaty with Germany until 1921. By then, many nations had joined the League of Nations. Without the United States, however, the League had limited power and influence. In the years ahead, the League would be unable to live up to its goals of protecting members against aggression.[35]

PART VI

*The Great Depression
and World War II*

36

Causes of the Stock Market Crash

Following the stock market crash in 1929, the United States was stricken by an economic depression unparalleled in world history. Breadlines, stories of people losing everything, Franklin Delano Roosevelt's New Deal, and the rise of fascist dictators: textbooks are replete with these familiar stories. While U.S. history textbooks have debated what caused the economic crash, there has never been a single consensus among them.

1933

Written just four years after the stock market crash, this passage claimed that the real culprit was the return to the gold standard. Considering when this textbook was written and published, it is also interesting to note the optimistic tone it offered its students.

World-Wide Business Depression Causes "Hard Times"

This statement is by no means belied by the fact that in 1930 millions were thrown out of work. The business depression of that year was world-wide, and cannot be blamed upon conditions peculiar to the United States. It was in part a reaction from too rapid business expansion, and in part the result of a general decline in commodity prices following the return of many countries to the gold standard. With the increased demand for gold the value of that metal rose, and so each dollar purchased more in wheat, or iron, or leather. Falling prices have a depressing effect on business, however, bringing reduced production, unemployment, and the other accompaniments of "hard times." When there has been a general adjustment to the new price level, the American industrial machine will get under way with full steam once more, the idle will be drawn back to work, and a new era of prosperity will open.[1]

1944

The historiography of the crash has usually focused on Herbert Hoover as the wrong man at the wrong time. Portrayed as aloof and unsympathetic to the common man, Hoover has generally received negative reviews for his reaction to this situation. When this textbook was published, Roosevelt was heading toward his fourth presidential reelection, the U.S. economy had rebounded, and the chances of victory in World War II did not seem as discouraging as it had three years earlier. From a historiographical standpoint, Hoover's reputation never really stood a chance.

In the autumn of 1929, just as the country seemed safe and sound on the "high plateau of permanent prosperity," except for farmers, the business boom attributed to Republican statecraft burst with a resounding crash. The prime stocks of the leading corporations fell nearly forty points on the average in a single day, October 29, when more than 16,000,000 shares were dumped on the market at the New York Stock Exchange. This panic was followed by the explosion of banks, railway companies, and private concerns, by increasing woes among farmers already in straits, by the closing of factories, shops, and offices, and by a steep decline in the opportunities of employment for artists, writers, musicians, architects, engineers, playwrights, and teachers—indeed the whole white-collar class—from New York to California. In the opening months of 1933, it was estimated, 12,000,000 men and women were out of work. Ruin and hunger, if not starvation, haunted not only the shacks of tenants and sharecroppers on the land, not only the back streets inhabited by industrial and professional classes, but also the grand avenues of great cities.

For a moment leaders in business and politics thought that this was "Just another panic." President Hoover said: "We have passed through no less than fifteen major depressions in the last century. . . . We have come out of each . . . into a period of prosperity greater than ever before. We shall do so this time." But as the depression dragged through tedious months and into years, belief in "prosperity just around the corner" turned into doubt or despair. As this revulsion of feeling intensified, trust in the "natural" and "normal" processes of "recovery" declined, and leaders in the economic, intellectual, and moral life of the nation vehemently declared their unwillingness to endure the crisis with pious resignation as a visitation of God or of natural forces beyond human control. Long years of research, debate, agitation, and legislative gains in respect of social improvement had prepared multitudes of Americans for a different attitude toward poverty, unemployment, and misery in "God's own country."²

1974

Students were informed in the early 1970s that while there were arguably a number of causes for the stock market crash, in the end the rich and powerful in the United States really did not seem to be hurt by all that had transpired.

The depression in the United States was touched off by distress in the New York Stock Exchange. For several years the prices of stocks had been rising. People bought stocks because they thought they could get rich easily. They gambled on the stock market by buying on margin, that is, buying on credit from brokers. This kind of speculation was all right only so long as stock prices continued to climb, as nearly everybody expected they would.

Outside the market there were signs that prosperity was weakening. Much of the prosperity had been founded on the construction and automobile industries. In 1925, the construction of homes had reached a value of 5 billion dollars; in 1929, the value fell to 3 billion. By 1929, too, sales of automobiles and related products had declined. Some stock operators began to quietly dispose of their holdings. In September 1929, the stock market broke and then recovered. On October 24, called "Black Thursday," prices broke sharply, and many investors lost money. On the following day, President Hoover assured the people that what had happened was not very serious.

Then, on Tuesday, October 29, the big crash came. In a day of wild trading, a day that turned out to be the most devastating in the history of the Stock Exchange, nearly 16.5 million shares of stock exchanged hands. The frenzied selling went on for two weeks, until the value of the stocks on the Wall Street exchange had declined about 40 percent.

Leaders in government and business tried to bolster sagging spirits. When men and women everywhere were being wiped out financially, John D. Rockefeller, for example, came out with an optimistic statement. He said that the country was sound and added that "my son and I have for some days been purchasing sound common stocks." Many people applauded Rockefeller, but Eddie Cantor, a popular comedian, commented later, "Sure, who else had any money left?"

The mighty crash on Wall Street brought the prosperity of the twenties to a disastrous end. Although the crash was not the only cause of the Great Depression that followed, it was a contributing factor.[3]

1999

At the end of the twentieth century, students began to read more detailed accounts of what happened to the American economy and its impact on U.S. citizens. Future historiographers will probably have no difficulty in reading within this text a cautionary tale of the 1990s' "Internet bubble" and the "speculative frenzy" that occurred at that time.

Speculation

As prices rose, more and more people began speculating. Speculation is engaging in a risky business venture on the chance that a quick or sizable profit can be made.

People bought shares they thought would rise in price quickly, and after prices went up they would sell the stocks for a profit.

To maximize the potential profits on their investments, speculators commonly bought stock on margin. To buy stock in this way one made a small cash down payment and borrowed the rest from a stockbroker. For example, for $2,000 a person could buy 100 shares on margin rather than pay cash for 10 shares of stock at $200 per share. The purchaser simply put down 10 percent of the price (or $20 per share) and borrowed the other $18,000 from a broker, who would then hold the shares of stock as collateral for the loan. So long as prices continued to rise, investors could sell the stock later, repay the loan, and reap the profit.

STOCK MARKET BEGINS TO DECLINE

Some bankers, brokers, and economists were concerned, however, because they knew the stocks for many companies were greatly overpriced in comparison to the earnings and profits the companies were making. Yet most investors were swept along on the tide of the day's optimism. Meanwhile, the market continued its dizzying climb. By the end of 1929, brokers' loans to those who had bought on margin exceeded $7 billion. The Federal Reserve Board tried to restore stability to the market by advising banks not to loan money for buying stocks on margin, but few banks listened.

In September 1929, the market started to waver as some professional speculators sensed danger and began to pull out, and prices slipped. Late in October real disaster struck. On Thursday, October 24, almost 13 million shares of stocks were frantically traded. As stocks' values dropped below the amounts borrowed to purchase them, brokers demanded that investors repay their loans. If they could not, the brokers offered the stock for sale.

BLACK TUESDAY

Recognizing what was going on, investment bankers tried to shore up market prices by purchasing as many shares as they could. The effort was not enough to stabilize an overvalued market. On October 29—Black Tuesday—the bottom fell out. Some 16 million shares were sold, causing such a collapse that by mid-November the average price of securities had been cut nearly in half. This cost investors about $30 billion, a sum that represented almost one-third of the value of all goods and services produced in the United States in 1929. The loss was equal to the total wages of all Americans that year. About 1.5 million Americans had been involved in purchasing stock. Many investors lost their entire life savings.

It was the failure of banks that hit people the hardest. Banks loaned money to brokerage houses, which in turn bought stock themselves or loaned money to investors for speculative stock purchases. When loan payments were not forthcoming, many banks went bankrupt. In the aftermath, millions of people who had never bought stock but had trustingly kept their money in savings accounts lost everything as the banks closed. The collapse of the stock market was only a prelude to a catastrophic economic decline from which the United States did not recover for 12 years. The causes of the Great Depression were so complex that economists have debated the issue ever since.[4]

37

Social Security Act

Today, Social Security is a political football, but U.S. history textbooks have sung its praises since the 1940s. Indeed, textbooks have called the concept of Social Security a "bold" initiative, a "supreme achievement," or something that "few people seriously question."

1948

Although both FDR and his New Deal were things of the past, many of his ideas and political appointees were still entrenched in Washington, DC, in 1948. The memory of the late president, the victory in World War II, and the end of the Great Depression were still very much part of the political and cultural landscape.

The Social Security Act

Chief among these laws of the summer of 1935 was the Social Security Act of August 14, which President Roosevelt himself, on signing, declared to be the "supreme achievement" of his administration. It was an attempt to remedy the glaring inequalities between great wealth and dire poverty, in which, according to a report of the Brookings Institution at Washington, 36,000 families at the top of the social scale received an income equal to that of 22,000,000 families at the bottom; and over 70 percent of the families of America had an income of less than $2,500 a year. The act had two main parts: direct aid for certain classes of needy or disabled persons (such as invalid mothers, crippled or homeless children, the blind, and those too poor to afford medical attention), and a system of insurance against old age and unemployment. The Federal government was to match state appropriations dollar for dollar up to $15 a month per person to persons temporarily out of jobs. And, finally, a compulsory old-age insurance fund, contributed to by employers alike, was to provide pensions after 1942 (later changed to January 1, 1940) for employees who had reached the age of 65, whether in need or not. The Social Security Act was subjected to severe criticism, both because many classes of workers (such as agricultural hands, domestic servants, and small-store employees) were excluded from its benefits, and because of the huge sums of money that would be impounded in the Treasury from the compulsory contributions to old-age insurance.[5]

1966

The roots of the upbeat view of Social Security in this section may well be a reflection of the optimism generated by President Lyndon Johnson's Great Society proposals of the mid-1960s.

Social Security for the People

In another of its fundamental reform measures, the New Deal boldly attacked the problem of individual security. The Social Security Act of 1935 had three major goals. First, it provided unemployment insurance for individuals who lost their jobs. The money for this purpose was raised by a payroll tax on employers in businesses employing more than 8 workers. The unemployment insurance fund was administered by state insurance systems, in co-operation with the federal government.

A second goal of the Social Security Act was to provide old-age pensions ranging from $10 to $85 a month for persons over sixty-five. The money for this purpose was raised by a payroll tax on employers and a social security tax on the wages of employees. A third goal of the Social Security Act was to help the handicapped—the blind, the deaf-mutes, the crippled, the aged, and dependent children. Federal pensions up to $20 a month were available for needy persons over sixty-five, provided that the states appropriated an equal amount. Federal funds were also available for those states which sought to protect the welfare of needy children, the blind, the crippled, and other handicapped people. All of the provisions of the Social Security Act were administered by the Social Security Board.

President Roosevelt considered the Social Security Act "a cornerstone in a structure which is being built." It was admittedly only a beginning; excluded from its provisions were public employees, farm laborers, domestic servants, and employees of religious, charitable, and nonprofit educational institutions. Nevertheless, by 1937 nearly 21 million workers were entitled to unemployment benefits, and 36 million workers to old-age pensions.[6]

1994

Written immediately after the Reagan and Bush administrations, and just before the "Republican Revolution" in the 1994 midterm elections, one might have thought that students would have been reading about the ills of government programs on society. On the contrary, this textbook referred to Social Security in fairly glowing terms, all the while criticizing those who opposed it.

Incomparably more important was the success of New Dealers in the field of unemployment insurance and old-age pensions. Their greatest victory was the epochal Social Security Act of 1935—one of the most complicated and far-reaching laws ever to pass Congress. To cushion future depressions, the measure provided for federal-state unemployment insurance. To provide security for old age, specified categories of retired workers were to receive regular payments from Washington. These payments ranged from $10 to $85 a month (later raised) and were financed by a payroll tax on both employers and employees. Provision was also made for the blind, the physically handicapped, delinquent children, and other dependents.

Republican opposition to the sweeping new legislation was bitter. "Social Security," insisted Hoover, "must be built upon a cult of work, not a cult of leisure." The GOP national chairman falsely charged that every worker would have to wear a metal dog tag for life.

Social Security was largely inspired by the example of some of the more highly industrialized nations of Europe. In the agricultural America of an earlier day, there had always been farm chores for all ages, and the large family had cared for its own dependents. But in an urbanized economy, at the mercy of boom-or-bust cycles, the government was now recognizing its responsibility for the welfare of its citizens. By 1939 over 45 million people were eligible for Social Security benefits, and in subsequent years further categories of workers were added and the payments to them were periodically increased.[7]

38

The Bataan Death March

On December 8, 1941 (December 7 in Hawaii), just hours after the bombing of Pearl Harbor, the Japanese military invaded the Philippine Islands. The fighting in the Philippines was a disaster for the U.S. and Filipino military. Believing that they were soon going to be resupplied by an American convoy of navy ships, which never came, the soldiers held out against the Japanese for four months with few, if any, rations, little ammunition, and no chance of being rescued. With no other options the American and Filipino forces were forced to capitulate. After the surrender, the Japanese began to round up prisoners and marched the starving, exhausted men fifty-five miles in the hot tropical sun, beating, torturing, and killing their captives along the way.

Following World War II, U.S. history textbooks almost always glorified the war, but the story of the "losers" in the Philippines, forgotten about by their government during the effort, seemed to have suffered the same curse when it came to our postwar textbooks.

1946

In the aftermath of the war, students were given little information about the fighting and suffering in the Philippines.

The ensuing months were indeed a stiff measure of the staying power of the American nation. Instead of collapsing, as some optimists had freely predicted, Japan continued to win impressive victories. A full-fledged invasion force was launched at the Philippine Islands.[8]

1961

Although this textbook selection actually mentioned the Bataan Death March, it offered neither details nor an explanation of what happened to the troops after their imprisonment.

Guam and Wake Island were quickly conquered in spite of the heroic resistance of American troops there. The Japanese landed in the Philippines and captured Manila, the capital, in less than a month. The American commander, General Douglas MacArthur, retreated to Bataan Peninsula. There he set up headquarters in the fortress of Corregidor on Manila Bay. For more than three months American troops held out against Japanese attacks. Food ran short, and the number of sick and wounded grew. At last the men of Bataan had to surrender and start a "death march" to Japanese prisons.[9]

1974

While still not going into any great detail, this textbook did inform students that these soldiers were an inspiration to the nation.

The only source of inspiration in the gloomy winter of 1941/42 came from Bataan and Corregidor in the Philippine Islands. There, outnumbered American and Filipino defenders held off the Japanese for five months. The death tolls at Bataan and Corregidor were staggering. A great number of the troops were Mexican Americans who had been stationed in the Philippines because, like many Filipinos, they spoke Spanish. Although the troops were captured, their fighting spirit inspired Americans at home.[10]

1995

While extremely brief, this selection gave some details as to what happened to the American and Filipino soldiers on the Bataan Peninsula.

Mistreatment of Prisoners

During the war, stories trickled out about the mistreatment of prisoners. Afterward, Americans learned horrifying details about brutal events
such as the *Bataan Death March*. After the Japanese captured the Philippines in 1942, they forced about 60,000 American and Filipino prisoners
to march 100 miles (160 km) with little food or water. About 10,000 people died or were killed.[11]

39

Japanese Internment

The story of Japanese American internment during World War II, though present in almost every U.S. history textbook from 1945 to the present, has only recently been given significant attention. And only of late have textbooks fully admitted that what happened to these citizens during the war was easily one of the greatest abuses of civil liberties and civil rights in American history.

1947

Written immediately after World War II, this textbook gave brief mention to the abuse of civil liberties.

Civil Liberties

World War II found less suppression of divergent views than had World War I. The one great restriction of personal liberties was the movement of people of Japanese ancestry from the Pacific Coast to the interior. The great majority of Americans were but little limited in expressing their views. The Supreme Court was liberal. The Office of War Information (OWI) was concerned most largely with foreign propaganda. A Director of Censorship prepared a code that was accepted voluntarily by the newspapers, although they could hardly refuse as long as the government controlled most of the sources of news. Reports from the war fronts were censored by the Army and Navy.[12]

1974

A quarter-century later, students learned that arguably the biggest issue with the Japanese American internment was the question of loyalty. Ironically, few, if any, textbooks during this time mention those Japanese Americans who served with distinction fighting with the 442 Regimental Combat Team during the war.

Violations of free speech and personal liberty were relatively few. Organized hate campaigns against Germans and Italians were rare. But an important exception to the government's good record on civil liberties was its treatment of Japanese Americans on the West Coast. In February 1942, Roosevelt authorized the army to exclude all persons of Japanese ancestry from "military areas" on the West Coast. Of the 112,000 persons affected by the order, 70,000 were American citizens born in the United States.

Later, the commanding general on the West Coast ordered the Japanese Americans to special camps surrounded by barbed wire and guarded by soldiers. Beginning in July 1942 some of the Nisei, citizens born in the United States of Japanese parents, were allowed to leave the camps to attend college, harvest crops, resettle in the Middle West, or volunteer for duty with the army. All first had to be cleared as loyal by the Federal Bureau of Investigation.

In December 1944, the Supreme Court ruled on two cases questioning the constitutionality of the evacuation. In one case, the Court said that the government's action was constitutional because it was prompted by "military necessity." In the other case, announced the same day, the Court said that the government could not keep a loyal citizen from returning to his or her home.[13]

1995

With U.S. history textbooks adopting a more multicultural perspective in the 1970s and following the 1980s' Reagan administration apology for the treatment of Japanese Americans during the war, the historiography of this story changed dramatically.

Relocation of Japanese Americans

The war brought suffering to many Japanese Americans. Most Japanese Americans lived on the West Coast or in Hawaii. Many of those on the West Coast were successful farmers and business people. For years, they had faced prejudice, in part because of their success.

After Pearl Harbor, many people on the West Coast questioned the loyalty of Japanese Americans. Japanese Americans, they said, might act as spies and help Japan invade the United States. No evidence of disloyalty existed. Yet the President agreed to move Japanese Americans to inland camps set up by the Wartime Relocation Agency (WRA). About 120,000 Japanese Americans were forced to sell their homes and businesses at great loss.

In WRA camps, Japanese Americans lived in crowded barracks behind barbed wire. Most were American citizens. They could not understand why they were singled out for such treatment. German Americans and Italian Americans were not sent to camps. Even Japanese Americans in Hawaii were not moved to camps.

In 1944, the Supreme Court ruled that the camps were a necessary wartime measure. Only after the Allies were certain of victory were Japanese Americans allowed to return to their homes.

LOYAL SERVICE AND A DELAYED APOLOGY

Even though they and their families were treated unfairly, thousands of Japanese American men served in the armed forces. Most were put in segregated units and sent to fight in Europe. There, they won many honors for bravery. The 442nd Nisei Regimental Combat Team became the most highly decorated military unit in United States history. Years later, Americans began to recognize the injustice that had been done to Japanese Americans. In 1988, Congress reviewed the government's wartime policy toward Japanese Americans. Lawmakers admitted that they could not right the wrong that had been done. They did, however, vote to apologize to Japanese Americans who had been driven from their homes in World War II. They also approved a payment of $20,000 to every survivor of the camps.[14]

40

Rosie the Riveter

During World War II, over six million women in the United States went into the industrial factories, most for the first time, and took over jobs that the men fighting overseas once held. With the U.S. industrial output twice that of the entire Axis powers combined, these women's contribution to the war effort was a profound one.

1944

Toward the war's end, many young men returned home with a desire to go back to their old jobs. While many felt that "Rosie the Riveter" had done a great service during wartime, it was now her duty to return home and allow men the chance to get back to work. This textbook argued that women working outside the home helped contribute to a series of societal ills.

In these circumstances, especially with so many mothers employed for long hours, by day or by night, outside the home, family life was not only shattered but hordes of young children were turned into the streets to fend for themselves. Older children left school in droves to work in factories for fabulous wages and, refusing to return to schools, took their lives into their own keeping. With children unguided by teachers or parents, juvenile delinquency and crimes increased to an extent that threatened the moral basis of American society. In August 1943, J. Edgar Hoover, head of the federal police force, exclaimed: "The tragedy revealed by our latest survey is found in the fact that the arrests of boys and girls seventeen years of age increased 17.7% [last year]. In reviewing the further trends for the past six months we find an 89% increase in the arrests of girls for offenses against common decency."

While various women's organizations were rejoicing in the equalities of opportunity, honors, and monetary rewards offered to women by the war and were pushing the recruiting of women for war work of all kinds, individual women, and to some extent organized women, began to appreciate the social peril of juvenile delinquency and also the problems of caring for the babies of mothers engaged in war work. Amid the pressures for complete concentration on war, therefore, women interested in social welfare urged that responsibility for looking after the children be mainly assumed by governments, federal, state, and local.

There was no doubt that families were undergoing disintegration; for men were being drafted for war, women drawn into the auxiliary armed forces, war production, and civilian defense, children of school age crowding into war industries, adolescents left to roam the streets for excitement, and the energies of parents distracted from the care of homes and children. The fact was indisputable and its social import was recognized by leaders in public affairs. It was discussed in newspapers, in meetings of organizations concerned with public welfare, in journals devoted to surveys of social and economic conditions, and in popular magazines. It was emphasized during debates in Congress over a proposal to defer pre–Pearl Harbor fathers.[15]

1950

Into the 1950s, the story of what women did on the home front during the war was often a barely mentioned topic in most U.S. history textbooks.

People did all sorts of extra or unusual jobs during the war. They helped as airplane spotters and air-raid wardens. They assisted in hospitals and in entertaining servicemen. Millions gave blood, which could be stored and shipped for use in saving the lives of the wounded. Women took jobs in shipyards, airplane factories, and in other types of work previously done chiefly by men.[16]

1966

In this selection, students not only read about the numerous and important roles women played during the war but also were given a brief background to women's struggles in this country.

During World War II, many more women than ever before disregarded the old saying that "woman's place is in the home." Actually this idea of "woman's place" had been diminishing for many years. In 1880, when most women agreed with men that woman's place was indeed in the home, only 2 1/2 million women were gainfully employed. By 1920, the number had risen to 5 million, and by 1940, to 11 million. It was the war, however, with its demands for manpower, that shattered most of the remaining prejudices against working women. By 1943, an additional 2 million women went to work in war plants, actually replacing men who had left for the armed services. And, for the first time, the American armed forces, which had previously used women only as nurses, now organized corps of women to substitute for men in non-combatant jobs. More than 250,000 women entered the Army (as Wacs), the Coast Guard (as Spars), the Navy (as Waves), and the Marine Corps. In the services, women worked as machinists, storekeepers, and office workers; they operated radios, and drove jeeps and trucks. When people recovered from their surprise at seeing women in these new roles, they began to speak of "the girl behind the man behind the gun."

Given the opportunity, women showed that they had the ability to work side by side with men, and to work just as effectively. By the end of the war, virtually the only jobs that remained closed to women were those that required extraordinary physical strength.[17]

1996

By the 1990s, students learned that women could not only handle this physical labor but that their work was also an inspiration to countless others. This textbook also

*added the presence of African American women to the narrative and briefly ex-
plained the role they played.*

Women in the war effort. The need for workers opened economic opportunities for women. Now, instead of being dissuaded from taking jobs
as they had been during the depression, they were urged to go to work. Six
million women joined the 12 million already in the labor force. They took
on a wide variety of jobs and surprised the men who had said they were too
weak and delicate to be lumberjacks, blast furnace operators, stevedores,
or blacksmiths. They proved that they could handle all these jobs. And
they also operated complex machines in shipyards and airplane factories.
Many for the first time could show their talents as doctors, dentists,
chemists, and lawyers. "Rosie the Riveter" became an inspiration for all
Americans.

Black women benefited, too. Before the war a greater percentage of
black women worked than white. But they were generally restricted to low-
paying jobs as domestic servants or farm laborers. When war came, they
found more interesting and better-paying jobs. Nearly half a million black
women who had worked as domestics left that work during the war to take
positions in factories.

When World War II ended, it seemed that once again women might be
forced to leave their jobs to make places for returning servicemen. But this
time a much larger proportion was offered work in peacetime production.
Prodded by war, the nation discovered its women and helped women discover themselves.[18]

41

The Bombing of Hiroshima
and Nagasaki

On August 6 and 9, 1945, the United States dropped two atomic bombs on the Japanese cities of Hiroshima and Nagasaki. The war in the Pacific quickly came to a close, and the United States found itself in the position of being the only global nuclear power. While there is no question as to what happened, over the past sixty years there has been much debate over whether or not the United States should have used this weapon.

1947

Immediately following World War II, U.S. history textbooks focused on the role of the atomic bombs in hurrying the end of the war. Few, if any, considered the bombs' impact on Japanese civilians, or dared to raise the question of their necessily in bringing the war to a close.

The Japanese war came to a climax early in 1945. The bloody conquests of Iwo Jima and Okinawa gave bases either for the direct invasion of Japan or for landings in China. The Chinese were having better success on the mainland. The end of the European war released large British and

American naval units, and also large and experienced armies. Russia finally declared war on Japan and invaded Manchuria. The United States unveiled its newest weapon, the atomic bomb, demonstrating twice—first at Hiroshima and then at Nagasaki—that a good-sized city could almost be erased from the map in one blinding flash. Confronted by this combination of forces Japan surrendered August 14—the formal surrender being accepted by General MacArthur on September 2, 1945.[19]

1954

As the nuclear arms race went into full swing, this text appeared to focus primarily on the development of the bombs themselves, somewhat apart from the broader strategic questions of their role in ending the war.

The Atomic Bomb

The real meaning of the ultimatum was made clear on August 6, 1945, when an American superfortress dropped a new kind of bomb over the Japanese city of Hiroshima. The possibility of the development of an atomic bomb had been clearly established by scientific discoveries made in 1939. Shortly after the United States became involved in the war, the development of the bomb was undertaken as a top-secret military project.

Leading atomic scientists of the world, including some who had come to this country as refugees from Axis oppression, were engaged in the project. In July, 1945, a test bomb was successfully exploded at Los Alamos, New Mexico. President Truman fully recognized the fearful potentialities of such a weapon. He considered its use justifiable as a means of bringing about a rapid conclusion of the war.

The single bomb dropped over Hiroshima, a city of 375,000, had an explosive power equal to that of twenty thousand tons of TNT. At one blow, the heart of the city was destroyed and three fifths of its population wiped out. Two days later a second and more powerful bomb was dropped on the city of Nagasaki. One-third of the city was destroyed.[20]

1966

Still in the shadow of the Cuban Missile Crisis, students in the mid-1960s had to con-template the possibility of a nuclear war. This selection let students know that a nu-clear holocaust might be the end result, if a "lasting peace" was not found.

On August 6, 1945, the first atomic bomb used in warfare was dropped from an American airplane onto the city of Hiroshima in Japan. Three days later, a second bomb fell on Nagasaki, another Japanese city. More than 150,000 Japanese died in the resulting holocausts. Thousands of others suffered dreadful after effects.

In February 1947, in *Harper's* Magazine, Secretary of War Henry L. Stimson wrote about the decision to use the bombs:

"The face of war is the face of death; death is an inevitable part of any order that a wartime leader gives. . . . War in the twentieth century has grown steadily more barbarous, more destructive, more debased in all its aspects. Now, with the release of atomic energy, man's ability to destroy himself is very nearly complete. The bombs dropped on Hiroshima and Nagasaki ended a war. They also made it wholly clear that we must never have another war. This is the lesson men and leaders everywhere must learn, and I believe that when they learn it they will find a way to lasting peace. There is no other choice." [21]

1995

In 1995, the Smithsonian Institution in Washington, DC, came under attack for its dis-play of the airplane that dropped the original atomic bomb on Hiroshima—the Enola Gay. Critics claimed that the exhibit was actually antiwar and brought into question the use of this bomb to end the war. The Smithsonian left the Enola Gay on display, yet with little or no interpretations attached—a stand it seems many textbooks have agreed with since 1945. Students in this 1990s' text, however, were given a number of possible interpretations as to why the bomb was used.

Triumph and Tragedy in the Pacific

The defeat of Japan was now only a matter of time. The United States had three possible ways to proceed. The military favored a full-scale invasion, beginning on the southernmost island of Kyushu in November 1945 and culminating with an assault on Honshu (the main island of Japan) and a climatic battle for Tokyo in 1946; casualties were expected to run into the hundreds of thousands. Diplomats suggested a negotiated peace, urging the United States to modify the unconditional surrender formula to permit Japan to retain the institution of the emperor. At Potsdam, Churchill and Truman did issue a call for surrender, warning Japan it faced utter destruction, but they made no mention of the emperor. . . .

Weather conditions on the morning of August 6 dictated the choice of Hiroshima as the bomb's target. The explosion incinerated 4 square miles of the city, instantly killing more than sixty thousand. Two days later, Russia entered the war against Japan, and the next day, August 9, the United States dropped a second bomb on Nagasaki. There were no more atomic bombs available, but no more were needed. The emperor personally broke a deadlock in the Japanese cabinet and persuaded his ministers to surrender unconditionally on August 14, 1945. Three weeks later, Japan signed a formal capitulation agreement on the decks of the battleship *Missouri* in Tokyo Bay to bring World War II to its official close.

Many years later, scholars charged that Truman had more in mind than defeating Japan when he decided to use the atomic bomb. Citing air force and naval officers who claimed Japan could be defeated by a blockade or by conventional air attacks, these revisionists suggested the real reason for dropping the bomb was to impress the Soviet Union with the fact that the United States had exclusive possession of the ultimate weapon. The available evidence indicates that while Truman and his associates were aware of the possible effect on the Soviet Union, their primary motive was to end World War II as quickly and effortlessly as possible. The saving of American lives, along with a desire for revenge for Pearl Harbor, were uppermost in the decision to bomb Hiroshima and Nagasaki. Yet in using the atomic bomb to defeat Japan, the United States virtually guaranteed a postwar arms race with the Soviet Union.[22]

PART VII

The Cold War and
Postwar America

42

The Marshall Plan

The economic side of the Truman Doctrine, the Marshall Plan, was America's effort to try to save much of Europe from financial ruin and being overrun by communism. Often portrayed as an example of America's altruistic spirit, some
critics have complained that the Marshall Plan was just another sign of U.S. imperialism in the twentieth century.

1957

*Throughout the rest of the postwar period students in the United States learned
about this historical event through the prism of the Cold War. Here is an especially
striking example.*

The Truman Doctrine and Marshall Plan Aided Europe

The rapid growth of Russian influence after World War II alarmed the
West. Our leaders realized that they must act quickly or all of Europe
might go Communistic. In 1947 President Truman urged Congress to
grant aid to European nations threatened by the Communists. The idea
became known as the *Truman Doctrine.* Under the plan Congress granted

400 million dollars to aid Greece and Turkey, whose independence was threatened by Russia.

Other European nations were in danger. Many of their factories and railroads lay in ruins. Thousands were hungry, cold, and out of work. Communist agents were busy in France, Belgium, Holland, and Italy urging people to overthrow their governments. What could be done? Secretary of State George Marshall offered a plan. The United States would supply tools, food, and money to help European nations rebuild their homes and industries. The nations must develop their own programs and prove they were willing to help themselves. This was the *Marshall Plan*. It was in many ways quite successful. The nations of Western Europe grasped eagerly at the chance to get on their feet again. In a few years they were producing big crops and their factories were working overtime. The Marshall Plan renewed the world's faith in freedom and democracy and helped the United States win many new friends.[1]

1966

In the mid-1960s, U.S. students learned that American kindness and benevolence were thwarted by the Soviet Union's Cold War fears.

The Communists Condemn the Marshall Plan and Counter with the Molotov Plan

"Our policy is not directed against any country or doctrine," Marshall had said in suggesting his plan. However, the U.S.S.R. refused Marshall Plan aid and made its satellites unhappy by forbidding them to accept such aid. It condemned the Marshall Plan as a scheme of "dollar imperialists" to place all Europe under the economic domination of the United States.

In 1949, the U.S.S.R. countered the Marshall Plan with the Molotov Plan, which aimed to bind the satellite countries more closely to the U.S.S.R. economically. The Marshall and Molotov Plans caused trade between Western and Eastern Europe to drop sharply.[2]

1992

While previous textbooks written and published during the Cold War usually viewed this topic as a "black-and-white" issue, by the early 1990s, with the Cold War con-

cluded, students began to learn that there were many more sides to the Marshall Plan.

The Marshall Plan

While military aid could help contain communism, Truman and his advisers knew it was only part of the answer. In June 1947 Secretary of State George Marshall suggested another way to bolster freedom—a plan for helping Europe rebuild.

The war had been over for two years, but Europeans were still struggling to survive. Cities and towns had been bombed into ruin. Roads and canals were destroyed. Worst of all, millions of people were sick, homeless, and hungry. In May 1947 Churchill lamented that Europe was "a rubble heap . . . a breeding ground of pestilence [disease] and hate."

Conditions like these were not only heartbreaking but also dangerous. Such terrible suffering provided ideal conditions for communism to grow, and already Communist parties were gathering strength in France and Italy. However, a ruined, starving Europe would drain the American economy—and American businesses desperately depended on European markets.

Marshall's plan involved spending billions of dollars to help put Europe, including the USSR, back on its feet. To qualify for the aid, nations had to agree to spend the dollars on goods from the United States. At first many conservatives in Congress disagreed with the plan, but events in eastern Europe soon changed their minds. The Soviets refused to take part in the plan, criticizing it as America's way of taking over Europe. In February 1948 the Communist party seized control of Czechoslovakia, completing the Soviet domination of eastern Europe.

Two months later Truman approved Congress's bill for $17 billion in aid to Europe over five years. Sixteen nations participated in the plan, and by 1952 they were more successful than anyone had dreamed. The Communist party in western Europe was severely weakened. Western European industries had increased their output by 64 percent, and American prosperity was ensured. At the same time, however, tensions with the Soviet Union continued to grow.[3]

43

Truman Fires MacArthur

When President Harry Truman left office in 1952, he was considered one of the least popular presidents in U.S. history. Over fifty years later his reputation has rebounded, with some historians placing him on the short list of great American presidents. One of the more controversial things Truman did while in office was to fire General Douglas MacArthur as overall commander of the United Nations' forces during the Korean War (1950–53). MacArthur was not only one of America's greatest war heroes from World War II but was also the darling of the conservative wing of the Republican Party, and thus, firing MacArthur caused a political storm in Washington, DC.

1954

Shortly after the firing took place, this U.S. history textbook treaded lightly, briefly discussing the controversy and making the claim that it had an impact on the 1952 presidential election—without indicating specifically what that impact might have been.

In April, 1952, in the midst of the conversations for truce negotiations, President Truman recalled General MacArthur. It had been known for some time that there was a lack of co-operation between the Far Eastern Command and Washington, but whose fault it was is still an argued point. The officials in Washington felt that MacArthur was not carrying out his instructions. On his return to America, MacArthur was invited to appear before Congress and before numerous audiences throughout the country. He vigorously attacked the administration's Far Eastern policy and proposed a plan of his own. The MacArthur incident influenced public opinion in America and affected the outcome of the election in 1952.[4]

1961

Making the point that this was a highly controversial issue, this selection took pains to vindicate Truman's decision, contending that MacArthur was overreaching his bounds.

General MacArthur Is Removed

After the intervention of Red China in Korea, a great difference of opinion developed between General MacArthur and the Truman administration on the conduct of the war. MacArthur favored bombing bases, supply routes, and industrial areas in China and Manchuria, blockading the coast of China, and using Chiang Kai-shek's troops in Formosa for an attack on the Chinese mainland.

The administration rejected these measures because it feared that they would lead to an all-out war between the United States and Red China and possibly touch off World War III. Furthermore, Europe was considered to be more important than the Far East. If the United States became involved in a full-scale war with China, the Russians would have a free hand in Europe. The administration's strategy, therefore, was to fight a limited war in Korea, keep communism north of the thirty-eighth parallel, and inflict severe punishment on North Korean and Chinese forces in order to force them to abandon their aggression.

On April 11, 1951, after General MacArthur had made a series of public statements frankly criticizing the administration's policy, President Truman suddenly removed him from his command and appointed General Matthew B. Ridgway to take his place. MacArthur's dismissal caused a great furor in the United States. Many Americans were violently critical of

Truman's action. Others defended the President's position with equal vigor.

During May and June, the Senate Military Affairs Committee held a series of open hearings at which the administration's military and civilian leaders appeared to explain and defend their policies in the Far East. They insisted that a limited war was the wisest course for the United States to pursue in Korea. At the same time, they made it clear that the United States would oppose Red China's efforts to be admitted to the United Nations and that she would take any measures necessary to prevent Red China from seizing Formosa. It was a long time, however, before the furor over the MacArthur dismissal died down in the United States.[5]

1995

By the mid-1990s, amid a notable revival of Truman's reputation, few textbooks questioned the wisdom of the president's decision to fire such a popular general as MacArthur.

Truman Fires MacArthur

MacArthur complained publicly that politicians in Washington were holding him back. "We must win," he insisted. "There is no substitute for victory." Angry that MacArthur was defying orders, Truman fired the general.

Many Americans were furious. They gave MacArthur a hero's welcome when he returned to the United States. Truman, however, strongly defended his action. He felt that MacArthur's statements undermined attempts to reach a peace settlement. Under the Constitution, he pointed out, the President is commander in chief. As commander in chief, it was Truman—not the general—who had power to make the key decisions about war and peace.[6]

44

McCarthyism

In the 1950s, when the fear of Communist subversion was a real (or perceived) threat for most Americans, a junior senator from Wisconsin, Joseph McCarthy, fanned the flames by claiming that there were Communists within the U.S. government. It then became his "mission" to root them out. With the frequent analogies to the witch hunts in colonial Salem, Massachusetts, McCarthy's story has usually been portrayed in U.S. history textbooks as an example of how paranoid and hysterical people had become in the early days of the Cold War.

1967

This textbook did not mince words about Senator McCarthy and his search for Communists. Not only were words such as "recklessly" and "panic" used to inform students about McCarthy's tactics; this author also went so far as to state that McCarthy did all of this "with no regard for truth."

A Panic About Security

In addition, a few Communists, keeping their party ties secret, as well as some Communist sympathizers, managed to work their way into government posts. There they served as spies for the Soviet Union.

Discovery of this handful of traitors was made at just the time that the Cold War began. Fear spread that there were numerous Soviet agents or sympathizers in the nation. The result was a hysteria much like that of the Alien and Sedition Acts of the 1790's and of the Red Scare following the first World War.

THE DRAGNET APPROACH

Prodded by public opinion, President Truman set up a loyalty check of federal employees. It was, in the main, a check on associations. The attorney general drew up a list of organizations in which Communists had figured. Government employees who had belonged to any of these organizations became suspects.

Stringent as it was, this measure failed to satisfy public opinion. Eisenhower, when he became President, issued additional orders. On the mere accusation of being a security risk, a federal employee could be fired. The justification offered was that it was better to lose thousands of loyal employees than take a chance on having one security risk on the payroll.

With greater fanfare, investigating committees of Congress and of state legislatures went hunting for Communists and "fellow travelers." The only purpose served by most of these investigations was to win publicity. Charges recklessly harmed many lives and careers.

MCCARTHYISM

In 1950 Senator Joseph R. McCarthy made this activity even more sensational. With no regard for truth, he applied the Communist label to State Department personnel, cabinet officers, generals, professors, librarians, and cleaning women.

Despite his brazenness, McCarthy went almost unchallenged. Believing that he had strong public support, politicians and newspapers feared even to criticize him. At last, when McCarthy charged that the army was honeycombed with Communists, President Eisenhower ordered the army to fight back. Two months of hearings, nationally televised, showed McCarthy as a fraud. The Senate then voted to censure him. The hearings, followed by the Senate vote, helped the nation regain its balance. Panic about home-grown Communists began to ebb. The hunt for Communists and "fellow travelers," now generally known as McCarthyism, diminished in fervor and scope.

The panic, however, left behind restrictions on American freedoms. In some states no one can be licensed as a barber, notary, or professional wrestler unless he swears that he has not been a Communist. Federal and state employees still have past associations checked. Applicants for many jobs in private industry have their political activities investigated.

Such practices narrow the freedoms which the Bill of Rights was set up to protect. It is an unhappy paradox that these practices were thought necessary on account of a Cold War commitment to protect freedom elsewhere in the world.[7]

1974

The authors of this textbook pulled no punches in informing students that McCarthy was "irresponsible," "unscrupulous," and a "bully."

The Hiss case had made the nation acutely aware of Communist subversion and had set off an anti-Communist crusade. In the campaign of 1948, some Republicans charged the Democratic party with being "soft on communism." But the person who most exploited and abused the Communist issue was Joseph R. McCarthy, a Republican senator from Wisconsin. His actions introduced a new word into the American language: McCarthyism, the making of indiscriminate and irresponsible charges of political disloyalty.

McCarthyism first appeared in February 1950, when the senator claimed that the State Department was "thoroughly infested with Communists." As chairman of the Permanent Subcommittee on Investigations, McCarthy accused and frightened many people over a period of four years. But he never proved his charges. Because of his unscrupulous methods and careless accusations, McCarthy caused much controversy.

Eisenhower's beliefs often differed from those of many members of his party. In his policies on civil liberties he tried to avoid splitting the party. Although Eisenhower disliked Senator Joseph McCarthy's methods, he tried to placate the senator. He stepped up the hunt for subversives in government and fired employees who were viewed as security risks. In August 1954, Congress passed the Communist Control Act. It outlawed the

Communist party. Many people criticized the Eisenhower administration for some of its security policies.

But some extreme conservatives—particularly McCarthy—claimed the administration did not go far enough. McCarthy even accused Eisenhower's choice as ambassador to the Soviet Union of being a "security risk." In December 1953, McCarthy accused the secretary of the army of shielding Communists in the army.

Later the army accused McCarthy of seeking special treatment for an assistant who had been drafted. In April 1954, Congress held hearings on the charges made by McCarthy and by the army. For more than a month the hearings were broadcast on nationwide television. Millions of Americans watched McCarthy bully and insult witnesses, among them high-ranking officers.

McCarthy began to lose his hold on the public, and in December 1954, the Republican-controlled Senate turned against him. It condemned him, by a vote of 67 to 22, for conduct unbecoming a senator. Eisenhower publicly expressed satisfaction with this blow at McCarthyism. The senator's influence dropped abruptly, never to return.[8]

1999

References to McCarthy's witch-hunt tactics and his spreading of paranoia are themes found in most U.S. history textbooks. Disliked by a Republican president and a Republican-led Congress that censured him, McCarthy's story will probably never be debated in textbooks since in the years following this event, there has been little partisan rancor over his deeds and legacy.

Increased fears of communist subversion were fertile ground for more reckless voices. At a Lincoln's Day speech in February 1950, Senator Joseph R. McCarthy of Wisconsin accused the Democratic party of "twenty years of treason." McCarthy charged that Roosevelt had deliberately sacrificed the navy at Pearl Harbor and had "sold out" to the Soviet Union at Yalta. In addition, McCarthy claimed to have a list of "card-carrying Communists" in the State Department.

While McCarthy never produced the list, nor a shred of evidence to support his charges, he ruined the careers of many government officials. A growing atmosphere of hysteria inspired other "witch-hunts." Private groups used the communist label to drive liberal professors out of colleges. They made sure books they believed to be subversive were removed from schools. They had many broadcasters, writers, and entertainers barred from television and kept many actors from working on the stage and in films. Years later a Senate committee determined that McCarthy's accusations and investigations had been groundless. The use of indiscriminate, unfounded political accusations to destroy or assassinate the character of one's opponent came, in time, to be known as McCarthyism.[9]

45

Desegregation and the Civil Rights Movement

In the first major attempt at desegregating a public school since the Supreme Court ruled on *Brown v. Board of Education,* the desegregation of Little Rock High School brought a number of explosive political issues to the forefront. First, what power does the federal government have over the states? And second, how would race relations be resolved in the South just one hundred years after the passage of the Thirteenth, Fourteenth, and Fifteenth Amendments?

1966

This passage admitted that by the 1960s, the problems of race and school desegregation were far from settled.

Education

In the 1950's the focus of attention was on the public schools. Although considerable progress was made toward desegregation in the District of Columbia and some of the border states, Virginia and parts of the deep South opposed the entire policy. In March 1956 a number of southern Congressmen voiced their opposition to the new policy in a "Declaration" in which they stated that the Supreme Court decision was a "clear abuse of judicial power." Then, in the autumn of 1957, President Eisenhower ordered federal troops to Little Rock, Arkansas, where violence had broken out when the school board permitted a few Negro boys and girls to attend a high school previously reserved for white students. The problem of school desegregation was still far from a solution when the Eisenhower administration drew to an end.[10]

1974

Twenty years after Brown v. Board of Education, this excerpt struck a pessimistic tone by informing students about the policy of "token desegregation" in the South.

Southern states had long enforced segregation of blacks and whites in trains, buses, restaurants, schools, and other public places. An 1896 Supreme Court decision was the legal basis for this practice.

After World War II, the Supreme Court heard a number of cases that challenged the "separate but equal" doctrine. The most important was that of Brown v. Board of Education of Topeka. In May 1954 the justices ruled unanimously that separate facilities in public education were by their nature unequal and kept blacks from enjoying educational rights on terms equal with whites. A year later, the Supreme Court required the southern states to integrate their schools "with all deliberate speed."

In the border states and in some of the large cities, authorities began admitting black and white children to the same schools. But in most of the South the decision met with bitter resistance that finally led to crisis.

In September 1957, Governor Orval Faubus of Arkansas challenged the authority of the federal government. He used all available means to keep black students out of Central High School, an all-white school in Little Rock. When local authorities did not control rioting there, President Eisenhower ordered paratroopers to Little Rock to protect the black students and to enforce the federal court's order. "Mob rule," he told the nation, "cannot be allowed to override the decisions of our courts."

Despite the President's use of the army, desegregation of schools in Arkansas was delayed for several years. Other southern states followed a policy of "token desegregation," allowing only a few blacks to enter white schools. By the beginning of 1961, a small percentage of the 3 million black children in the South were attending integrated classes, but no legal doctrine blocked further integration.[11]

1999

By the 1990s, the Civil Rights Movement was increasingly presented in its fullest national context, reflecting a more in-depth historical understanding of the period.

The state's governor, Orval Faubus, defied federal authority and sent National Guard troops to prevent the students from attending. President Eisenhower tried to persuade Governor Faubus to obey the court order. The governor withdrew the troops, but without their presence the African American students were exposed to an angry mob that threatened them with physical harm. Forced to act to maintain order, Eisenhower sent in 1,000 paratroopers and federalized, or put under the jurisdiction of the federal government, 10,000 members of the Arkansas National Guard to surround the school so that the students could enter safely.

As Daisy Bates, then the president of the Arkansas NAACP, later remembered:

" . . . the nine [African American] pupils marched solemnly through the doors of Central High School, surrounded by twenty-two soldiers. An Army helicopter circled overhead. Around the massive brick schoolhouse 350 paratroopers stood grimly at attention. . . . Within minutes a world that had been holding its breath learned that the nine pupils . . . had finally entered the 'never-never-land.' "

Troops remained in Little Rock for the rest of the year, however, and Central High School was closed for the 1958–1959 academic year.

As the Eisenhower administration drew to a close, the nation remained racially divided. Custom and years of intimidation kept many African Americans from voting. Between 1957 and 1960, the Justice Department brought only 10 suits to secure voting rights for African Americans. Only 25 percent of African American adults voted in states of the Deep South, and only 5 percent in Mississippi. The movement for civil rights was just beginning.[12]

46

The Bay of Pigs

John F. Kennedy has generally enjoyed a near-godlike mythology in U.S. history textbooks, owing in large measure to the circumstances of his assassination. It is interesting, then, to consider what was by all accounts a blatant screwup for President Kennedy—the Bay of Pigs invasion. Although planned by Eisenhower's CIA, this operation trained Cuban exiles to invade their former homeland and free it from the grips of a communist government lead by Fidel Castro. It ended in a well-publicized disaster in April 1961.

1975

This American "fiasco" was not only "humiliating," according to this textbook, but blame lays squarely at the feet of Kennedy and his decision to not use U.S. military forces.

In the continuing tensions of the Cold War, the closer relationship between Cuba and the Soviet Union seemed to threaten American security. President Eisenhower gave support to a secretly planned invasion of Cuba by anti-Communist Cuban exiles who had fled Cuba after Castro came to power. But before any such invasion took place, a new American President, John F. Kennedy, had taken office. President Kennedy was willing to continue American aid for the invasion project although he refused to allow direct American involvement. Operating without direct American military aid in combat, the invasion force of 1,400 Cuban exiles which landed at the Bay of Pigs in April 1961 was quickly and utterly defeated by Castro's forces.

The Bay of Pigs fiasco was a humiliating blow to American prestige and to the newly-inaugurated Kennedy administration. President Kennedy's relations with the Russians became more difficult, particularly because the young American President feared that Premier Khrushchev might interpret the Bay of Pigs failure as evidence of American weakness or lack of will.[13]

1986

Although this textbook explained that Kennedy did many good things in Latin America, it also took the time to tell students that the Bay of Pigs tainted the young president's image, at least for a brief period of time.

President Kennedy had stressed domestic economic issues in the 1960 campaign. But shortly after he took office, foreign problems began to occupy most of his time. During President Eisenhower's second term there had been a revolution in Cuba led by Fidel Castro. Castro set up a communist-type government on this island just 90 miles (144 kilometers) off the tip of Florida. He established close ties with the Soviet Union and took an unfriendly attitude toward the United States.

The Eisenhower administration had cut off trade with Cuba. Meanwhile, the Central Intelligence Agency (CIA), a government bureau created in 1947, began to train a small army of Cuban refugees. The plan was to have this force invade Cuba from Central America in order to overthrow Castro. Of course this was done in complete secrecy.

When Kennedy learned of the plan, he hesitated to allow the CIA to put it into effect. He had criticized Eisenhower for supporting conservative governments in Latin America only because they were anticommunist. Should he now encourage the overthrow of a government only because it was procommunist?

Kennedy was eager to develop good relations with Latin American countries and to help them improve the lives of their poor. In early 1961 he created the Peace Corps, an organization that sent volunteers to help the people of needy countries. He proposed what he called an Alliance for Progress to provide economic aid for Latin American countries. Nevertheless, Kennedy decided to go ahead with the CIA scheme. On April 17, 1961, the Cuban force was put ashore in western Cuba, at a place known as the Bay of Pigs. The invaders expected that the Cuban peasants would greet them with open arms. Instead they met only Castro's army. All of the invaders were captured or killed.

The Bay of Pigs dealt a terrible blow to the prestige of the United States and to Kennedy in particular. Was the youthful new President a reckless adventurer? Could he stand up strongly to his clever communist opponents? Citizens who had voted for Kennedy because they did not trust Nixon were especially shocked.[14]

1992

While textbooks have blamed the CIA and Eisenhower, and even admitted that the Bay of Pigs invasion put a blemish on Kennedy's time in office, none have gone so far as to claim that it was an outright bad decision.

Before leaving office Eisenhower had urged Kennedy to step up the training of La Brigada. Now in office Kennedy took the advice of CIA operatives and ordered La Brigada to land secretly in Cuba, inspire a popular uprising, and sweep Castro out of power.

The invasion on April 17, 1961, failed miserably. When the 1,500 commandos tried to land at the Bay of Pigs on Cuba's southern coast, they met disaster at every turn. Their boats ran aground on coral reefs; Kennedy cancelled their air support to keep U.S. involvement secret; and the promised uprising of the Cuban people never happened. Within two days Castro's forces killed several hundred members of La Brigada and captured nearly all the rest.

The Bay of Pigs was a dark moment for Kennedy. The action exposed an American plot to overthrow a neighbor's government, and the clumsy affair made the United States look weak, like a paper tiger.[15]

47

The Laotian Crisis

Just before Kennedy was sworn into office, President Eisenhower, at a White House meeting, warned Kennedy of the situation in Laos: "You may have to go in there and fight it out," he informed the newly elected President. Laos had become one of America's top global hot spots in the early 1960s. After the withdrawal of the French, the Laotians found themselves caught between the Soviet Union and the United States in an international Cold War struggle. At one point, Nikita Khrushchev even threatened nuclear war if the situation there continued to escalate. The Laotian Crisis usually is given little, if any, space in most U.S. history textbooks. The war in Vietnam and the Cold War on a larger scale usually overshadow the events in Laos and their importance to the Kennedy administration as well as America's foreign policy.

1966

Published less then five years after the Laotian Crisis caused such a stir for Kennedy, this textbook took the time to inform students about the events that transpired in Laos and why it was important for the United States to get involved. Interestingly, the authors of this textbook spent more time discussing Laos than Vietnam.

Continuing Conflict in Southeast Asia

Crises continued to develop in Asia, as well as in Latin America and Africa, during the 1960's. The possibility that Communist North Korea, supported by Red China and the U.S.S.R., might renew its aggression on South Korea remained a constant threat. But the major crisis areas were the new countries of Southeast Asia—Laos, Cambodia, and North and South Vietnam.

The tiny kingdom of Laos, with its swamps and jungles, was divided into three political factions—pro-Western, Communist, and neutral. In an effort to secure a strong pro-Western government, the United States poured several hundred million dollars into the country. Finally, faced with the failure of these efforts, the Kennedy administration reversed its policy. In July 1962, after lengthy negotiations with the Laotian factions and the Communist powers, a truly neutral government was established in Laos.

The United States also gave considerable military and economic aid to Cambodia in an effort to secure a pro-Western government. As in Laos, however, the policy failed. In the autumn of 1963, apparently yielding to strong pressures from the Communists, the Cambodian government asked the United States to withdraw its military and technical personnel.[16]

1974

By 1974, with the Vietnam War coming to an end, the American fear of Soviet aggression had not abated. In this passage, students learned that what matters is the fact that Kennedy stood strong against the Communist aggressors, forcing them, through military pressure, to come to the negotiating table.

Eisenhower's deepest Asian involvement came in Laos. The President sent economic and military aid in 1959 and 1960 to the kingdom of Laos. The Pathet Lao, a nationalist movement that received Communist support, fought this conservative government. The Pathet Lao claimed to represent the people of Laos and accused the United States of opposing national self-determination. Although the Pathet Lao was winning the civil war, the Eisenhower administration would not send United States troops to Laos. Eisenhower did not want to risk a war with Communist China, which supported the Pathet Lao.

In Laos, President Kennedy abandoned the Eisenhower policy of helping pro-Western regimes in anti-Communist wars. Kennedy accepted a
British plan for a cease-fire in the civil war in Laos and for a neutralist government that would be neither pro-Western nor Communist . . .

The Soviets, too, accepted this plan. In May 1962, however, it looked
as if Communists might overrun the nation. President Kennedy reacted
with a show of strength. He ordered the Seventh Fleet into the waters next
to Laos and stationed more than 5,000 combat troops in neighboring
Thailand. The Communist offensive ceased. In June, fourteen nations
signed agreements guaranteeing independence and neutrality for Laos.[17]

1994

*With the Cold War having concluded a few years earlier, students in the mid-1990s
learned that Kennedy did not always listen to his military advisers and actually preferred diplomacy over the use of the military.*

Sparsely populated Laos, freed of its French colonial overlords in 1954,
was festering dangerously by the time Kennedy came into office. The
Eisenhower administration had drenched this jungle kingdom with dollars
but failed to cleanse the country of an aggressive communist element. A
red Laos, many observers feared, would be a river on which the influence
of Communist China would flood into all of Southeast Asia.

As the Laotian civil war raged, Kennedy's military advisers seriously
considered sending in American troops. But the president found that he
had insufficient forces to put out the fire in Asia and still honor his commitments in Europe. Kennedy thus sought a diplomatic escape hatch in
the fourteen-power Geneva conference, which imposed a shaky peace in
Laos in 1962.[18]

PART VIII

The Vietnam Era

48

The Gulf of Tonkin

The textbook history of the Vietnam War has evolved rapidly over the space of thirty years. It is not surprising, then, that the immediate "cause" of the war—the alleged attack by North Vietnam on U.S. warships operating in the Gulf of Tonkin—showed itself to be the subject of much historical controversy.

1967

With the war in Vietnam still raging, American students learned in this history text-book that there was no question about the nature of the attack against U.S. ships in the Gulf of Tonkin and that unlike their French counterparts, the United States was in this war for the long haul.

The climactic test of American policy came in Southeast Asia. The weakness of the successive military governments that had attempted to establish their legitimacy after the death of Diem encouraged the National Liberation Front to step up its guerrilla campaign. Disorder forced Saigon into greater expenditures and more extensive recruitment of troops, which compounded its difficulties. Toward the end of 1963, the assassination of

President Kennedy and the mistaken assumption that the change of administration would confuse American policy encouraged the Vietcong in the belief that victory was near. Regular troops from North Vietnam moved south to give the *coup de grace* to the tottering regime in the South.

An attack on United States ships in the Gulf of Tonkin in 1964 was the occasion for the decision to honor American commitments even though that might involve a large-scale war in Asia. A resolution of Congress gave the President authority to resist aggression in Southeast Asia. The number of military personnel increased and the conflict deepened.

Hanoi, deceived by the belief that weariness over a remote conflict would compel the Americans to yield as the French had, refused to back down. There followed the game of escalation that the strategies had predicted. The United States bombed naval installations to retaliate against the incident in the Gulf. Air attacks upon North Vietnam and the full-scale use of American troops followed a Vietcong assault on the American camp at Pleiku in February 1965. The failure of the enemy to respond to the 37-day suspension of air strikes beginning on December 24, 1965, led in June 1966 to the bombing of oil depots near Hanoi and Haiphong. Meanwhile American troops, supplied with helicopters and heavy armaments, broke up the Vietcong main forces and began to strike at the guerrilla strongholds in the Mekong delta.

The objective of the United States was to make its power credible. It did not seek to destroy the Hanoi regime; rather, it used only as much force as would persuade the Communists that they had no hope of victory and had better negotiate peace.[1]

1982

In the 1980s, the historiography now emphasized that the United States had actually been involved militarily in the region before the "attacks" against American naval ships. Although this textbook made no claims that the Tonkin incident was falsified, it did argue that President Johnson "exaggerated" the crisis in order to deepen U.S. involvement.

By early 1964 the Viet Cong controlled nearly half of South Vietnam. Because the new Saigon government was shaky and seemed to be leaning toward neutralism, United States officials cooperated in a second coup. In neighboring Laos, American bombers hit supply routes connecting the Viet Cong with the North Vietnamese, thus widening the scope of the war. Then in August an incident in the Gulf of Tonkin, off the coast of North Vietnam, drew the United States even deeper into the Vietnamese quagmire. While assisting South Vietnamese raiders, the U.S.S. *Maddox* and C. *Turner Joy* were attacked by North Vietnamese boats.

Johnson seized the chance to go on national television and announce retaliatory air strikes above the 17th parallel. He exaggerated the crisis, comparing it to Greece and Turkey in 1947, Berlin in 1948, and Korea in 1950. On August 7 Congress obliged him with the Tonkin Gulf resolution, passed 466–0 in the House and 88–2 in the Senate following brief debate. Only Wayne Morse of Oregon and Ernest Gruening of Alaska dissented from the resolution's sweeping language. The document authorized the president to "take all necessary measures to repel any armed attack against the forces of the United States and to prevent further aggression." Over time the Tonkin Gulf resolution would come to serve as the declaration of war Congress never voted on. Only in 1970 would senators repeal it, realizing too late that they had surrendered their powers in the foreign policy process by giving the president wide latitude to conduct the war as he saw fit.[2]

1992

From discussing the "unprovoked attacks" against the United States to basically calling the president a liar, this selection made it clear that the Tonkin events served as a pretext for war.

The Gulf of Tonkin Resolution

In early August Johnson announced that North Vietnamese torpedo boats had attacked two U.S. destroyers patrolling in the Gulf of Tonkin off the coast of North Vietnam. Johnson angrily declared that Americans had been the victims of "unprovoked" attacks. He urged Congress to pass a resolution giving him authority to "take all necessary measures to repel any armed attack against the forces of the United States and to prevent further aggression." An alarmed Congress almost unanimously passed the so-called Gulf of Tonkin Resolution. The resolution was not a declaration of war, but it authorized Johnson to widen the war. The resolution, he said, "was like grandma's nightshirt—it covered everything."

Few Americans questioned the president's account of the incident. Years later, however, it was revealed that Johnson had withheld the truth from the public and Congress. The American warships had been helping South Vietnamese commandos raid two North Vietnamese islands the night of the attacks.[3]

49

The Counterculture

Few aspects of the 1960s have cast such a long shadow as the counterculture movement. Liberals and conservatives (political, social, and cultural) have used the hippies and the various images of them as backdrops to a broad range of public controversial issues over the past thirty years. High school students, however, have been intrigued by this group that thumbed its nose at authority, used illegal drugs, "made love not war," and listened to rock music.

All of this has created a number of challenges for textbook authors when writing about the counterculture movement.

1974

In a matter-of-fact style, this U.S. history textbook offered an excellent explanation of who the "hippies" were and what they believed, but it did not take a stand regarding their impact on society.

The style setters of the sixties were the hippies. They were the spiritual descendants of the Beat Generation of the late 1940's and 1950's. "Beatniks" rejected materialism and dabbled in mysticism. In the late 1950's, some of the beatniks moved to the Haight-Ashbury district of San Francisco, a neighborhood of Victorian houses. Members of a new generation were attracted to the area and took up some of the beatnik characteristics while rejecting others. These were "hippies," sometimes called flower children.

Hippies rejected some aspects of materialism—such as pursuing a career—while embracing other aspects—such as working long enough to buy a stereo set or a car. Pursuing a philosophy that stressed love and sharing, some hippies lived together in communal apartments and houses. Many smoked marijuana and experimented with other drugs. The hippies' hair flowed long and often uncombed; men were bearded; men and women wore patched jeans and army or navy surplus jackets.

Although the hippie movement attracted only a small minority of youth, its impact was great. Young people everywhere took up the dress and hair styles, if not the drug attitudes and philosophy, of the flower children. Young people dressing and acting as hippies could be seen hitchhiking on highways to San Francisco, Big Sur, Chicago, New York, and elsewhere. Often they would be packed into a camper painted with flowers or exotic designs. Typically, they would have a dog or two and a guitar. These were America's gypsy children.

Many nonhippies took to drugs. Like the hippies, they believed that marijuana was less dangerous than the alcohol their parents' generation drank. The use of marijuana became widespread. Drug users became younger and younger, and drugs of all kinds were widely used by high school and college students.[4]

1982

In the more conservative 1980s, this textbook emphasized that students who followed the hippy lifestyle were a small minority, and one that was looked down on by middle-class parents.

While some youths sought alternative experiences through drugs and music, others tried to construct alternative ways of life. Among the most conspicuous were the hippies who were drawn to the San Francisco Bay area. In the Haight-Ashbury section of the city, "flower children" created an urban subculture as distinctive as that of any Chinatown or Little Italy.

"Hashbury" inspired numerous other communal living experiments. Throughout the country, hitchhikers hit the road in search of communes, America, and themselves.

Just as the New Left attracted a minority of students, so the counter-culture represented only a small proportion of American youth. But to dis-concerted middle-class parents, hippies seemed to be everywhere. Parents carped about long hair, love beads, and patched jeans. They complained that "acid rock" was deafeningly loud, discordant, and even savage. And they feared their children would suffer lifelong damage from drugs. Per-haps most disturbing to parents were the casual sexual mores their chil-dren adopted, partly as a result of the availability of birth-control pills. For many young people, living together was no longer equivalent to living in sin. And as attitudes toward premarital sex changed, so did notions about pornography, nudity, homosexuality, sex roles, and familial relationships.[5]

1995

This textbook offered students a discussion of such topics as the sexual revolution and drug use, topics that would not have been found in high school history text-books prior to the 1970s.

People's appearances reflected the changes that were taking place. The hippies of the 1960s—men and women who self-consciously rejected con ventional norms—tried to look different. Women chose freer fashions, such as miniskirts and loose-fitting dresses. Men let their hair grow long and wore beards. Many hippies adopted the dress of working people, which seemed somehow more "authentic" than the school clothes of mid-dle-class youth. Therefore, men and women wore jeans, muslin (plain-woven cotton) shirts, and other simple garments that were intended to look handmade.

THE SEXUAL REVOLUTION

The new views about sexual behavior advanced by the counterculture were labeled "the sexual revolution." The young people who led this revo-lution demanded more freedom to make personal choices. Some argued that sex should be separated from its traditional ties to family life. Lynn

Ferrin, who moved to San Francisco to become part of the counterculture in California, remembered her feelings at the time:

> I was among the women in that whole vanguard of sexual freedom who were very excited by being free women. . . . In my circles, you wouldn't think of getting married, settling down with one person. The suburbs and the station wagon full of Cub Scouts became something you didn't want anything to do with.

The sexual revolution in the counterculture led to more open discussion of sexual subjects. Newspapers, magazines, and books published articles that might not have been printed, even in the recent past. The 1962 book by Helen Gurley Brown, *Sex and the Single Girl*, became a best-seller. In 1966 William H. Masters and Virginia E. Johnson shocked many people when they published *Human Sexual Response,* a report on their scientific studies of sexuality. Novels like D. H. Lawrence's *Lady Chatterly's Lover,* which had been banned in the United States since 1928 for being too explicit, now became available.

Many men and women also experimented with new living patterns. Some hippies rejected traditional relationships and lived together in communal groups. More and more people simply lived together as couples, without getting married.

THE DRUG SCENE

Also part of the 1960s counterculture were psychedelic drugs, which are drugs that cause the brain to behave abnormally. As a result, the brain produces hallucinations and other altered perceptions of reality. The beatniks had experimented with drugs a decade before, but they had been in the minority. Now drug use became more widespread among the nation's youth.

One early proponent of psychedelic drug use was researcher Timothy Leary, who worked at Harvard University with Richard Alpert on the chemical compound lysergic acid diethylamide, commonly known as LSD. The two men were fired from their research posts for using undergraduates in experiments with the drug. Leary then began to preach that drugs could help free the mind. He advised listeners, "Tune in, turn on, drop out."

Soldiers who had used drugs in Vietnam brought them home when their tours of duty were completed. Marijuana became common among middle-class college students. Todd Gitlin, a radical activist who became president of SDS, explained that "the point was to open up a new space, an *inner* space, so that we could space out, live for the sheer exultant point of living."

On the other side of the drug issue, however, was serious danger. Overdoses and deaths from accidents that occurred while under the influence of drugs caused concern in many quarters. Three leading musicians—Janis Joplin, Jim Morrison, and Jimi Hendrix—died of complications from drug overdoses. They were not the only ones. Their deaths represented the tragic excesses to which some people were driven by their reliance on drugs as an escape.[6]

50

Nixon in China

When dealing with President Richard Nixon, U.S. history textbooks usually focus on the Watergate scandal and his eventual resignation. Increasingly, however, historians have acknowledged the significance of Nixon's 1972 trip to China, an event that laid the groundwork for future relations between the two superpowers.

1975

This U.S. history textbook looked at Nixon's trip to China not only as another political move during the Cold War but also as a step toward ending the Vietnam War.

Throughout 1972, however, President Nixon seemed determined to pursue his own course of diplomacy and to make no concessions to his critics. In February he made a historic trip to China to talk to the leaders of Communist China and in May he visited Moscow. Both Communist states, now hostile to each other, welcomed the American President because each wanted better relations with the United States as a counterweight to the other. Both visits gave Nixon the opportunity to urge China and the Soviet Union to bring pressure on North Vietnam to end the war on terms acceptable to the United States. Possibly such pressures influenced the North Vietnamese to begin serious negotiations for a settlement in October of 1972. But even as the possibility of peace seemed near, the Vietnam War went into a final spasm of agony when President Nixon ordered an all-out bombing campaign against Hanoi because some new snags in the Paris talks seemed to doom a settlement on terms the United States could accept.[7]

1987

In this U.S. history textbook, the authors went so far as to claim that Nixon's visit to China was "an extraordinary diplomatic feat."

Nixon Makes New Overtures to the Soviet Union and China

Once President Nixon had awed his critics by moving toward peace in Vietnam, he was ready to make the diplomatic moves for which he would be long remembered. Nixon knew that American power was vastly overcommitted in the world. He knew, too, that the United States could no longer police the entire globe. But rather than simply reduce the American role in the world, the President and Henry Kissinger decided to take advantage of the divisions between the other major powers to maintain American supremacy. First and foremost in their plans was a desire to take advantage of the deep hostility between the two great communist powers, the Soviet Union and China.

Nixon hoped to use U.S. technological know-how and agricultural surpluses, both of which were badly needed by the Soviet Union and China, to shape those nations' policies. By holding out the bait of increased trade, the President hoped to gain access to the vast Chinese and Soviet markets for U.S. business. He also hoped to gain Soviet and Chinese help in bringing North Vietnam to the bargaining table.

In July 1971 Nixon, a person who had made his political reputation by taking a hard line against communism, stunned the world. He told a vast television audience that he had accepted an invitation to visit China. Conservative Republicans were shocked. They could not believe that this was the same Richard Nixon who had blamed China for the Korean War or who had fought so hard to keep China out of the United Nations. In February 1972 President Nixon visited the Chinese capital, Beijing. A new era in American diplomatic relations was underway.

The new relationship between China and the United States upset the Soviet Union, which had long been engaged in a war of words with China. Anticipating Soviet concern, Nixon visited the Soviet Union in 1972. In a televised address in Moscow, the President expressed the need for friendship and arms reduction as a part of a détente (relaxation of tensions) between the two superpowers. The visit also gave a significant boost to Strategic Arms Limitation Talks (SALT) between Washington and Moscow. The result was the SALT I treaty, ratified by the Senate in 1972, placing limitations on existing nuclear weapons.

The President had accomplished an extraordinary diplomatic feat. He had gained communist cooperation at a time when the United States was at war with communist North Vietnam. At the same time, he had made it clear to the world that national interest had become more important than ideology in U.S. foreign policy.[8]

5 1
_____

The Modern Feminist Movement

The feminist movement is often portrayed in U.S. history textbooks as a spin-off of the Civil Rights Movement. The presentation of this history has changed dramatically over the past forty years, reflecting not only the changing status of women in American society but also the increasing sophistication of women's history and the growing prominence of women in the history profession.

1966

Published the same year that the National Organization for Women was organized, this textbook discussed how women's roles were changing, but it did not mention the feminist movement as such.

The Changing Role of Women

One of the remarkable changes in America during the postwar years was the increasingly important role women were playing in the work life of the nation. The contrast with earlier years was striking. Where in 1910, for example, men made up most of the nation's work force, by the 1960's more than one-third of all gainfully employed workers were women.

Although the entrance of women into the work force had been gaining momentum since the beginning of the century, two major developments greatly speeded the process. First, the demand for manpower during World War II broke down many deeply rooted prejudices and gave women a chance to show that they could do as well as men in a great many different kinds of jobs. Second, and far more significant, the rapidly expanding economy created thousands of new jobs, nearly all of which called for skilled manpower rather than for muscle and brawn.

A large percentage of the gainfully employed women were married. A steadily growing number were entering the professions of medicine, law, education, religion, and the various fields of science and engineering. More and more were occupying positions of leadership in business and government formerly held only by men.

The movement of women into the work life of the nation actually represented a great social revolution. As one result of this development, the traditional patterns of family life were being altered, and the larger framework of society itself was being transformed.

The changing role of women was only one of the revolutionary developments that were transforming older ways of life. Even more far-reaching was the revolution that was transforming the relationships of Negroes and white persons in American society.[9]

1978

Published while the "women's liberation movement" was in full swing, this selection gave a short list of its demands.

Women Demand Equal Rights

In 1972 Congress approved another proposed amendment to the Constitution—the Twenty-Seventh Amendment—and sent it to the states for ratification. Called the "Women's Rights Amendment," it states that "equality of rights under the law shall not be denied or abridged by the United States or any State on account of sex."

Most Americans thought that the battle for equality between the sexes had been won in 1920, when women finally gained the right to vote. But the experience of many women, both at home and in the world of work, proved otherwise. Women found that they were usually offered lower paying and less-rewarding jobs; that they were paid lower wages than men doing similar work; and that they were seldom promoted to executive positions. Most men, they argued, wanted to keep women in the home and confine their activities to family chores. A number of women's organizations were formed, and in the last decade the "women's liberation movement" has gained wide publicity. These organizations are demanding "equal pay for equal work," day-care centers for the children of working mothers, and maternity leaves without loss of jobs for women who were having children.

By early 1974 the proposed Twenty-Seventh Amendment had been ratified by over thirty states. But it cannot become a part of the Constitution until two years after it has been approved by 38 of the states.[10]

1995

In comparison to earlier decades, by the 1990s the story of the feminist movement had expanded exponentially in U.S. history textbooks. What was once relegated to a brief paragraph or two had now exploded into pages of information, with the requisite photographs of women working in a variety of fields.

Active as they were in the civil rights movement and antiwar movements, women soon learned the male leaders of these causes were little different from corporate executives—they expected women to fix the food and type the communiqués while the men made the decisions. Understandably, women soon realized they could only achieve respect and equality by mounting their own protest.

In some ways, the position of women in American society was worse in the 1960s than it had been in the 1920s. After forty years, there was a lower percentage of women enrolled in the nation's colleges and professional schools. Women were still relegated to stereotyped occupations like nursing and teaching; there were few female lawyers and even fewer women doctors. And gender roles, as portrayed on television commercials, continued to call for the husband to be the breadwinner and the wife to be the homemaker. . . .

The 1964 Civil Rights Act helped women attack economic inequality head-on by making it illegal to discriminate in employment on the basis of sex. Women filed suit for equal wages, demanded that companies provide day care for their infants and preschool children, and entered politics to lobby against laws which—in the guise of protection to a weaker sex— were unfair to women. As the women's liberation movement grew, its advocates began to attack laws banning abortion and waged a campaign to toughen the enforcement of rape laws.

The women's movement met with many of the same obstacles as other protest groups in the 1960s. The moderate leadership of the National Organization for Women (NOW), founded by Betty Friedan in 1966, soon was challenged by those with more extreme views.[11]

52

The Camp David Accords

Before 9/11, U.S. history textbooks usually only looked at the Middle East as it re-lated to the formation of Israel in 1948 and the oil crisis of the 1970s. In the 1980s and 1990s, textbooks began to add more information about the region, but usu-ally cast it in terms of U.S. foreign policy challenges. Still, the only positive image conveyed to American students about the Middle East seems to be when the United States brokers a peace agreement.

1987

In what is otherwise usually portrayed as a dismal presidency, Jimmy Carter got credit in this selection for the peace treaty he helped broker. Every textbook pub-lished since the early 1980s tells this story, which is uniformly accompanied by the picture of Carter shaking hands with Anwar Sadat and Menachem Begin.

The Middle East Settlement Becomes Carter's Greatest Foreign Policy Success

President Carter's greatest foreign policy success came in the Middle East. The Arab countries and the Palestine Liberation Organization

(PLO) were pledged to destroy Israel. But Egypt, the most powerful of the Arab nations, began to take a new position on Israel.

First, Egyptian President Anwar Sadat removed all Soviet advisers from his country and established closer relations with the United States. Sadat also decided that solving Egypt's extremely severe economic problems was more important than destroying Israel. The next development came when Muammar el-Qaddafi, the leader of Egypt's oil-rich neighbor, Libya, made several attempts at overthrowing Sadat. When the Israeli secret service, the Mossad, saved Sadat from assassination by one of Qaddafi's gunmen, the stage was set for a historic development. Egypt became the first Arab nation to recognize the right of Israel to exist.

Egypt was bitterly criticized by other Arab states for breaking ranks. Cut off from the rest of the Arab world and exposed to military and economic pressure from Libya and Saudi Arabia, Egypt needed to conclude a treaty with Israel that would bring glory to Sadat by returning to Arab hands the land that Israel had captured in the 1967 Six-Days' War.

Negotiations between Sadat and Israeli Prime Minister Menachem Begin began in November 1977 but, by August of 1978, they had broken down. At this moment President Carter stepped in. He invited both Sadat and Begin to the Camp David presidential retreat in the mountains of western Maryland. There, in 13 grueling days of negotiations, Carter was able to convince the two leaders to sign on September 12, 1978, an agreement called the Camp David Accords, which paved the way for peace in the Middle East. Carter was widely hailed for his success at Camp David. It was the President's finest moment.[12]

1995

While Carter's reputation as a world political leader has vastly improved since his electoral defeat in 1980, he continues to get trounced in U.S. history textbooks.

The inconclusive results of the 1973 October War gave Henry Kissinger the opportunity to play the role of peacemaker in the troubled Middle East. Shuttling back and forth between Cairo and Jerusalem, and then to Damascus, the secretary of state finally succeeded in arranging a pullback of Israeli forces in both the Sinai and the Golan Heights. Although he failed to achieve his goal of an Arab-Israeli settlement,

Kissinger had succeeded in demonstrating that the United States could play the role of neutral mediator between the Israelis and Arabs. And equally important, he had detached Egypt from dependence on the Soviet Union, thereby weakening Russian influence in the Middle East.

In November 1977, Egyptian president Anwar Sadat stunned the world by traveling to Jerusalem in an effort to reach agreement directly with Israel. The next year, Carter invited both Sadat and Israeli prime minister Menachem Begin to negotiate under his guidance at Camp David. For thirteen days, President Carter met with Sadat and Begin, finally emerging with the ambiguous Camp David Accords. A framework for negotiations, rather than an actual peace settlement, the Camp David agreements dealt gingerly with the problem of Palestinian autonomy in the West Bank and Gaza Strip areas.

In 1979, Israel and Egypt signed a peace treaty that provided for the gradual return of the entire Sinai to Egypt but left the fate of the Palestine Arabs vague and unsettled. By excluding both the Palestine Liberation Organization (PLO) and the Soviet Union from the negotiations, the United States alienated Egypt from the other Arab nations and drove the more radical states closer to the Soviet Union.

Any sense of progress in the Middle East as a result of Camp David was quickly offset in 1979 with the outbreak of the Iranian Revolution.[13]

53

The Reagan Revolution

The Reagan revolution, which helped usher in a period of conservative politics in the United States, officially began in 1981 when Reagan was sworn into office. Reagan promised a hard-line toward Communism, supply-side economics, financial cuts in many government-funded programs, and a return to improved social and moral values. History textbooks, in fact, have come increasingly under attack since 1981 by conservatives, who argue that high school history textbooks have consistently downgraded the roles of white men, the military, and the U.S. government, all the while overglamorizing the roles of minorities, women, and other political ideologies deemed detrimental to America's youth.

1982

Written during the first year of the Reagan administration, this U.S. history textbook had a whiff of journalism about it, explaining both how Reagan was elected and what this new president hoped to accomplish while in office.

In 1980 Reagan triumphed easily over moderate Republicans like Representative John Anderson of Illinois, Senator Howard Baker of Tennessee, and former CIA director George Bush of Texas. And his appeal to the voters in the presidential campaign was much more widespread than observers had predicted. He promised economy in government and a balanced budget, and he committed himself to "supply-side" economics, or tax reductions to businesses to encourage capital investment. But while he planned to slash federal spending, Reagan also pledged to cut income taxes and boost the defense budget—a feat John Anderson said could only be done with mirrors. Reagan's stand against abortion and the ERA recommended him to the profamily movement.

Indeed, his candidacy united the old right wing with the new. The old right, explained one fund raiser, had never been very interested in social issues. "But when political conservative leaders began to reach out and strike an alliance with social conservatives—the pro-life people, the anti-ERA people, the evangelical and born-again Christians, the people concerned about gay rights, prayer in the schools, sex in the movies or whatever—that's when this whole movement began to come alive. It's happened in a big way just in the last two years, and it's just exploding."

As election day approached, some political analysts thought they detected a resurgence of support for Carter. Polls predicted a Reagan victory by 3 to 5 percent, a small margin given the country's problems. But on election day voters gave Reagan and his running mate, George Bush, 51 percent of the vote to 41 percent for Carter and 7 percent for Anderson. Reagan's sweep was nationwide; Carter carried only six states and the District of Columbia. Although the vote was partially an affirmation of Reagan's conservatism, it also signified deep dissatisfaction with Carter.[14]

1999

This lengthy section tried to offer an evenhanded assessment of Reagan and his policies. It gave credence to both his successes and to complaints from his opponents.

The hostage crisis became a key issue in Carter's bid for reelection. Carter fought off a strong challenge from Senator Edward Kennedy of Massachusetts for the Democratic nomination. As Election Day grew near, however, the American people became increasingly impatient with the situation in Iran.

The Republicans chose former California governor Ronald Reagan as their candidate. Reagan's chief opponents in the primaries were two moderate Republicans, former United Nations Ambassador George Bush and Illinois Representative John Anderson. After his nomination, Reagan picked Bush as his running mate.

The Republicans adopted a conservative platform calling for reductions in taxes and government spending in order to restore prosperity. The party did endorse higher defense spending to strengthen the role of the United States in world affairs.

Throughout the campaign, Reagan hammered at Carter's lack of leadership and the nation's weak economy. He promised voters economic growth and development. On Election Day, Reagan claimed victory with 51 percent of the popular vote and 489 electoral votes. Carter won 41 percent, with 49 electoral votes. John Anderson and other candidates of minor parties split the rest of the vote. The conservative tide that elected Reagan resulted in a Republican Senate and reduced the Democratic House of Representatives.

President Carter's failure to obtain release of the hostages sealed his defeat. Only after Ronald Reagan was sworn in on January 20, 1981, did Iran release the Americans, ending their 444 days in captivity.

Reagan's election indicated a significant conservative shift in Americans' political convictions. In addition to support from traditionally conservative groups such as fundamentalist Christians and antifeminists, many groups that had historically voted Democratic broke with their party and supported Reagan. These included former liberals, blue-collar workers, ethnic voters, and Southerners, who became known as "Reagan Democrats." The 69-year-old Reagan also attracted many older voters.

As a whole, the Reagan conservatives believed that the federal government should withdraw from most areas of domestic life.

They were against liberal social programs and government restrictions on business. In foreign policy, they favored a strong military to stand against communism. President Reagan acted quickly to limit the size of the federal government. His first act as President was to place a freeze on the hiring of federal employees. At the same time, he began to ease government controls on many business activities. He set up a task force headed by Vice President Bush to review federal regulations. As President,

Reagan moved to fulfill his campaign promise to get the economy going again. In February 1981, he told Americans:

> Since 1960 our government has spent $5.1 trillion. Our debt has grown to $648 billion. Prices have exploded by 178 percent. . . . [We] know we must act and act now. We must not be timid. . . .

To take care of the problem, Reagan proposed a new economic program, which came to be called "Reaganomics."

CUTTING TAXES

The first part of the President's program was to make deep cuts in federal taxes. He predicted that income tax reductions would increase consumer spending and would also encourage investments, especially by the wealthy. Similarly, cuts in corporate taxes would allow companies to expand production and hire more workers. Reagan's beliefs were based on an economic theory called supply-side economics, which claimed that the economy could best be stimulated by increasing the supply of goods rather than the demand.

REDUCING GOVERNMENT SPENDING

The second part of Reagan's program was to reduce government spending by ending federal job-training programs and cutting back the amount of federal money going into Medicare, food stamps, and education. Critics predicted that Reagan's proposal would cause great suffering for the economically disadvantaged. Reagan denied this, claiming that there would always be a "safety net" of government aid for truly needy Americans.

RESULTS OF REAGANOMICS

Although the President faced opposition to his proposals, he had personal qualities that helped to promote his position: a great ability to communicate with his audience and a sense of humor. In March 1981, when he was shot and seriously wounded, the President's aides visited him in the hospital. They assured him that the business of government was continuing as usual. "What makes you think I'd be happy about that?" Reagan quipped.

With his great popularity and shrewd handling of Congress, Reagan soon got much of his economic program passed. The final bill included $39 billion in tax cuts and a 25 percent cut in income taxes. The results of Reaganomics, however, were not quite what the President had hoped. Spending cuts, together with high interest rates, brought inflation down, but at first the cure was painful.[15]

NOTES

EDITOR'S NOTE

1. Frances Fitzgerald, *America Revised: History Schoolbooks in the Twentieth Century* (Boston: Little, Brown, 1979), 7.

INTRODUCTION

1. Benjamin F. Walker, *Curriculum Evolution as Portrayed Through Old Textbooks* (Terre Haute, IN: Curriculum Research and Development Center, 1976), 67.
2. Ibid., 2.
3. Charles Carpenter, *History of American Schoolbooks* (Philadelphia: University of Pennsylvania Press, 1963), 16–17.
4. John A. Nietz, *The Evolution of American Secondary School Textbooks; Rhetoric & Literature, Algebra, Geometry, Natural History (Zoology), Botany, Natural Philosophy (Physics), Chemistry, Latin and Greek, French, German & World History as Taught in American Latin Grammar School Academics and Early High Schools Before 1900* (Rutland, VT: C.E. Tuttle Co., 1966), 265.
5. Ibid., 267–68.
6. Ibid., 7.
7. D. Antonio Cantu and Warren Wilson, *Teaching History in the Digital Classroom* (New York: M.E. Sharpe, 2003), 4–5.
8. Nietz, *The Evolution of American Secondary School Textbooks*, 247.
9. These four publishing firms are Pearson, a British company; Vivendi Universal, a French company; Reed Elsevier, a British-Dutch company; and McGraw-Hill, the only U.S.-owned textbook publisher.
10. Frances Fitzgerald, *America Revised: History Schoolbooks in the Twentieth Century* (Boston: Little, Brown, 1979), 21–22.
11. Some argue this trend actually goes all the way back to the Reconstruction pe-

riod, when southern states adopted textbooks in order to give their own view of history.

1. EXPLORATION AND COLONIZATION

1. William Robertson, *The History of the Discovery and Conquest of America* (New York: Harper and Brothers, 1844), 243–44.

2. Harper's School History, *Narrative of the General Course of History* (New York: Harper and Brothers, 1856), 314–18.

3. William H. Seavey, *History of the United States of America: For the Use of Schools* (Boston: Brewer and Tileston, 1874), 21, 24.

4. Barnes Historical Series, *A Brief History of the United States* (New York: A.S. Barnes and Company, 1880), 13–14.

5. John Fiske, *A History of the United States for Schools* (Boston: Houghton Mifflin Company, 1899), 2–8.

6. James A. James and Albert Hart Sanford, *American History* (New York: Charles Scribner's Sons, 1912), 98–101.

7. John Bach McMaster, *A School History of the United States* (New York: American Book Company, 1916), 69–70.

8. David Saville Muzzey, *An American History* (Boston: Ginn and Company, 1920), 20.

9. Wilbur F. Gordy, *History of the United States* (New York: Charles Scribner's Sons, 1927), 17–22.

10. Paul F. Boller and E. Jean Tilford, *This Is Our Nation* (St. Louis, MO: Webster Publishing Co., 1961), 26–27.

11. John A. Garraty, *American History* (Orlando, FL: Harcourt Brace Jovanovich, 1986), 3–5.

12. Samuel G. Goodrich, *Lights and Shadows of American History* (Boston: Bradbury, Soden and Co., 1844), 34–38.

13. Mary Elise Thalheimer, *The Eclectic History of the United States* (New York: Van Antwerp, Bragg and Co., 1881), 10–12.

14. Lawton B. Evans, *The Essential Facts of American History* (Chicago: Benj. H. Sandborn and Co., 1914), 4–6.

15. Everett Augspurger and Robert A. McLemore, *Our Nation's Story* (Chicago: Laidlaw Brothers, 1954), 60–61.

16. James West Davidson and Michael B. Stoff, *The American Nation* (Englewood Cliffs, NJ: Prentice Hall, 1995), 54.

17. Noah Webster, *An American Selection of Lessons in Reading and Speaking* (Boston: Isaiah Thomas and Ebenezer T. Andrews, 1794), 85.

18. Salma Hale, *History of the United States, from Their First Settlement as Colonies, to the Close of the War with Great Britain in 1815* (Keene, NH: J. and J.W. Prentiss, 1830), 10.

19. John J. Anderson, *A Popular School History of the United States* (New York: Clark and Maynard Publishers, 1880), 21–22.

20. Leon Canfield et al., *The United States in the Making* (Boston: Houghton Mifflin Company, 1946), 11.

21. Davidson and Stoff, *The American Nation*, 68–70.

22. John Frost, *History of the United States: For the Use of Common Schools* (Philadelphia: Thomas, Cowperthwait, and Co., 1842), 20–22.

23. Augusta B. Berard, *School History of the United States* (Philadelphia: H. Cowperthwait and Co., 1855), 94–95.

24. William H. Seavey, *History of the United States of America: For the Use of Schools* (Boston: Brewer and Tileston, 1874), 15.

25. Fiske, *A History of the United States for Schools,* 51–52.

26. Thomas M. Marshall, *American History* (New York: Macmillan, 1933), 58.

27. Davidson and Stoff, *The American Nation,* 75.

28. Noah Webster, *An American Selection of Lessons in Reading and Speaking: Calculated to Improve the Minds and Refine the Taste of Youth* (Salem, MA: Cushing and Appleton, 1805), 92–94.

29. Frost, *History of the United States: For the Use of Common Schools,* 36.

30. Samuel G. Goodrich, *A Pictorial History of the United States with Notices of Other Portions of America North and South* (Philadelphia: E.H. Butler & Co., 1866), 40–43.

31. John J. Anderson, *A Grammar School History of the United States* (New York: Clark and Maynard, 1872), 19.

32. David H. Montgomery, *The Leading Facts of American History* (Boston: Ginn and Company, 1897), 53–54.

33. Herbert R. Cornish and Thomas H. Hughes, *History of the United States for Schools* (New York: Hinds, Hayden and Eldridge, Inc., 1936), 36.

34. Howard B. Wilder, Robert P. Ludlum, and Harriett McCune Brown, *This Is America's Story,* 4th ed. (Boston: Houghton Mifflin Co., 1978), 74, 76.

35. Robert A. Divine et al., *America Past and Present* (New York: HarperCollins College Publishers, 1995), 36.

36. Webster, *An American Selection of Lessons in Reading and Speaking* (1794), 92.

37. Samuel G. Goodrich, *Peter Parley's Common School History* (Philadelphia: William Marshall and Company, 1838), 338–39.

38. Goodrich, *Lights and Shadows of American History,* 207–9, 212–13.

39. Berard, *School History of the United States,* 13–14.

40. Cornish and Hughes, *History of the United States for Schools,* 35, 43–44.

41. Margaret S. Branson, *America's Heritage* (Lexington, MA: Ginn and Company, 1986), 50–51.

42. Webster, *An American Selection of Lessons in Reading and Speaking* (1794), 96–97.

43. Charles Prentiss, *History of the United States of America; With a Brief Account of Some of the Principal Empire & States of Ancient & Modern Times* (Keene, NH: John Prentiss, 1821), 74.

44. Berard, *School History of the United States,* 65–66.

45. Anderson, *A Popular School History of the United States,* 92–93.

46. Evans, *The Essential Facts of American History,* 87.

47. Hale, *History of the United States* (1830), 32–33.

48. Berard, *School History of the United States,* 16–17.

49. Seavey, *History of the United States of America,* 41

50. Evans, *The Essential Facts of American History,* 70–71.

51. Charles A. Beard and Mary R. Beard, *A Basic History of the United States* (New York: Doubleday, Doran and Company, 1944), 20–21.

52. Divine, *America Past and Present,* 49.

53. John Prentiss, *History of the United States of America,* 2nd ed. (Keene, NH: John Prentiss, 1823), 47–48.

54. Berard, *School History of the United States,* 34–35.

55. Goodrich, *A Pictorial History of the United States,* 100–101.

56. James and Sanford, *American History,* 94.

57. Cornish and Hughes, *History of the United States for Schools,* 72.

58. Mary Beth Norton et al., *A People and a Nation: A History of the United States* (Boston: Houghton Mifflin Company, 1982), 42–43.

2. THE AMERICAN REVOLUTION

1. John Prentiss, *History of the United States of America; With a Brief Account of Some of the Principal Empire & States of Ancient and Modern Times* (Keene, NH: John Prentiss, 1821), 126–27.

2. A.B. Berard, *School History of the United States* (Philadelphia: H. Cowperthwait & Co., 1855), 90–91.

3. Samuel G. Goodrich, *A Pictorial History of the United States with Notices of Other Portions of America North and South* (Philadelphia: E.H. Butler & Co., 1866, 150–51.

4. John Fiske, *A History of the United States for Schools* (Boston: Houghton Mifflin Company, 1899), 168–69.

5. Herbert R. Cornish and Thomas H. Hughes, *History of the United States for Schools* (New York: Hinds, Hayden and Eldridge, Inc., 1936), 93–95.

6. Howard B. Wilder, Robert P. Ludlum, and Harriett McCune Brown, *This Is America's Story* (Boston: Houghton Mifflin Co., 1950), 120–21.

7. Lewis Paul Todd and Merle Curti, *Rise of the American Nation,* 2nd ed. (New York: Harcourt, Brace and World, Inc., 1966), 49.

8. Mary Beth Norton et al., *A People and a Nation: A History of the United States* (Boston: Houghton Mifflin Company, 1982), 88–89.

9. John Prentiss, *History of the United States of America,* 2nd ed. (Keene, NH: John Prentiss, 1823), 141–42.

10. Berard, *School History of the United States,* 113–15.

11. Harper's School History, *Narrative of the General Course of History* (New York: Harper and Brothers, 1856), 368–69.

12. Goodrich, *A Pictorial History of the United States,* 176–77.

13. John J. Anderson, *A Popular School History of the United States* (New York: Clark and Maynard Publishers, 1880), 127–28.

14. Cornish and Hughes, *History of the United States for Schools,* 116.

15. Daniel J. Boorstin and Brooks M. Kelley, *A History of the United States* (Upper Saddle River, NJ: Prentice Hall, 1996), 81.

16. Noah Webster, *An American Selection of Lessons in Reading and Speaking,* 5th ed. (Boston: Isaiah Thomas and Ebenezer T. Andrews, 1794), 123–24.

17. Salma Hale, *History of the United States, from Their First Settlement as Colonies, to the Close of the War with Great Britain in 1815* (Keene NH: J. and J.W. Prentiss, 1830), 147.

18. Samuel G. Goodrich, *Lights and Shadows of American History* (Boston: Bradbury, Soden and Co., 1844), 257–58.

19. Fiske, *A History of the United States for Schools,* 203–5.

20. Charles A. Beard and Mary R. Beard, *A Basic History of the United States* (New York: Doubleday, Doran and Company, 1944), 103–4.

21. Howard B. Wilder, Robert P. Ludlum, and Harriett McCune Brown, *This Is America's Story,* 4th ed. (Boston: Houghton Mifflin Co., 1978), 151–53.

22. David A. Ritchie, *American History: The Modern Era Since 1865* (New York: Glencoe McGraw-Hill, 1999), 47.

23. Jesse Olney, *A History of the United States, on a New Plan, Adapted to the Capacity of Youth* (New Haven, CT: Durrie and Peck, 1851), 156.

24. Goodrich, *A Pictorial History of the United States*, 246–47.

25. Emerson David Fite, *History of the United States* (New York: Henry Holt and Company, 1916), 152–53.

26. William Grimshaw, *History of the United States from Their Settlement as Colonies, to the Peace with Mexico, in 1848* (Philadelphia: Lippincott, Grambo, and Co., 1851), 178–79.

27. *A Popular History of the United States of America* (New York: A.S. Barnes and Company, 1878), 261–62.

28. James W. Davidson and Michael B. Stoff, *The American Nation* (Englewood Cliffs, NJ: Prentice Hall, 1995), 177–79.

3. THE NEW NATION

1. *Outlines of American History: From the First Discovery to the Present Time* (Philadelphia: Thomas, Cowperthwait and Co., 1845), 139–40.

2. William H. Seavey, *History of the United States of America; For the Use of Schools* (Boston: Brewer and Tileston, 1874), 182.

3. Henry William Elson and Cornelia Eliza MacMullan, *The Story of Our Country* (New York: Thompson Brown Company, 1911), 70–72.

4. Thomas M. Marshall, *American History* (New York: Macmillan, 1933), 266.

5. Richard N. Current, Alexander DeConde, and Harris L. Dante, *United States History: Search for Freedom* (Glenview, IL.: Scott, Foresman and Company, 1974), 129–30.

6. Andrew Cayton, Elisabeth Israels Perry, and Allen M. Winkler, *America: Pathways to the Present* (Englewood Cliffs, NJ: Prentice Hall, 1995), 96.

7. *A Popular History of the United States of America* (New York: A.S. Barnes and Company, 1878), 409.

8. Henry W. Elson, *Side Lights on American History* (New York: Macmillan, 1900), 168–73.

9. David Saville Muzzey, *An American History* (Boston: Ginn and Company, 1920), 206–8.

10. Charles A. Beard and Mary R. Beard, *A Basic History of the United States* (New York: Doubleday, Doran and Company, 1944), 177–78.

11. Paul F. Boller and E. Jean Tilford, *This Is Our Nation* (St. Louis, MO: Webster Publishing Co., 1961), 217.

12. David A. Ritchie, *American History: The Modern Era Since 1865* (New York: Glencoe McGraw-Hill, 1999), 146.

13. *Outlines of American History*, 151.

14. Elson, *Side Lights on American History*, 208–22.

15. Mary Beth Norton et al., *A People and a Nation: A History of the United States* (Boston: Houghton Mifflin Company, 1982), 329.

16. Marcius Willson, *History of the United States, for the Use of Schools* (New York: Mark H. Newman & Co., 1849), 336–37.

17. Alexander Johnston, *A History of the United States for Schools* (New York: Henry Holt and Company, 1889), 210–11.

18. Emerson David Fite, *History of the United States* (New York: Henry Holt and Company, 1916), 275–76.

19. Ruth Wood Gavin and William A. Hamm, *The American Story: A History of the United States of America* (Boston: D.C. Heath and Company, 1947), 212–13.

20. Current, DeConde, and Dante, *United States History*, 164–65.

21. Cayton, Perry, and Winkler, *America*, 117–18.

22. Samuel G. Goodrich, *A Pictorial History of the United States with Notices of Other Portions of America North and South* (Philadelphia: E.H. Butler and Co., 1866), 438–39.

23. David H. Montgomery, *The Leading Facts of American History* (Boston: Ginn & Company, 1897), 249–50.

24. Beard and Beard, *A Basic History of the United States,* 191–92.

25. Lewis Paul Todd and Merle Curti, *Rise of the American Nation,* 2nd ed. (New York: Harcourt, Brace & World, Inc., 1966), 326–27.

26. Cayton, Perry, and Winkler, *America,* 151.

27. George P. Quackenbos, *Illustrated School History of the United States* (New York: D. Appleton and Co., 1867), 421.

28. *A Popular History of the United States of America,* 445.

29. John Fiske, *A History of the United States for Schools* (Boston: Houghton Mifflin Company, 1899), 337.

30. Albert Bushnell Hart, *Essentials in American History: From Discovery to the Present Day* (New York: American Book Company, 1905), 330–31.

31. Fite, *History of the United States,* 277–78.

32. Howard B. Wilder, Robert P. Ludlum, and Harriett McCune Brown, *This Is America's Story* (Boston: Houghton Mifflin Co., 1950), 341.

33. Boller and Tilford, *This Is Our Nation,* 272.

34. Robert A. Divine et al., *America Past and Present* (New York: HarperCollins College Publishers, 1995), 347.

35. Willson, *History of the United States, for the Use of Schools,* 346–47.

36. John J. Anderson, *A Popular School History of the United States* (New York: Clark and Maynard Publishers, 1880), 241–42.

37. Elson and MacMullan, *The Story of Our Country,* 132–33.

38. Todd and Curti, *Rise of the American Nation,* 323–24.

39. James W. Davidson and Michael B. Stoff, *The American Nation* (Englewood Cliffs, NJ: Prentice Hall, 1995), 366.

4. THE CIVIL WAR ERA

1. William Grimshaw, *History of the United States from Their First Settlement as Colonies, to the Peace with Mexico, in 1848* (Philadelphia: Lippincott, Grambo, and Co., 1851), 300–301.

2. Harper's School History, *Narrative of the General Course of History* (New York: Harper & Brothers, 1856), 446–47, 450.

3. Alexander Johnston, *A History of the United States for Schools* (New York: Henry Holt and Company, 1889), 24, 59.

4. Henry W. Elson, *Side Lights on American History* (New York: Macmillan, 1900), 149–55.

5. Thomas M. Marshall, *American History* (New York: Macmillan, 1933), 340–42.

6. Howard B. Wilder, Robert P. Ludlum, and Harriett McCune Brown, *This Is America's Story* (Boston: Houghton Mifflin Co., 1950), 286–87.

7. Paul F. Boller and E. Jean Tilford, *This Is Our Nation* (St. Louis, MO: Webster Publishing Co., 1961), 243.

8. Richard N. Current, Alexander DeConde, and Harris L. Dante, *United States History: Search for Freedom* (Glenview, IL: Scott, Foresman and Company, 1974), 170–71.

9. Andrew Cayton, Elisabeth Israels Perry, and Allen M. Winkler, *America: Pathways to the Present* (Englewood Cliffs, NJ: Prentice Hall, 1995), 109.

10. Samuel G. Goodrich, *A Pictorial History of the United States with Notices of Other Portions of America North and South* (Philadelphia: E.H. Butler and Co., 1866), 469.

11. John Fiske, *A History of the United States for Schools* (Boston: Houghton Mifflin Company, 1899), 366–67.

12. Emerson David Fite, *History of the United States* (New York: Henry Holt and Company, 1916), 381–82.

13. Wilder, Ludlum, and Brown, *This Is America's Story*, 371, 373.

14. Robert A. Divine et al., *America Past and Present* (New York: HarperCollins College Publishers, 1995), 438.

15. William H. Seavey, *History of the United States of America; For the use of Schools* (Boston: Brewer and Tileston, 1874), 226.

16. Fiske, *A History of the United States for Schools*, 367–68.

17. James A. James and Albert Hart Sanford, *American History* (New York: Charles Scribner's Sons, 1912), 364–65.

18. Lewis Paul Todd and Merle Curti, *Rise of the American Nation*, 2nd ed. (New York: Harcourt, Brace & World, Inc., 1966), 363.

19. John A. Garraty, *American History* (Orlando, FL: Harcourt Brace Jovanovich, 1986), 442–44.

20. Cayton, Perry, and Winkler, *America*, 181.

21. Seavey, *History of the United States of America*, 274–75.

22. Johnston, *A History of the United States for Schools*, 325.

23. Fiske, *A History of the United States for Schools*, 406.

24. Thomas A. Bailey and David M. Kennedy, *The American Pageant: A History of the Republic* (Lexington, MA: D.C. Heath and Company, 1994), 600.

25. John Andrew Doyle, *History of the United States* (New York: Henry Holt and Company, 1876), 376–77.

26. Henry William Elson and Cornelia Eliza MacMullan, *The Story of Our Country* (New York: Thompson Brown Company, 1911), 219–23.

27. Ibid.

28. Marshall, *American History*, 440.

29. John M. Blum et al., *The National Experience: A History of the United States* (New York: Harcourt Brace Jovanovich, 1973), 353–54.

30. Cayton, Perry, and Winkler, *America*, 215.

31. *A Popular History of the United States of America* (New York: A.S. Barnes & Company, 1878), 604–5, 608.

32. David H. Montgomery, *The Leading Facts of American History* (Boston: Ginn & Company, 1897), 328–29.

33. James and Sanford, *American History*, 414–16.

34. Thomas Jefferson Wertenbaker and Donald E. Smith, *The United States of America: A History*, (New York: Charles Scribner's Sons, 1933), 417–18.

35. Wilder, Ludlum, and Brown, *This Is America's Story*, 371, 398–99.

36. Current DeConde, and Dante, *United States History*, 289–91.

37. Cayton, Perry, and Winkler, *America*, 237–38.

38. Johnston, *A History of the United States for Schools*, 382.

39. Lawton B. Evans, *The Essential Facts of American History* (Chicago: Benj. H. Sanborn & Co., 1914), 440–41.

40. Fite, *History of the United States*, 416–18.

41. Herbert R. Cornish and Thomas H. Hughes, *History of the United States for Schools* (New York: Hinds, Hayden & Eldridge, Inc. 1936), 345, 348–50.

42. David Saville Muzzey, *A History of Our Country: A Textbook for High School Students* (Boston: Ginn and Company, 1948), 433–34.
43. Boller and Tilford, *This Is Our Nation*, 342–43.
44. Daniel J. Boorstin and Brooks Mather Kelley, *A History of the United States* (Upper Saddle River, NJ: Prentice Hall, 1996), 373–74.

5. INDUSTRIALIZATION, IMPERIALISM, AND WAR

1. James A. James and Albert Hart Sanford, *American History* (New York: Charles Scribner's Sons, 1912), 493.
2. David Saville Muzzey, *An American History* (Boston: Ginn and Company, 1920), 441–42.
3. Lewis Paul Todd and Merle Curti, *Rise of the American Nation*, 2nd ed. (New York: Harcourt, Brace & World, Inc., 1966), 499–500.
4. Mary Beth Norton et al., *A People and a Nation: A History of the United States* (Boston: Houghton Mifflin Company, 1982), 489.
5. Robert A. Divine et al., *America Past and Present* (New York: HarperCollins College Publishers, 1995), 612.
6. Albert Bushnell Hart, *Essentials in American History: From Discovery to the Present Day* (New York: American Book Company, 1905), 536.
7. Emerson David Fite, *History of the United States* (New York: Henry Holt and Company, 1916), 433–34.
8. Thomas J. Wertenbaker and Donald E. Smith, *The United States of America: A History* (New York: Charles Scribner's Sons, 1933), 595–96.
9. Herbert R. Cornish and Thomas H. Hughes, *History of the United States for Schools* (New York: Hinds, Hayden and Eldridge, Inc., 1936), 35.
10. Howard B. Wilder, Robert P. Ludlum, and Harriett McCune Brown, *This Is America's Story* (Boston: Houghton Mifflin Co., 1950), 371, 373.
11. Paul F. Boller and E. Jean Tilford, *This Is Our Nation* (St. Louis, MO: Webster Publishing Co., 1961), 660–61.
12. John A. Garraty, *American History* (Orlando, FL: Harcourt Brace Jovanovich, 1986), 568–72.
13. Muzzey, *An American History*, 533.
14. Wertenbaker and Smith, *The United States of America*, 522–23.
15. Boller and Tilford, *This Is Our Nation*, 259–60.
16. Howard B. Wilder, Robert P. Ludlum, and Harriett McCune Brown, *This Is America's Story*, 4th ed. (Boston: Houghton Mifflin Co., 1978), 544.
17. James W. Davidson and Michael B. Stoff, *The American Nation* (Englewood Cliffs, NJ: Prentice Hall, 1995), 607–8.
18. Hart, *Essentials in American History*, 552.
19. Muzzey, *An American History*, 452.
20. Wertenbaker and Smith, *The United States of America*, 488–89.
21. Glen W. Moon and Don C. Cline, *Story of Our Land and People* (New York: Holt, Rinehart and Winston, 1961), 583–84.
22. Garraty, *American History*, 621–22.
23. Joel D. Steele and Esther Baker Steele, *Barnes's School History of the United States* (New York: American Book Company, 1903), 350–51.
24. John Bach McMaster, *A School History of the United States* (New York: American Book Company, 1916), 477–78.
25. Wilbur F. Gordy, *History of the United States* (New York: Charles Scribner's Sons, 1927), 428, 430–33.

26. Wilder, Ludlum, and Brown, *This Is America's Story*, 371, 551.
27. Moon and Cline, *Story of Our Land and People*, 586–87.
28. Daniel J. Boorstin and Brooks Mather Kelley, *A History of the United States* (Upper Saddle River, NJ: Prentice Hall, 1996), 514–15.
29. Muzzey, *An American History*, 518.
30. David Saville Muzzey, *A History of Our Country: A Textbook for High School Students* (Boston: Ginn and Company, 1948), 694–95.
31. Norton, *A People and a Nation*, 654–55.
32. Muzzey, *An American History*, 526–28.
33. George Earl Freeland and James Truslow Adams, *America's Progress in Civilization* (New York: Charles Scribner's Sons, 1946), 499–502.
34. Todd and Curti, *Rise of the American Nation*, 634–36.
35. Davidson and Stoff, *The American Nation*, 668–71.

6. THE GREAT DEPRESSION AND WORLD WAR II

1. Thomas Jefferson Wertenbaker and Donald E. Smith, *The United States of America: A History* (New York: Charles Scribner's Sons, 1933), 611–12.
2. Charles A. Beard and Mary R. Beard, *A Basic History of the United States* (New York: Doubleday, Doran and Company, 1944), 452–53.
3. Richard N. Current, Alexander DeConde, and Harris L. Dante, *United States History: Search for Freedom* (Glenview, IL: Scott, Foresman and Company, 1974), 470.
4. David A. Ritchie, *American History: The Modern Era Since 1865* (New York: Glencoe McGraw-Hill, 1999), 514–17.
5. David Saville Muzzey, *A History of Our Country: A Textbook for High School Students* (Boston: Ginn and Company, 1948), 847–48.
6. Lewis Paul Todd and Merle Curti, *Rise of the American Nation*, 2nd ed. (New York: Harcourt, Brace and World, Inc., 1966), 678–79.
7. Thomas A. Bailey and David M. Kennedy, *The American Pageant: A History of the Republic* (Lexington, MA: D.C. Heath and Company, 1994), 811–12.
8. Leon Canfield et al., *The United States in the Making* (Boston: Houghton Mifflin Co., 1946), 870.
9. Glen W. Moon and Don C. Cline, *Story of Our Land and People* (New York: Holt, Rinehart and Winston, 1957), 49.
10. Current, DeConde, and Dante, *United States History*, 552, 554.
11. James W. Davidson and Michael B. Stoff, *The American Nation* (Englewood Cliffs, NJ: Prentice Hall, 1995), 760.
12. Robert Riegel and Helen Haugh, *The United States of America: A History* (New York: Charles Scribner's Sons, 1947), 784.
13. Current, DeConde, and Dante, *United States History*, 542.
14. Davidson and Stoff, *The American Nation*, 750–52.
15. Beard and Beard, *A Basic History of the United States*, 474–75.
16. Howard B. Wilder, Robert P. Ludlum, and Harriett McCune Brown, *This Is America's Story* (Boston: Houghton Mifflin Co., 1950), 615–16.
17. Todd and Curti, *Rise of the American Nation*, 727.
18. Daniel J. Boorstin and Brooks Mather Kelley, *A History of the United States* (Upper Saddle River, NJ: Prentice Hall, 1996), 677–78.
19. Riegel and Haugh, *The United States of America*, 794.
20. Everett Augspurger and Robert A. McLemore, *Our Nation's Story* (Laidlaw Brothers, 1954), 736–37.

21. Todd and Curti, *Rise of the American Nation,* 739.

22. Robert A. Divine et al., *America Past and Present* (New York: HarperCollins College Publishers, 1995), 844–45.

7. THE COLD WAR AND POSTWAR AMERICA

1. Glen W. Moon and Don C. Cline, *Story of Our Land and People* (New York: Holt, Rinehart and Winston, 1961), 603–4.

2. Nathaniel Platt and Muriel Jean Drummond, *Our Nation from Its Creation,* 2nd ed. (Englewood Cliffs, NJ: Prentice Hall, 1966), 827.

3. Gary B. Nash, *American Odyssey: The United States in the Twentieth Century* (Lake Forest, IL: Glencoe Macmillan, 1992), 466.

4. Everett Augspurger and Robert A. McLemore, *Our Nation's Story* (Chicago: Laidlaw Brothers, 1954), 786.

5. Paul F. Boller and E. Jean Tilford, *This Is Our Nation* (St. Louis, MO: Webster Publishing Co., 1961), 655–56.

6. James W. Davidson and Michael B. Stoff, *The American Nation* (Englewood Cliffs, NJ: Prentice Hall, 1995), 780.

7. John W. Caughney, John Hope Franklin, and Ernest May, *Land of the Free: A History of the United States* (Pasadena, CA: Franklin Publications, Inc., 1967), 610–12.

8. Richard N. Current, Alexander DeConde, and Harris L. Dante, *United States History: Search for Freedom* (Glenview, IL: Scott, Foresman and Company, 1974), 577–78, 589–90.

9. David A. Ritchie, *American History: The Modern Era Since 1865* (New York: Glencoe McGraw-Hill, 1999), 628.

10. Lewis Paul Todd and Merle Curti, *Rise of the American Nation,* 2nd ed. (New York: Harcourt, Brace & World, Inc., 1966), 805.

11. Current, DeConde, and Dante, *United States History,* 599–600.

12. Ritchie, *American History,* 674.

13. Martin W. Sandler, Edwin C. Rozwenc, and Edward C. Martin, *The People Make a Nation* (Boston: Allyn and Bacon, Inc., 1975), 520.

14. John A. Garraty, *American History* (Orlando, FL: Harcourt Brace Jovanovich, 1986), 840–41.

15. Nash, *American Odyssey,* 488.

16. Todd and Curti, *Rise of the American Nation,* 789.

17. Current, DeConde, and Dante, *United States History,* 592–93, 639.

18. Thomas A. Bailey and David M. Kennedy, *The American Pageant: A History of the Republic* (Lexington, MA: D.C. Heath and Company, 1994), 933–34.

8. THE VIETNAM ERA

1. Oscar Handlin, *America: A History* (New York: Holt, Rinehart and Winston, 1967), 1045–47.

2. Mary Beth Norton et al., *A People and a Nation: A History of the United States* (Boston: Houghton Mifflin Company, 1982), 907.

3. Gary B. Nash, *American Odyssey: The United States in the Twentieth Century* (Lake Forest, IL: Glencoe Macmillan, 1992), 657–58.

4. Richard N. Current, Alexander DeConde, and Harris L. Dante, *United States History: Search for Freedom* (Glenview, IL: Scott, Foresman and Company, 1974), 648.

5. Norton, *A People and a Nation,* 941–42.

6. Andrew Cayton, Elisabeth Israels Perry, and Allen M. Winkler, *America: Pathways to the Present* (Englewood Cliffs, NJ: Prentice Hall, 1995), 729–30.

7. Martin W. Sandler, Edwin C. Rozwenc, and Edward C. Martin, *The People Make a Nation* (Boston: Allyn and Bacon, Inc., 1975), 541.

8. Carol Berkin and Leonard Wood, *Land of Promise: A History of the United States*, 2nd ed. (Glenview, IL: Scott, Foresman and Company, 1987), 794.

9. Lewis Paul Todd and Merle Curti, *Rise of the American Nation*, 2nd ed. (New York: Harcourt, Brace & World, Inc., 1966), 803.

10. Howard B. Wilder, Robert P. Ludlum, and Harriett McCune Brown, *This Is America's Story*, 4th ed. (Boston: Houghton Mifflin Co., 1978), 714.

11. Robert A. Divine et al., *America Past and Present* (New York: HarperCollins College Publishers, 1995), 942–43.

12. Berkin and Wood, *Land of Promise*, 810.

13. Divine, *America Past and Present*, 965–66.

14. Norton, *A People and a Nation*, 979–81.

15. Donald A. Ritchie, *American History: The Modern Era Since 1865* (New York: Glencoe McGraw-Hill, 1999), 753–56.

BIBLIOGRAPHY

A Brief History of the United States. New York: A.S. Barnes and Company, 1880.

Anderson, J.J. *The United States Reader: Embracing Selections from Eminent American Historians, Orators, Statesmen and Poets, with Explanatory Observations, Notes, etc.* New York: Clark and Maynard, 1873.

————. *A Popular School History of the United States, in Which Are Inserted as Part of the Narrative Selections from the Writings of Eminent American Historians, and Other American Writers of Note.* New York: Clark & Maynard Publishers, 1880.

A Popular History of the United States of America. New York: A.S. Barnes and Company, 1878.

Augsperger, Everett, and Robert A. McLemore. *Our Nation's Story.* Chicago: Laidlaw Brothers, 1954.

Bailey, T.A., and D.M. Kennedy. *The American Pageant: A History of the Republic.* Lexington, MA: D.C. Heath and Company, 1994.

Beard, C.A., and W.C. Bagley. *The History of the American People.* New York: Macmillan, 1920.

Beard, C.A., and M.R. Beard. *A Basic History of the United States.* New York: Doubleday, Doran and Company, 1944.

Belford, R.J. *A History of the United States in Chronological Order from A.D. 432 to the Present Time.* New York: World, 1886.

Berard, A.B. *School History of the United States.* Philadelphia: H. Cowperthwait & Co., 1855.

Berkin, C., and L. Wood. *Land of Promise: A History of the United States.* 2nd ed. Glenview, IL: Scott, Foresman and Company, 1987.

Blum, J.M., et al. *The National Experience: A History of the United States.* New York: Harcourt Brace Jovanovich, 1973.

Boller, P.F., and E.J. Tilford. *This Is Our Nation*. St. Louis, MO: Webster Publishing Co., 1961.

Boorstin, D.J., and B.M. Kelley. *A History of the United States*. Upper Saddle River, NJ: Prentice Hall, 1996.

Branson, M.S. *America's Heritage*. Lexington, MA: Ginn and Company, 1986.

Campbell, L.J. *A Concise History of the United States Based on Seavey's Goodrich's History*. Boston: Brewer and Tileston, 1874.

Cantu, D.A., and W. Wilson. *Teaching History in the Digital Classroom*. New York: M.E. Sharpe, 2003.

Carpenter, C. *History of American Schoolbooks*. Philadelphia: University of Pennsylvania Press, 1963.

Caughney, J.W., J.H. Franklin, and E. May. *Land of the Free: A History of the United States*. Pasadena, CA: Franklin Publications, Inc., 1967.

Cayton, A., E.I. Perry, and A.M. Winkler. *America: Pathways to the Present*. Englewood Cliffs, NJ: Prentice Hall, 1995.

Cornish, H.R., and T.H. Hughes. *History of the United States for Schools*. New York: Hinds, Hayden & Eldridge, Inc., 1936.

Creery, W.R. *Catechism of the History of the United States; with Questions on the Constitution of the United States and the Constitution of Maryland, Also a List of Presidents, Vice Presidents and Cabinet Officers, from the Formation of the Government to the Year 1869, Inclusive*. Baltimore, MD: Baltimore Publishing Co., 1869.

Current, R.N., A. DeConde, and H.L. Dante. *United States History: Search for Freedom*. Glenview, IL: Scott, Foresman and Company, 1974.

Darby, W., and T. Dwight Jr. *A New Gazetteer of the United States of America*. Hartford, CT: Edward Hopkins, 1833.

Davidson, J.W., and M.B. Stoff. *The American Nation*. Englewood Cliffs, NJ: Prentice Hall, 1995.

Divine, R.A., et al. *America Past and Present*. New York: HarperCollins College Publishers, 1995.

Doyle, J.A. *History of the United States*. New York: Henry Holt and Company, 1876.

Elson, H.W. *Side Lights on American History*. New York: Macmillan, 1900.

———. *Modern Times and the Living Past*. New York: American Book Company, 1935.

Elson, H.W., and C.E. MacMullan. *The Story of Our Country*. New York: Thompson Brown and Company, 1911.

Emerson, J. *Questions and Supplement to Goodrich's History of the United States*. Boston: Jenks, Palmer & Co., 1851.

Evans, L.B. *The Essential Facts of American History*. Chicago: Benj. H. Sanborn and Co., 1914.

Fiske, J. *A History of the United States for Schools*. Boston: Houghton Mifflin Company, 1899.

———. *The Critical Period of American History: 1783–1789*. Boston: Houghton Mifflin Company, 1899.

Fite, E.D. *History of the United States*. New York: Henry Holt and Company, 1916.

Fitzgerald, F. *America Revised: History Schoolbooks in the Twentieth Century*. Boston: Little, Brown, 1979.

Foster, E.G. *A History of the United States*. Topeka, KS: Historical Publishing Company, 1914.

Freeland, G.E., and J.T. Adams. *America's Progress in Civilization*. New York: Charles Scribner's Sons, 1946.

Frost, J. *History of the United States: For the Use of Common Schools*. Philadelphia: Thomas, Cowperthwait, & Co., 1842.

Gammell, W., and J.B. Moore. *Makers of American History*. New York: University Society, Inc., 1904.

Garraty, J.A. *American History*. Orlando, FL: Harcourt Brace Jovanovich, 1986.

Gavin, R.W., and W.A. Hamm. *The American Story: A History of the United States of America*. Boston: D.C. Heath and Company, 1947.

Goodrich, C.A. *A History of the United States of America on a Plan Adapted to the Capacity of Youths, and Designed to Aid the Memory by Systematic Arrangement and Interesting Associations*. 35th ed. Boston: Richardson, Lord & Hobrook, 1822.

———. *Questions on the Enlarged and Improved Edition of Goodrich's School History of the United States*. Boston: Jenks & Palmer, 1846.

———. *History of the United States of America; for the Use of Schools*. Boston: Brewer and Tileston, 1874.

Goodrich, S.G. *Peter Parley's Common School History*. Philadelphia: William Marshall and Company, 1838.

———. *Lights and Shadows of American History*. Boston: Bradbury, Soden and Co., 1844.

———. *A Pictorial History of the United States with Notices of Other Portions of America North and South*. Philadelphia: E.H. Butler & Co., 1866.

Gordy, W.F. *History of the United States*. New York: Charles Scribner's Sons, 1927.

Grimshaw, W. *History of the United States from Their First Settlement as Colonies, to the Peace with Mexico, in 1848. Comprising Every Important Political Event; with a Progressive View of the Aborigines; Population, Agriculture, and Commercial; of the Arts, Sciences, and Literature; and Occasional Biographies of the Most Remarkable Colonists, Writers and Philosophers, Warriors and Statesmen*. Philadelphia: Lippincott, Grambo, & Co., 1851.

Guernsey, E. *History of the United States of America, Designed for Schools. Extending from the Discovery of America by Columbus to the Present Time; with Numerous Maps and Engravings, Together with a Notice of American Antiquities, and the Indian Tribes*. 3rd ed. New York: Cady and Burgess, 1848.

Hale, S. *History of the United States, from Their First Settlement as Colonies, to the Close of the War with Great Britain in 1815*. Keene, NH: J. and J.W. Prentiss, 1830.

———. *History of the United States, from Their First Settlement as Colonies, to the Close of the War with Great Britain in 1815*. Keene, NH: J. and J.W. Prentiss, 1833.

Hale, S.S.R., and A.R. Baker. *School History of the United States; Containing Chronological Notices, and an Outline of Topics for a More Extended Course of Study; Together with Copious Notes*. Boston: William Pierce, 1836.

Handlin, O. *America: A History*. New York: Holt, Rinehart and Winston, 1967.

Harper's School History. Narrative of the General Course of History from the Earliest Periods to the Establishment of the American Constitution. New York: Harper & Brothers, 1856.

Hart, A.B. *Essentials in American History: From Discovery to the Present Day*. New York: American Book Company, 1905.

Hicks, J.D. *The American Nation: A History of the United States from 1865 to the Present*. Boston: Houghton Mifflin Company, 1946.

Hughes, R.O. *Problems of American Democracy*. Boston: Allyn and Bacon, 1922.

———. *The Making of Today's World*. Boston: Allyn and Bacon, 1955.

James, J.A. and A.H. Sanford. *American History.* New York: Charles Scribner's Sons, 1912.

Johnston, A. *A History of the United States for Schools with an Introductory History of the Discovery and English Colonization of North America with Maps, Plans, Illustrations, and Questions.* New York: Henry Holt and Company, 1889.

Jordan, W.D., et al. *The United States.* 5th ed. Englewood Cliffs, NJ: Prentice Hall, 1982.

Lossing, B.J. *An Outline History of the United States, for Public and Other Schools; from the Earliest Period to the Present Time.* New York: Sheldon & Company, 1875.

Marshall, T.M. *American History.* New York: Macmillan, 1933.

McMaster, J.B. *A School History of the United States.* New York: American Book Company, 1916.

Montgomery, D.H. *The Leading Facts of American History.* Boston: Ginn and Company, 1897.

Moon, G.W., and D.C. Cline. *Story of Our Land and People.* New York: Holt, Rinehart and Winston, 1961.

Muzzey, D.S. *An American History.* Boston: Ginn and Company, 1920.

———. *A History of Our Country: A Textbook for High School Students.* Boston: Ginn and Company, 1948.

Myers, P.V.N. *A General History for Colleges and High Schools.* Boston: Ginn & Company, 1904.

Nash, G.B. *American Odyssey: The United States in the Twentieth Century.* Lake Forest, IL: Glencoe Macmillan, 1992.

Nietz, J.A. *The Evolution of American Secondary School Textbooks: Rhetoric & Literature, Algebra, Geometry, Natural History (Zoology), Botany, Natural Philosophy (Physics), Chemistry, Latin and Greek, French, German & World History as Taught in American Latin Grammar School Academies and Early High Schools Before 1900.* Rutland, VT: C.E. Tuttle Co, 1966.

Norton, M.B., et al. *A People and a Nation: A History of the United States.* Boston: Houghton Mifflin Company, 1982.

Olney, J. *A History of the United States, on a New Plan; Adapted to the Capacity of Youth.* New Haven, CT: Durrie & Peck, 1851.

Outlines of American History: From the First Discovery to the Present Time. For Families and Schools. With Numerous Engravings, and Questions for the Examination of Pupils. Philadelphia: Thomas, Cowperthwait & Co., 1845.

Platt, N., and M.J. Drummond. *Our Nation from Its Creation.* 2nd ed. Englewood Cliffs, NJ: Prentice Hall, 1966.

Prentiss, C. *History of the United States of America; With a Brief Account of Some of the Principal Empires & States of Ancient & Modern Times. For the Use of Schools and Families.* Keene, NH: John Prentiss, 1821.

———. *History of the United States of America; With a Brief Account of Some of the Principal Empires and States of Ancient and Modern Times. For the Use of Schools and Families.* 2nd ed. Keene, NH: John Prentiss, 1823.

Quackenbos, G.P. *Illustrated School History of the United States and the Adjacent Parts of America, from the Earliest Discoveries to the Present Time: Embracing a Full Account of the Aborigines; Biographical Notices of Distinguished Men; Numerous Maps, Plans of Battle-Fields, and Pictorial Illustrations; and Other Features Calculated to Give Our Youth Correct Ideas of Their Country's Past and Present, and a Taste for General Historical Reading.* New York: D. Appleton & Co., 1867.

Ridpath, J.C. *History of the United States, Prepared Especially for Schools: On a New and Comprehensive Plan, Embracing the Features of Lyman's Historical Chart (Grammar School Edition)*. Cincinnati, OH: Jones Brothers & Co., 1878.

Ritchie, D.A. *American History: The Modern Era Since 1865*. New York: Glencoe Mc-Graw-Hill, 1999.

Robertson, W. *The History of the Discovery and Conquest of America*. New York: Harper and Brothers, 1844.

Russell, J. *A History of the United States of America, from the Period of the Discovery to the Present Time: Arranged for the Use of Schools, with Questions for the Examination of Students*. Philadelphia: Hogan & Thompson, 1841.

Sandler, M.W., E.C. Rozwenc, and E.C. Martin. *The People Make a Nation*. Boston: Allyn and Bacon, Inc., 1975.

Scott, D.B. *A School History of the United States, from the Discovery of America to the Year 1877*. New York: Harper & Brothers, 1877.

Steele, J.D., and E.B. Steele. *A Brief History of the United States*. New York: American Book Company, 1885.

—— ——. *Barnes's School History of the United States: Being a Revision of a Brief History of the United States*. New York: American Book Company, 1903.

Swan, W.D. *First Lessons in the History of the United States. Compiled for the Use of Common Schools*. Boston: Hickling, Swan, and Brown, 1856.

Swinton, W. *A Condensed School History of the United States, Constructed for Definite Results in Recitation and Containing a New Method of Topical Reviews*. New York: American Book Company, 1871.

————. *First Lessons in Our Country's History: Bringing out Its Salient Points, and Aiming to Combine Simplicity with Sense*. New York: Ivison, Blakeman, Taylor & Company, 1879.

Taylor, E. *The Model History: A Brief Account of the American People for Schools*. Chicago: Scott, Foresman & Co., 1897.

Thalheimer, M.E. *The Eclectic History of the United States*. New York: Van Antwerp, Bragg & Co., 1881.

The American's Guide: Comprising the Declaration of Independence; the Articles of Confederation; the Constitution of the United States, and the Constitutions of the Several States Composing the Union. Philadelphia: Hogan & Thompson, 1821.

Todd, L.P., and M. Curti. *Rise of the American Nation*. 2nd ed. New York: Harcourt, Brace & World, Inc., 1966.

Townsend, H. *Our America: The Story of Our Country; How It Grew from Little Colonies to a Great Nation*. Boston: Allyn and Bacon, 1945.

Trainer, J. *United States History by the Brace System: A Study of the History of the United States for the Use of Teacher and Pupil*. Chicago: A. Flanagan, 1883.

Vannest, C.G., and H.L. Smith. *Socialized History of the United States*. New York: Charles Scribner's Sons, 1936.

Venable, W.H. *A School History of the United States*. Cincinnati, OH: Wilson, Hinkle & Co., 1872.

Walker, B.F. *Curriculum Evolution as Portrayed Through Old Textbooks*. Terre Haute, IN: Curriculum Research and Development Center, 1976.

Webster, N. *An American Selection of Lessons in Reading and Speaking: Calculated to Improve the Minds and Refine the Taste of Youth and Also to Instruct Them in the Geography, History, and Politics of the United States*. 5th ed. Boston: Isaiah Thomas and Ebenezer T. Andrews, 1794.

————. *An American Selection of Lessons in Reading and Speaking: Calculated to Improve the Minds and Refine the Taste of Youth and Also to Instruct Them in the Geography, History, and Politics of the United States*. Newburyport, MA: Edward Little and Co., 1805.

————. *History of the United States to Which Is Prefixed a Brief Historical Account of Our [English] Ancestors, from the Dispersion at Babel, to Their Migration to America and of the Conquest of South America, by the Spaniards*. 3rd ed. New Haven, CT: Durrie & Peck, 1832.

Wertenbaker, T.J., and D.E. Smith. *The United States of America: A History*. New York: Charles Scribner's Sons, 1933.

West, R., and W.M. West. *The New World's Foundations in the Old*. Boston: Allyn and Bacon, 1942.

West, W.M. *American History and Government*. Boston: Allyn and Bacon, 1913.

Wilder, H.B., R.P. Ludlum, and H.M. Brown. *This Is America's Story*. Boston: Houghton Mifflin Co., 1950.

————. *This Is America's Story*. 4th ed. Boston: Houghton Mifflin Co., 1978.

Willard, E. *Abridged History of the United States; or, Republic of America*. Philadelphia: A.S. Barnes & Co., 1844.

————. *History of the United States, or Republic of America: with a Chronological Table and a Series of Progressive Maps*. New York: A.S. Barnes & Co., 1856.

Willson, M. *History of the United States, for the Use of Schools*. New York: Mark H. Newman & Co., 1849.

————. *History of the United States, From the Earliest Discoveries to the Present Time. With Additions, Containing History of the British American Provinces, History of Mexico, and the Constitution of the United States, with Explanatory Notes and Questions*. 55th ed. New York: Ivison & Phinney, 1857.

Woodburn, J.A., and T.F. Moran. *The Makers of America*. New York: Longmans, Green and Co., 1924.

PERMISSIONS

I am grateful for permission to reproduce the following copyrighted material (in cases where copyright information is omitted for works not in the public domain, every effort has been made to contact the copyright holders; any omissions will be corrected in subsequent reprintings):

Excerpts from *A People and a Nation,* Second Edition, by Mary Beth Norton, David M. Katzman, Paul D. Escott, Howard P. Chudacoff, Thomas G. Patterson, and William M. Tuttle, Jr. Reproduced by permission of Houghton Mifflin Company.

Excerpts from *The American Pageant: A History of the Republic,* Tenth Edition, by Thomas A Bailey and David M. Kennedy. Reproduced by permission of Houghton Mifflin Company.

Excerpts from *Story of Our Land and People* by Glen W. Moon and Don C. Cline. Reproduced by permission of Harcourt, Inc.

Excerpts from *Rise of the American Nation,* Second Edition, by Lewis Paul Todd and Merle Curti. Reproduced by permission of Harcourt, Inc.

Excerpts from *American History,* Revised Edition, by John Garraty. Reproduced by permission of Harcourt, Inc.

INDEX

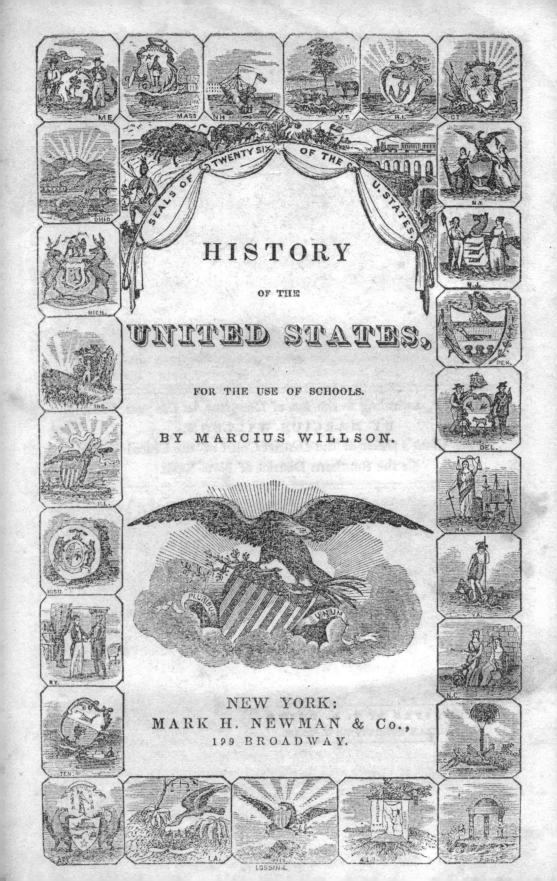

SEALS OF TWENTY SIX OF THE U. STATES

HISTORY

OF THE

UNITED STATES,

FOR THE USE OF SCHOOLS.

BY MARCIUS WILLSON.

E PLURIBUS UNUM

NEW YORK:
MARK H. NEWMAN & Co.,
199 BROADWAY.